Cape Verde

Christmas 2022

To My ~~Darling~~ Fishers —
Wishing you a very
Happy Christmas and
happy travels!
There aren't many books
on Cape Verde — nor nice maps.
This book will provide you
with an overload of information!! Hopefully you
can find something that
will enhance a ~~bot~~ of
your stay with info??
Much much
big love and hugs
Tom and Barbara
✗   ✗

NATIONS OF THE MODERN WORLD: AFRICA

Larry W. Bowman, *Series Editor*

CAPE VERDE

Crioulo Colony to Independent Nation

RICHARD A. LOBBAN, JR.

Routledge
Taylor & Francis Group
New York London

To the loving memory of my father,
who passed away while this was being written,
and to my mother, whose wisdom and guidance
will always be appreciated

Nations of the Modern World: Africa

First published 1995 by Westview Press

Published 2018 by Routledge
711 Third Avenue, New York, NY 10017, USA
2 Park Square, Milton Park, Abingdon, Oxon OX14 4RN

Routledge is an imprint of the Taylor & Francis Group, an informa business

Copyright © 1995 Taylor & Francis

Library of Congress Cataloging-in-Publication Data
Lobban, Richard.
    Cape Verde : Crioulo colony to independent nation / Richard A. Lobban, Jr.
        p.   cm. — (Nations of the modern world. Africa)
    Includes bibliographical references and index.
    ISBN 0-8133-8451-6   ISBN 0-8133-3562-0
    1. Cape Verde—History.   I. Title.   II. Series.
DT671.C25L62   1995
966.58—dc20   94-45834
                                                                            CIP

ISBN 13: 978-0-8133-3562-9 (pbk)

Contents

4 RADICALS, SOLDIERS, AND DEMOCRATS: POLITICS IN CAPE VERDE — 87

5 PEASANTS, SOCIALISTS, AND CAPITALISTS: ECONOMICS IN CAPE VERDE — 125

6 CONCLUSION: CAPE VERDE AT THE END OF THE TWENTIETH CENTURY — 145

Tables and Illustrations

PHOTOGRAPHS

Preface and Acknowledgments

THIS BOOK REPRESENTS a long evolutionary process that began in 1964 in Dar es Salaam, Tanzania, when I built and taught in a school for refugees from southern and Portuguese Africa. My involvement in the struggle against Portuguese colonialism was inspired by Eduardo Mondlane, a neighbor and the founder of the Frente de Libertaçāo de Moçambique (FRELIMO), the liberation movement in Mozambique. Later, while working as a staff journalist for *Southern Africa Magazine* (published in New York) in the early 1970s, I covered the nationalist war in Guinea-Bissau firsthand by crossing that nation on foot and by dugout canoe. For this unique opportunity I thank the Partido Africano da Independência da Guiné e Cabo Verde (PAIGC) for providing a military guard for my travel in contested areas in Guinea-Bissau during 1973. Likewise, I am grateful to the respective PAIGC governments for the practical support they provided for my travels in Guinea-Bissau and Cape Verde in 1975 and to the Movimento para Democracia (MpD) government of Cape Verde for allowing me to consult archives and libraries and speak with government officials, members of the opposition Partido Africano da Independência de Cabo Verde (PAICV), and other citizens of the independent Republic of Cape Verde in 1992. In the field of African studies, such freedoms are not granted automatically.

This book has also evolved over more than two decades of writing and teaching about Cape Verde and West Africa at Rhode Island College, which houses the widely recognized and often visited Cape Verdean Studies Special Collection. In many ways over many years, I am especially grateful for the collegial interaction, support and encouragement, and intellectual stimulation provided by Deirdre Meintel, Marilyn Halter, Marlene Lopes, and Waltraud Coli. Deirdre has pioneered in the complex anthropology of colonial Cape Verde. Marilyn and I coauthored a historical reference book on the islands, and her outlook has contributed substantially to the present work. Marlene and I are now writing the third edition of that work, and as the reference librarian of the Cape Verdean Studies Special Collection, she has endlessly shared ideas, information, and citations with me. Waltraud and I have coauthored a history of Cape Verdeans in Rhode Island, a project that grew out of her master's thesis on Cape Verdean ethnicity at Rhode Island College.

I have gained much from the fruitful collaboration of each of these friends and colleagues. It would be difficult to acknowledge all the ways in which they have assisted me, but I believe this book is the result of a collective intellectual effort for which I credit my friends; however, I accept the blame for all remaining errors.

The names of those in and around the Cape Verdean–American community who offered valuable assistance are too many to be noted in full, but several individuals deserve special recognition. I am especially grateful to Claire Andrade-Watkins, Ron Barboza, Matt Barros, David Baxter, Sam Beck, Vanessa Brito, Joe Cardosa, Mindy Carvalho, Tony Da Moura, Francisco Fernandes, Virginia Goncalves, Katherine Hagedorn, Susan Hurley-Glowa, Oling Jackson, Danny Lima, José Lopes, Luís Lopes, Thomas Lopes, Fatima Monteiro, Eva Nelson, Albert Pereira, Maria Rodrigues, João Rosário, Yvonne Smart, and João Soares. Within the formally recognized Cape Verdean Sub-Committee of the Rhode Island Heritage Commission there has been a solid base of encouragement and support. Two bibliographer-librarians also deserve special recognition: Paul Cyr at the New Bedford (Massachusetts) Public Library and Gretchen Walsh at the African Studies Center at Boston University. Appreciation is also extended to Robert Tidwell, who provided critical advice in computer processing and tolerated my endless questions. The original maps in this book were professionally drafted by cartographer Richard E. Grant, to whom I offer much gratitude.

In Cape Verde, appreciation goes to many as well: For their special assistance in the recent or distant past, I thank José Maria Almeida, José Araujo, Humberto Cardosa, Francisco Fernandes, John Grabowski, Ross Jaax, Terry McNamara, Lineu Miranda, António Neves, Henrique and Pedro Pires, João Pires and his family, Helena Ruivo, and Joe Sconce.

My knowledge of the ethnomusicology of Cape Verde was significantly advanced by my association with Peter Manuel, Susan Hurley-Glowa, and Katherine Hagedorn. Nelson Kasfir at Dartmouth College has been very helpful in sharpening my focus on the development of democracy and political systems in Africa.

Very important financial assistance for the research done in 1992 was provided by the West Africa Research Association at the Smithsonian Institution. Without this, the critical update of information about Cape Verde would simply not have been possible. To this was added generous financial support from the Rhode Island College Faculty Research Fund. I am most grateful for their help in underwriting the considerable travel costs incurred in research in the remote Cape Verdean archipelago. This allowed me to study some of the important transformations that have emerged in the period of plural democracy in Cape Verde. At Westview Press, Senior Editor Barbara Ellington, Assistant Editor Kathleen McClung, and Series Editor Larry Bowman have also provided constructive advice. Editorial scrutiny by Marianne Fluehr is very gratefully acknowledged.

Thanks also to Carolyn and Josina Fluehr-Lobban for putting up with me during the many months that passed while working on this project. A very special thank-you goes to Nichola Fluehr-Lobban, my eleven-year-old daughter and "research assistant" who accompanied me during my five-week stay in Cape Verde in the summer of 1992.

Richard A. Lobban, Jr.
Pawtuxet Village, Rhode Island

1

INTRODUCTION

THE CAPE VERDE ISLANDS are not well known to the world at large. There are only nine significant islands in this West African and Atlantic archipelago, and their combined population is only one-third of a million. Yet these islands are remarkably complex in their history and composition. Indeed, such a simple matter as conceptualizing their location is more difficult than one might expect.[1]

Although the islands may have been visited before the Portuguese arrived, Cape Verdean history essentially starts with the settlers from Portugal and their slaves in the 1460s. From that point forward, for more than five centuries, the islands' history was characterized by Portuguese colonialism and a synthesis of the *Crioulo* culture. Throughout this period, the Portuguese regarded Cape Verde as an integral part of metropolitan Portugal; its position was much like that of the state of Hawaii in relation to the mainland United States. The islands have also been at the center of major oceanic crossroads. Today, they are home to Portuguese, Nigerians, Guineans, Senegalese, and other West Africans. The diverse Cape Verdean population also includes descendants of Spaniards, English, Italians, Brazilians, Sephardic Jews, Lebanese, Dutch, Germans, Americans, and even Japanese and Chinese. Much of the islands' genetic ancestry can be traced to African groups who spoke the Fula, Mandinka, and various Senegambian languages. The "purely" Portuguese have always been in the minority, but it is largely from them that the dominant language, culture, and politics have been derived. To characterize Cape Verde as a society descended from slaves is correct to a degree, but it is also a society descended from slavers, free citizens, and refugees.

Like most modern populations, the fundamental essence of the Cape Verdean people reflects enduring patterns of connection to all continents across the oceans. In this respect, Cape Verde is like a miniature version of any multiethnic modern state. To focus on Cape Verde, one must use a wide-angle lens to see the critical linkages to Europe, West Africa, and the New World and find all the points

1

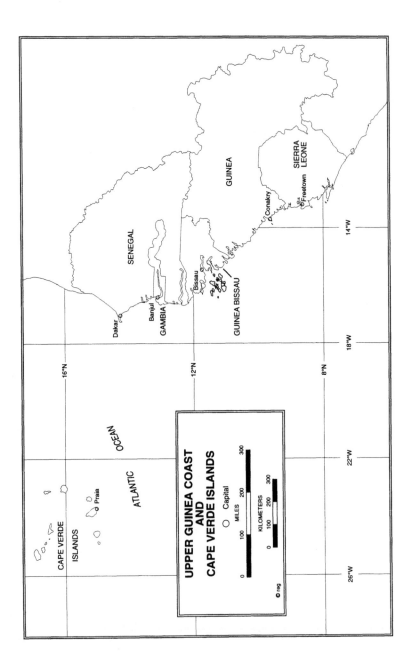

UPPER GUINEA COAST
AND
CAPE VERDE ISLANDS

of origin, articulation, and destination of the Cape Verdean people. A view of Europe, especially Portugal, is required to detect the roots of the political and economic power that dominated Cape Verde for the vast part of its history.[2] The ties to West Africa must be explored as well, not only because so many thousands of Cape Verdean ancestors came from the Upper Guinea coast but also because Cape Verde was the official, formal, and effective command post on the Guinea coast for the Portuguese until the late nineteenth century. Moreover, most grants to Portuguese or Brazilian trading monopolies in Cape Verde simultaneously included the "Rivers of Guinea."[3]

For simplicity, I use the term *Guinea-Bissau* ("Rivers of Guinea") to refer to today's Republic of Guinea-Bissau, which was known as Portuguese Guinea in colonial times. By using this term, I also distinguish this nation from neighboring Guinea-Conakry. However, for the longest part of the history of Cape Verde, the colonial administration included both the islands and steadily diminishing portions of the Upper Guinea coast. The last remaining part of Portuguese territory in this region was in Guinea-Bissau.

In the following chapters, I will describe the many ways in which the histories, peoples, and policies of these two lands are linked. Even the war of national independence, waged from 1963 to 1974 in Guinea-Bissau, had as its central goal the joint liberation and administration of the two lands. The strategy of the nationalist movement and political party—the Partido Africano da Independência da Guiné e Cabo Verde (PAIGC)—was to struggle for independence in the forests of Guinea and pressure the Portuguese in Lisbon to release their historical hold on the Cape Verde Islands. The connections between these regions are also revealed in the fact that some of the leading Portuguese military officers who were defeated in Guinea, Angola, and Mozambique were the same men who toppled colonial fascism in Lisbon and negotiated the independence of Cape Verde some months later. The majority of the top revolutionary leaders in Guinea were of Cape Verdean origin, including Amilcar Cabral, Luís Cabral, Aristides Pereira, and Pedro Pires, all of whom fought in the forests of Guinea-Bissau. Pereira was the first president of Cape Verde, and Pires was the first prime minister of the ruling party—the Partido Africano da Independência de Cabo Verde (PAICV)—from 1975 to 1991.

To understand Cape Verde (or Armenia, Hong Kong, Ireland, Israel, Palestine, or Scotland), one must also study its diaspora communities: The connections to the economy and power relations of the wider world are essential. In all these cases, the majority of the people claiming a common nationality do not live in the very nation that is the focus of their sentimental and even political allegiance. In the case of Cape Verde, linkages to the port towns of Europe, to São Tomé, to the coast of West Africa, to Brazil and the Antilles, and especially to New England are vital to the nation's history.

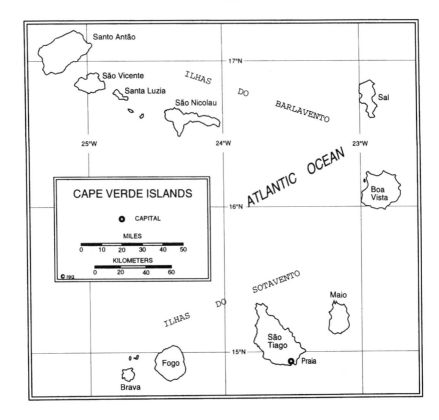

Geographic Location

Despite the term *Verde* ("green") in its name, Cape Verde (or Cabo Verde, in Portuguese) was named not for its verdant plant growth or agriculture but for its juxtaposition to Cap Vert (a French name) on the African coast—a point that had been reached by the Portuguese almost twenty years before the islands themselves were discovered. Although some think that the islands were named for their greenness, the fifteenth-century diaries of Christopher Columbus specifically noted the dry and barren Cape Verdean landscape; he considered the land's name a misnomer.

The Cape Verdean archipelago lies within a grid from 283 to 448 miles (452.8 to 716.8 km) off the coast of Senegal, or from 14°48' to 17°12' north latitude and 22°41' to 25°22' west longitude. Such data seem straightforward and clear today. But early Portuguese navigators believed the islands were "just downstream" in the Canary current, and even in twentieth-century Portuguese books, the islands are conceptualized as being located 1,900 miles (3,040 km) south-southwest of Lisbon. In the eighteenth century, when the interests of Brazilian slavers essen-

Village of Cova de Joana, Brava Island (Photo by Waltraud Berger Coli)

tially ruled Cape Verde, the archipelago's location could be reasonably defined as 1,500 miles (2,400 km) north-northeast of Brazil. The point here is that the location of Cape Verde was conceptualized primarily by outsiders, according to the interests they had in the islands, and even some modern Cape Verdeans are as likely to focus on its location relative to Europe or New England rather than to the nearby African coast. Many of the complex issues of Cape Verdean ethnicity and identity relate to this sense of location. Clearly, the question of location involves more than longitude and latitude; it is also a matter of attitude and self-consciousness.

Climate

One might imagine that an African republic of oceanic islands would be lush and moist, but the Cape Verdean archipelago is better understood as a western extension of the Sahara Desert. In fact, the islands are extremely dry and have long been troubled by cycles of prolonged drought. The two-season weather cycle of this region is caused by the north-south movement of the Inter-Tropical Convergence Zone (ITCZ). The ITCZ is associated with hot, dry winters north of the zone and hot, wet summer weather to the south of the zone. The clashing weather fronts of the ITCZ in the region of Cape Verde also spawn hurricanes that regularly torment the Caribbean and the east coast of the United States in the late summer months.[4]

The ITCZ usually reaches only the southernmost Cape Verde Islands. In some years, it falls short of them, and there is simply no rain in the archipelago; in other years, this ITCZ front moves farther north, and the drought cycle is broken. Historically, drought cycles in Cape Verde have caused great hardships—including famine and many deaths—and led to endless waves of emigration. Seldom is the rainfall adequate for extensive, self-sufficient agriculture, particularly because much of the terrain is rocky and steep. With adequate rainfall, water conservation, and careful irrigation, there is some potential for agriculture, and in recent decades, widespread improvements have been made in this respect. Still, Cape Verdeans must import much of their food supply, thereby consuming precious foreign cash reserves.

There is also a microclimatic variation on islands with higher elevations (the highest is 9,281 feet, or 2,821.4 m). At such elevations, the moisture of passing clouds can condense at lower temperatures by the process of orographic, or pluvogenic, cooling, which can cause rain at higher elevations. In turn, this gives rise to some small but permanent springs and streams. But the flatter islands are notorious for their very low levels of annual rainfall. Yearly variation in temperature is not great: It is seldom cooler than 68°F (22°C) or hotter than 80°F (27°C).

Altogether, there are twenty-one islands and islets in Cape Verde, but only nine are regularly inhabited. These include Santo Antão, São Vicente (with its port of Mindelo), São Nicolau, Sal (with its international airport), Boa Vista, Maio, São Tiago (with the capital, Praia), Fogo, and Brava. The islands together only cover 1,557 square miles (4,033 square kilometers)—just a little more territory than Rhode Island. The terrain is overwhelmingly rocky and volcanic, and there is very little topsoil, given the drought conditions and severe wind and water erosion. At best, only 1.65 percent of the land is arable, and much of this has been abused by absentee landowners and worn down by overgrazing (especially by sheep and goats).

The general appearance of the islands resembles a lunar landscape, with towering rocky peaks on some islands and gravelly, sandy soils. The land is deeply eroded, and there are extensive areas of very sparse settlement. Some of these volcanic islands, such as Sal, are almost flat; others are mountainous. Fogo, for example, rises to a majestic cone and has experienced numerous eruptions in historical times.

Linkages to the Wider World

The Cape Verde Islands have been both isolated from yet remarkably connected to the major events of world history. Their remote location, hundreds of miles from the nearest continent, has naturally made them vulnerable to neglect, oversight,

ILHA DE SÃO TIAGO

Tarrafal

Chão Bom

23° N
30'

ATLANTIC OCEAN

Pedra Badejo

Assomada +
1394 m

15° W
00'

Legend

Cidade Velha

Praia

★   Capital

●   Cities

——— Major Roads

—·— Other Roads

Kilometers

0   10   20   30

© reg

and abuse. But the islands were also integrally linked to wider events, such as the golden age of Portuguese discovery, the voyages of Columbus and Vasco da Gama, the pirate attacks by Francis Drake, and the provision of coal and fuel for the British empire. Cape Verde was critical in the slave trade, and it was visited by such famed U.S. ships as *Old Ironsides.* The islands also hosted the American Africa Squadron, used by the U.S. Navy for anti–slave trade patrols, and they figured in Charles Darwin's theory of biological evolution. In the liberation war fought against Portuguese colonial rule in Guinea-Bissau, Cape Verde played a much more significant role than one might expect. Clearly, this was due to the strategic location of the archipelago: Sailors, slavers, colonialists, scientists, flyers, and others enjoyed the security of the islands and also found their location convenient for long-range travel to the farthest corners of the globe.

Following the struggles led by Amilcar Cabral, one of Africa's great twentieth-century revolutionary thinkers and a Cape Verdean, this island republic gained its independence in 1975. The theories and practices of Cabral are widely considered

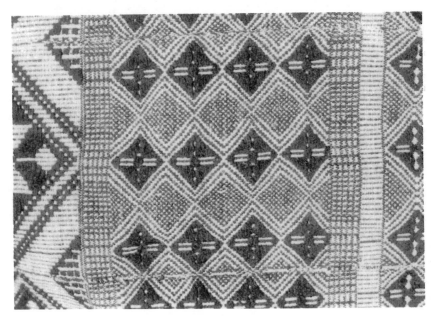

Cape Verdean pano, *used in dress, dance, and the slave trade (Photo by Waltraud Berger Coli)*

to equal those of Kwame Nkrumah, Julius Nyerere, Fidel Castro, and Ho Chi Minh.[5] Most recently, Cape Verde has witnessed the birth of plural democracy, which resulted in a peaceful transition from the former ruling party—the PAICV—to the opposition party that now governs—the Movimento para Democracia (MpD). Cape Verde is regarded as a model democracy in West Africa, a region where one-party states, military rule, and civil war are not uncommon. During the 1992 elections in Angola, Cape Verdeans were specially selected by the Organization of African Unity (OAU) to play a supervisory role, and in the same year, Cape Verdean diplomats served on the United Nations Security Council.

The most enduring resource and export of Cape Verde has been its people. Cape Verdeans have long been a people on the move—traders on the Guinea coast, colonial administrators for Portugal, revolutionaries in the national liberation of Africa, sailors and whalers on U.S. schooners and barks, laborers in the cranberry bogs of Cape Cod or the cocoa plantations of São Tomé and Principé, and merchant mariners around the world. Remittances sent home by Cape Verdeans living and working in the nation's long-lasting diaspora have been vital in sustaining the islands' population.[6]

The natural resources in the archipelago also include the products of the sea—diverse species of fish, turtles, and whales. And providing supplies and repairs for passing ships has been an important part of the economy for centuries. Prominent among traditional Cape Verdean crafts are the handwoven *panos*, cotton cloths that served as a basic unit of currency in slave and coastal trade. Cape Verdean livestock, especially horses, had a similar function, and other domestic animals were used for ship supply and hide production. The islands' other natural resources—salt, cotton, puzzolane, coffee, bananas, indigo, and urzella—had varying importance over the years. Tourism in this land of sun and sand, where there is little crime and no terrorism, will certainly be important in future development.

This book provides a more detailed account of the historical features of the islands, from discovery and settlement to the slave trade and independence. The growth of Cape Verdean culture is also investigated. In the chapters that follow, I will describe the evolution of contemporary Cape Verde and look closely at the unique problems and solutions of this area's economic and political development.

2

THE HISTORICAL SETTING

THE CAPE VERDE ISLANDS were uninhabited when they were first reached by the Portuguese in the 1450s. However, given the very close cultural ties between the islands and both Portugal and West Africa, it is worthwhile to consider the long history of these latter areas. The early European settlers and their African slaves imported diverse cultural values, genetic bonds, and various musical and linguistic traditions to the islands. Indeed, the process of becoming and being Cape Verdean fundamentally reflects these earlier origins and the geographic context.

The Earliest Times

From an anthropological perspective, the search for roots can begin with antiquity. All human beings find their hominid ancestry leading back to eastern and southern Africa's savannas millions of years ago. The poorly developed ancient archaeology of the West African savanna has not produced early hominid fossils, but it is not unreasonable to assume that our ancestors ranged there as well. Saharan rock paintings show hunters and gatherers in a much wetter Sahara before 5000 B.C.

Perhaps as early as 3000 to 4000 B.C., agriculture based on rain-fed cultivation of millet and sorghum emerged in the West African savanna, especially along the fertile banks of the Senegal and Niger Rivers. Livestock-herding ancestors of the Saharan Berbers were probably present by 3000 B.C., judging from their images in other rock paintings and from their relatives in North Africa.

Small-scale but permanently settled village society in the savanna emerged in about the second millennium B.C., with livestock, hides, handicrafts, pottery, and some agricultural surplus. Meanwhile, the forested regions of coastal West Africa were likely inhabited by relatively dispersed hunting and fishing peoples. Beginning in the first millennium B.C., some of the Sahelian or savanna grassland crops, such as millet, sorghum, watermelon, and sesame, were spreading into the forest regions. By the end of that millennium, crops in the forested areas also included the more important southeast Asian crops, such as wet rice, yams, bananas, mangos, and sugarcane; these had arrived in East Africa by ship and through trade and were later dispersed by West African farmers. With the development of iron smelting and the manufacture of farm tools and weapons, these foods could be more effectively cultivated, resulting in an explosive spread of savanna peoples into the forests in the centuries after Christ. There, they assimilated, enslaved, or were absorbed by the original coastal inhabitants. Consequently, the culturolinguistic groups of the Upper Guinea coast became notably diversified and dispersed.[1]

As early as the seventh century B.C., Phoenician navigators sailing from either Carthage or the Red Sea were likely the first non-Africans to circumnavigate the African continent.[2] Fragmentary reports suggest that they were also the first to sight the Cape Verde Islands or Hesperides, where they noted a smoking volcanic island that could well correspond to Fogo.[3]

Beyond the Straits of Gibraltar, the Phoenician voyagers established archaeologically documented trade settlements on the Atlantic coasts of Africa and Portugal. In Portugal, the Phoenicians had settlements in the Algarve, Tagus, and Alentejo areas and exposed the ancient Portuguese to the technology they would later use to explore the oceans.[4] Parts of Sahelian West Africa were brought into contact with the Mediterranean world through the famed "silent barter trade." (In this trading system, an individual left his or her goods in an appointed place, then, after other goods of equal value were deposited there, the individuals would gather those goods and depart.) Apparently, the Phoenicians acquired ivory, elephants, hides, gold, and slaves.

At the brutal end of the Third Punic War in 146 B.C., the Romans replaced the Phoenicians on land and sea; now Rome's ships sailed the Mediterranean and Atlantic, and one Roman report spoke of sailors reaching West Africa and beyond.[5] Romans were rather insecure about travel to the West African savanna, even with newly introduced camels, but some Sahelian products reached Roman North Africa through Jewish intermediaries. In the south, the salt trade was conducted on a modest scale.[6]

Roman rule of Portugal and Spain had deep and enduring effects on culture and language; this is obvious in urban layouts, aquaducts, and place-names. At first, Christianity was opposed by the Roman Empire, but official conversion in A.D. 312 brought this religion to the Iberian Peninsula, where it has remained dominant. However, in the subsequent collapse of the Roman Empire in A.D. 476, the entire region from North Africa to Western Europe fell into such disarray that Berbers and Africans in the savanna and Suevi, Visigoth, and Jewish peoples in

Iberia found both insecurity and a risky but tempting opportunity.[7] In Sahelian West Africa, religions blended a traditional animism, the worship of ancestors, and a syncretic use of certain Hebrew and Christian icons. The trading states of Tekrur and Ghana were located at this ecological and cultural nexus between the savanna and the desert. The ancient West African and West European ancestors of modern Cape Verdeans were already positioning themselves.

Into the great power vacuum in the mid–seventh century swept Arab armies, bearing the new messianic religion of Islam. They advanced rapidly across North Africa and crossed the Straits of Gibraltar in A.D. 711. Upon entering Europe, the Moors began some seven centuries of occupation on the Iberian Peninsula and advanced deep into France until they were halted at the Battle of Poitiers in A.D. 732. For many centuries to come, crusading Europeans sought to reverse and avenge these Moorish conquests.

Strengthened by their religious purpose and military success, the North African Muslims also turned their attention southward across the vast Sahara. Ghana was first noted on an Arab map of A.D. 770 by Muhammad ibn Ibrahim Al-Fazari, who stimulated interest in this "land of gold." The Almoravids, or Islamized Berbers and Arabs, who were already occupying Portugal then sought to spread Islam to Sahelian African states—whose people sought gold and slaves from the hilly, forested lands still farther southwest.[8] The conversion fervor brought the first Muslim emperor to the Malian throne in A.D. 1050. In 1076, Muslim forces completed their conquest of Ghana, thereby controlling the entire Maghreb as well as most of Iberia.[9]

The process of Islamizing Europe and Africa prompted two very different reactions. In Spain and Portugal, the final result was Christian revivalism, the Crusades, and more centuries of religious rivalry. By the late eleventh century, the Spaniards had already driven the Moors from northern Spain, and the Portuguese were similarly mobilized. Christian resistance to Islam and the religious revival movement would subsequently add to the political justification for fifteenth-century Portuguese exploration and expansion.

In Africa, by contrast, Islam deepened its roots. Even when the Almoravid control of ancient Ghana collapsed in A.D. 1135, Islam survived and became more entrenched. Muslims were also active in the Atlantic; eleventh-century Moorish sailors reportedly reached Sal Island in Cape Verde for salt supplies. The Muslim scholar 'Abd Allah Muhammad Al-Idrisi cites Arab travelers from Lisbon who went to the Canary Islands in the first half of the twelfth century and met Arabic-speakers there.[10] Two Chinese writers from the twelfth and thirteenth centuries even claim that Arabs sailed west across the Atlantic from Casablanca for 100 days to reach a land called "Mu-lan-pi," which may have been the New World.[11] The wide circulation of such information suggests the Portuguese were aware of the Canaries and perhaps even of Cape Verde.

Although their power in Iberia began to slip in the twelfth century, Moors still held major towns in southern Spain. In Portugal, the erosion of Moorish control was accelerated in A.D. 1143 when an independent monarchy was created, led by the country's first Christian king, Afonso I (1112–1185). During the reign of Afonso III (1248–1279), the Portuguese launched the Reconquista in the name of Christ. This was further consolidated by King Afonso IV, who ruled from 1325 to 1357.[12]

Jewish cartographers in thirteenth- and fourteenth-century Spain made detailed descriptions of the Moroccan coast and Saharan interior. In 1375, the *Catalan Atlas* was published in Majorca, Spain, and is usually attributed to the famed Jewish cartographer Abraham Cresques; this map shows the locations of the Canaries and the Atlantic coast of Morocco.[13]

A fascinating tale from the historian of Mali Ibn Fadl Allah Al-Umari related that a great fleet of ships, perhaps under the command of Aboubacar II (son of the great Mansa Musa), traveled from Malian territory on the Senegambian coast westward across the Atlantic; however, no independent confirmation of this voyage is available.[14] By the late fourteenth century, as the Portuguese sought to learn more of the huge ocean that washed their shores, their imagination turned seaward. They hoped to either circumvent or combat their Moorish enemies in the Maghreb—and to begin to discover a new world.

In 1380, far to the south along the coast of Senegal and Gambia, the African kingdoms of the Wolof and Serer were becoming independent of a weakening Mali Empire. These kingdoms and Mali had expanded southward to trap decentralized Senegambian people against the coast. There, these Africans would soon meet the Portuguese who were entering the same region from the ocean.

The Golden Age of Portuguese Maritime Exploration

The expulsion of the Moors in 1139 and the replacement of the Burgundian dynasty of Portugal in 1389 by the House of Avis (Knights of Calatrava) sweetened Portuguese dreams of maritime expansion. Other motivating factors included the relatively small size of Portugal and its limited natural resources, especially of gold—a commodity that was believed to be abundant in Guinea. The search for a shorter route to Asia that would bypass the Arabs was yet another motivation. The cultural and demographic resurrection following the plague epidemics may also have added to the new impetus to look outward. Human curiosity stimulated by the oral records of earlier Arab mariners and thoughts of great, unseen African empires—endowed with unimaginable supplies of gold—tempted the Portuguese adventurers even more.

From a technical point of view, the long Portuguese association with the Phoenicians and Moors led to substantial maritime innovations and designs, such as the carracks, the barcas, and the lateen sail of the caravel; navigational advances included the compass, quadrant, sextant, astrolabe, and pilot books, as well as a better understanding of astronomy and more precise cartography.

Venetian and Genoan merchants were already conducting their own exploration, as a 1403 Genoan map of North Africa indicates. Similarly, the French traveler Anselme d'Isalquier from Toulouse had pioneered in crossing the Sahara to reach Gao in 1413. At last, at the start of the fifteenth century, the irresistable impulse for oceanic exploration launched Portuguese ships, to begin the exploration of the Atlantic coast of northwestern Africa.[15]

This great Portuguese plunge into maritime exploration was taken mainly during the reign of João I (1385–1433), especially by his son, Prince Henrique (Henry). Prince Henry was emboldened to plan attacks against additional Moorish lands following his capture of Ceuta, across from Gibraltar in 1415. His chronicler, Gomes Eannes de Azurara, wrote a detailed account of this campaign in his book *Key to the Mediterranean*. The great epoch of fifteenth-century Portuguese exploration along the coast of Africa was now under way.[16]

Portuguese, Genoan, and Venetian merchant explorers and, later, settlers sailing from the Algarve region and from Lisbon were contracted to embark on these new voyages. The maritime history of West Africa at this period typically includes information on the pilots chartered and supported by Prince Henry the Navigator, although the prince probably did not sail farther than Ceuta. However, in 1434, sailing for Prince Henry, Captain Gil Eannes reached Cape Bojador in the former Spanish Sahara, just south of the Canaries. Encouraged by their newfound reach, the Portuguese tried to seize Tangiers two years later, but they suffered defeat in this effort. They resumed their military initiative under the long reign of Afonso V, from 1438 to 1481. Within this military context, the Portuguese took their first Muslim slaves or war captives from Morocco and Mauritania in the early 1440s. The slaves then saw domestic service in Portugal or labored in sugarcane plantations in the Madeira and Canary Islands. In this respect, the Portuguese were following an established practice for war captives taken by or from their Muslim foes.

Captain Antão Gonçalves, the first Portuguese slave raider and trader of record, made five voyages south of Cape Bojador from 1441 to 1447. In 1443, he and other captains serving Prince Henry were granted monopolies for regional trade farther south. By 1446, the Portuguese reached the coast of Guinea-Bissau. But Captain Nuño Tristão discovered his trading and slaving missions there were unwelcomed and opposed, and in about 1447, he was killed on the Upper Guinea coast by inhabitants resisting his slaving efforts. The same year saw a Genoan traveler, Antonio Malfante, cross the Sahara as far south as Tuat.[17] Another Genoan, Antonio Usodimare, and the Venetian Alvise Cadamosto sailed their three caravels into the

Senegal and Gambia Rivers in hopes of reaching Mali from the west.[18] Later, in the 1460s, Cadamosto, still employed by the Portuguese, navigated farther southward into unknown coastal waters.[19] In 1469, the Florentine trader Bendetto Dei reached Timbuktu by traveling completely across the Sahara. The Portuguese hoped that an easy sail down the coast to Arguin Island, along modern Mauritania, would give them good access for overland travel to Mali and its fabled land of gold. Even after this approach was abandoned, raiding and trading for slaves at Arguin continued.

By 1448, the Portuguese had shipped a minimum of 1,000 slaves from Africa. They soon determined that the slaving business would be best served by building a fortified *feitoria* (the residence of a *feitor*, or factor, who represented royal commercial interests) at Arguin Island to provide military and economic security for the *feitor*, or official agent of the Portuguese Crown. Other early traders like Diogo Gomes and Cadamosto went as far as Senegal for slaves. There, the Wolof and Serer kingdoms waged endless war against their neighbors to seize slaves, which they traded for cloth, beads, and muskets. Turning again to Gomes Eannes de Azurara in his 1453 *Cronica de Guiné*, one finds early, detailed accounts of enslaving Africans as well as the African resistance to and collaboration with the early slavers.

The slave trade involved more than just the economic value of the slaves. In their war against the Moors, the Iberian powers benefited when slaves were diverted to Cape Verdean and coastal markets: As more slaves passed through Portuguese hands, there were fewer available on the Moorish trans-Saharan routes, which undermined the economy of Portugal's African rivals. Trapped in between, the African slaves were captured, abused, and shipped off in either case. The redirection in the slave trade also steadily increased the overall inequities between African and European powers as the Europeans bought or bargained for slaves at low prices and sold high. They also removed a substantial portion of the African workforce, which was then used in European and New World development. In addition, slaving generated an atmosphere of protracted regional instability and insecurity.

It is significant that a half century *before* Columbus's pioneering travels and practices in the New World, two patterns had already begun. The first combined the ever-expanding slave trade and the lust for gold. The second involved the Spanish and Portuguese policies of genocide, which were applied in the Canaries and quickly extinguished the native Guanache. Sadly, these twin forces of slavery and genocide became established features of that age.

At the dawn of the discovery of the Cape Verde Islands, the relations between Christian Portugal and the Muslim world of northwest Africa were founded on deep religious, economic, and political rivalries. Ultimately, the nascent European mercantilism of the fifteenth-century would come to dominate by virtue of Europe's advantages in maritime exploration and innovation. The land-based Muslims of Africa and the Maghreb never effectively competed with the seafaring Portuguese.

The Discovery and Settlement of Cape Verde

It is possible that Cape Verde was visited by Phoenicians, Moorish Arabs, and Lebou fishermen from Senegal, but the first Portuguese sighting of the islands occurred in the mid–fifteenth century. This sighting was made either by the Genoan António da Noli in July 1455, by his fellow Genoan Usodimare, or by the Venetian Cadamosto in May 1456; although not Portuguese, these merchant explorers sailed under the Portuguese flag. In any case, after four more years, the Genoan brothers António and Bartolomeu da Noli and the Portuguese Diogo Afonso and Diogo Gomes completed charting the Sotavento ("southern," "leeward") Islands. The year 1460 is usually offered as the date of first settlement because this is when António da Noli was appointed *capitão* ("captain") of São Tiago Island.

Among the Barlavento ("northern," "windward") Islands, the easternmost Boa Vista was among the first reached by Da Noli and Gomes in 1460. Originally known as São Cristovão, it is the third largest island in the archipelago. The remaining westerly islands of the Barlavento group were reached in 1461–1462 during the voyages of Diogo Afonso. In São Tiago, the largest island with regular water supplies and fertile valleys, attention turned to the small capital town of Ribeira Grande. Afonso was appointed as the second *capitão* for São Tiago in September 1462. Diogo Afonso, a nephew and heir of Prince Henry, was titled as the squire of Prince Fernando, who was the brother of Portuguese King Afonso V. Such was the tight network of kinship among the feudal rulers of Cape Verde.

Da Noli was more or less loyal to Afonso V, and in exchange for this loyalty, he and his successors were given notable latitude in conducting freelance commerce in sugar plantations, in slave smuggling, and in making grants to Castilian merchants interested in the Cape Verdean plant dye known as orchil.[20]

Prince Henry's death in 1462 marked a turning point, as the age of Portuguese exploration of the African coast and Cape Verde gave way to the new age of Portuguese colonization, which quickly began in earnest. The Portuguese imported not only a feudal class structure to Cape Verde but also farmers from the Algarve region of Portugal, as well as Portuguese criminals, exiles, and Jews who were officially persecuted under the Inquisition. But slaves from the African coast always arrived in far greater numbers. The Portuguese masters soon began having sexual relations with their African slaves, which led to the creation of the majority Crioulo population. In one remarkable incident during these rough times, *capitão* Bartolomeu da Noli murdered a Franciscan priest named Rogerio in a dispute over a woman.

From the beginning, Cape Verde was operated on a plantation system modeled after that already developed in the Canaries and Madeiras. Land was immediately cleared to plant sugarcane and cotton; slaves were assigned to weave cotton, gather indigo, or labor in the salt flats of Sal and Maio. For domestic slaves, life may have been less harsh, but it was equally degrading and paternalistic.

Cape Verdeans placed a special value on slaves skilled in spinning, weaving, and dyeing cotton. Wolof women slaves were highly regarded as spinners, and Wolof men were the weavers, as was the custom among the Mande and Senegambian groups. The weavers produced six cloth strips of parallel design that were then sewn together to make a variety of *pano* or *barafula* ("trade cloths"); these cloths were reexported to the coast as a standard currency in slave trading.

In 1480, another Portuguese *capitão* was appointed to control the slave production system in Fogo, but it was not until 1510 that the *capitania* system was functioning effectively there. A 1515 census of Cape Verde's largest town—Ribeira Grande in São Tiago—found only eighty Portuguese families there but a far greater population of slaves. The intimate, long-standing, and functional relationship between the Cape Verde Islands and the African coast was thus present from the very first settlement.

Seeking to attract additional settlers to Cape Verde in the early 1460s, the Portuguese Crown provided some incentive by briefly allowing free trade in slaves and other coastal goods. However, the Crown soon suspended this liberal concession because Portugal's leaders feared they were losing too much wealth and because settlement of the islands was now established. In Lisbon, the king officially inaugurated the joint administration of Cape Verde and the Guinea coast on 12 June 1466. Under this royal authority, King Afonso V granted a trade monopoly to Lisbon merchant Fernão Gomes for the period 1468 to 1474, requiring that any ivory gathered during the lease period be sold exclusively to the Crown at a fixed price. In return, Gomes had to pay 200 milreis each year and further explore 100 leagues of West African coastline to the east of Sierra Leone. Gomes's role in extending coastal exploration led to the decisions to build a fortress at Al Mina and establish diplomatic ties with the Kingdom of Benin on the Lower Guinea coast. Gomes's charter excluded the Crown trade reserved on the uppermost Guinea coast, directly across from the Cape Verde Islands.

The Wolof and Senegambian political structure was described in detail by Cadamosto, who was intrigued with the rituals and habits of these people. He found the rituals both unusual and disgusting,[21] which helped lay the foundation for some of the racist stereotypes that were later developed by Europeans. Nevertheless, hoping to find African allies in the slave trade, the Crown made direct contact with members of the Wolof royalty who visited Lisbon in 1488. Upon their return to Senegal, however, some of these Wolofs were murdered by their Portuguese guards who perhaps feared they would be commercial rivals.

Meanwhile, in 1475, relations between Spain and Portugal worsened, ultimately leading to the Luso-Spanish War. During this conflict, Castilian captain Carlos de Valera sailed boldly down the African coast to sack São Tiago in 1476 and seize *capitão* António da Noli; da Noli, the flexible merchant adventurer, quickly changed his allegiance from Portugal to Spain. When the war ended in 1479 under the Papal Treaty of Alçacovas, Spain and Portugal demarcated specific domains for future trade and exploration. Portugal was compelled to relinquish the Canary Islands to Spain, but it retained the Madeiras, the Azores, and the Cape Verde Islands. In the mid–sixteenth century, Spain still generally observed the papal ruling (which normally kept Spanish ships away from the African coast), and harsh measures were imposed by Portuguese King João II against any Spanish interlopers.[22]

The explorations begun by Fernão Gomes could now be carried on by Diego da Azambuja, a Portuguese knight under the reign of King João II (1477 and 1481–1495). Azambuja was charged with extending the West African coastal exploration, trading for gold, and rapidly constructing the São Jorge Al Mina fortress on the Gold Coast. Construction materials and specialist craftsmen were brought in from Portugal in December 1481 in ten *caravelas,* accompanied by some 500 soldiers. Christopher Columbus, then sailing for the Portuguese, was probably a pilot on one of these ships, and he most likely made a stop in Cape Verde at this time. The construction project, designed to guard the Portuguese trade in slaves and gold for the next century and a half, was completed by the end of 1482. The gold from Al Mina and elsewhere on the Guinea coast would be vital in rebuilding the Portuguese economy and financing additional explorations.

In these early days and for a long time thereafter, Cape Verde served as Portugal's regional command center, dominating the West African maritime trade that extracted tens of thousands of slaves, tons of ivory, and immeasurable quantities of gold, hides, spices, woods, grain, and dyes. This great wealth attracted others: The Spanish, French, Dutch, and English would follow, challenge, and eventually overtake the weaker Portuguese. Papal authority kept the others away for several decades, but by 1477, the Spanish moved into the Canaries to complete the extermination of the native Guanache population and to keep the Portuguese from returning. Jealously competitive French sailors were seen in Cape Verdean waters as early as 1483.

Two years later, Portuguese sailors were at the mouth of the Congo River. Bartolomeu Dias sailed further south and finally reached the Cape of Good Hope in 1487. The elder brother of Christopher Columbus, Bartolomeu Columbus, sailed on the Dias voyage, during which Cape Verde likely served as a port of call.

Struggle to Control the African Coast

Africa in the fifteenth century was beset with problems. On one hand, Africans faced the grave dilemma of being either slaves or slavers. On the other, the lust for

The Cape Verde Islands (below and right of fish) were known as the Gorgades in the Hesperides Sea in this detail of a map drawn by Flemish cartographer Abraham Oretlius in 1570 (Library of Congress)

the wealth that could be derived from slaves and gold caused deep suspicions between the Portuguese and the Spanish, both of whom still feared the Muslims. Indeed, when Christopher Columbus shifted his loyalty from Portugal to Spain in the early 1490s, a royal *cedula* (the official sailing instructions), issued under papal authority, specifically ordered him to sail directly west and avoid Portuguese waters. Although papal authority was sufficient at first, the Spanish, English, French, Dutch, and Danes nevertheless quarreled endlessly for the "right" to carry away African slaves, gold, and other products.

Pope Alexander VI was aware of the potential for expanding conflict between Portugal and Spain. Therefore, on 4 May 1493, he called upon representatives of both Crowns to recognize the papal treaty that established Portuguese and Spanish territorial domains on the east and west, respectively, of a longitudinal line 100 leagues west of Cape Verde. After further exploration was completed by the following year, the Treaty of Tordesillas of 7 June 1494 adjusted this division to a line 370 leagues west of Cape Verde. These two treaties corrected the inequities that Spain had found in the 1479 Treaty of Alçacovas, which had favored Portugal. Importantly, Cape Verde was a key reference point in both.

By now, the Portuguese were already sailing onward to the Indian Ocean. In 1497, Vasco da Gama stopped at Sal and São Tiago in the Cape Verde Islands at the start of his voyage past the Horn of Africa and on to India. António da Noli, the famed *capitão* of São Tiago, died in the islands the same year. Christopher Columbus stopped in Cape Verde in 1498 on his third trip to the New World, and Amerigo Vespucci was there one year later. The heyday of the great navigators also saw the publication of books such as *Esmeraldo de Situ Orbis,* written by Duarte Pacheco Pereira between 1505 and 1508. In this book, Pereira compiled the latest information on global navigation and described the products and wealth of the Guinea coast. Another book, *Regimento do Cruzeiro do Sol,* written by Alvise Cadamosto in 1506 (the year of Columbus's death), gave astrological charts for navigation below the equator.

Meanwhile, the Muslim maritime threat to the Spanish and Portuguese Christians had lessened—but it was not eliminated. Consequently, as da Gama was returning from India with his diminished crew, he deliberately burned one ship in Cape Verdean waters to prevent it from falling into Muslim hands. In 1501, Ottoman sailors captured seven Spanish ships off the coast of Spain, near Valencia. It was then that the Ottomans first acquired knowledge of the New World and Atlantic archipelagos. The famous map drawn in 1513 by the Turk Piri Reis showed the Cape Verde Islands with notable precision in location, and the Portuguese names for the islands were given, written in Arabic script.

Under the authority of a papal bull in 1533, the Portuguese elevated the town of Ribeira Grande to the status of *cidade* ("city") and created a regional bishopric in Cape Verde. Parallel to the civil authority, this bishopric regulated religious matters over the islands and along the coast wherever the Portuguese were based. From these early days until the late nineteenth century, the islands were inseparable from the coast in their linked economies, political and religious administration, cultural borrowings, and human connections.

Although papal orders initially managed to keep the Spanish somewhat restricted on the coast, the English began to interlope in the 1540s when Captain William Hawkins began to raid and trade for slaves and other commodities. With the desire for gold, ivory, wax, and slaves steadily mounting, the French were also ready to challenge the Portuguese and English. In 1542, French naval raiders attacked the Cape Verde Islands to loot and to test the Portuguese military, which was simultaneously engaged in combat with Muslims battling Portugal's allies in distant Christian Ethiopia.

The formal arrival of the bishop of Cape Verde and the Guinea coast in 1550 did little to curb the mounting European hunger for regional treasures and trade. The Dutch entered the arena in the 1550s by seizing Portuguese *feitorias* at Arguin, at Gorée, and at São Jorge Al Mina. Little by little, the English, French, and Dutch began a long process of eroding Portuguese control of both the Upper and Lower Guinea coasts, which the Portuguese had monopolized for approximately a century.

By the sixteenth century, the pattern of governance and settlement in Cape Verde had crystallized into a more effective and permanent *capitania* system with a slave plantation economy. The evolving communities in the Cape Verde Islands deepened their roots through small-scale agriculture, maritime support activities, and a modest export trade. Reluctantly, they became habituated to attacks by their European rivals, just as they had grown accustomed to the periodic cycles of disease, drought, and famine.

On the coast, the trade competition intensified. The formal Crown claims of Portugal rested on papal bulls of the fifteenth century, but the Portuguese could not effectively control the coast, which was populated by smugglers, free-booters, and *lançados*. (The *lançados*, or "outcasts," were Luso-African traders who made up the core of *Crioulo* culture.) In 1562, John Hawkins, the son of William, substantially enlarged the scope of English slave raiding and trading with the backing of the Crown; he also looted six Portuguese ships in coastal waters. This brought wealth to Hawkins and to the royal English privy purse, and it presented a direct challenge to the Portuguese Crown.

In 1564, Portugal's king abolished the hereditary position of *capitão* of São Tiago after the death of the last man to hold this office. Then, to strengthen his weakened position, he made the post of governor a term appointment—an early step toward more centralization of Lisbon's power. A few years later, in 1576, this evolution was continued when the Cape Verde Islands became Portuguese "provinces," thereby further reducing the semiautonomous status of the land grants awarded to earlier *capitanias*. Nonetheless, given their strategic position, the Cape Verde Islands continued as the administrative and religious headquarters for the Portuguese who were left on the Upper Guinea coast.

Meanwhile, Portugal's royal house was about to suffer two grave reverses. First, King Sebastião was killed in battle during his failed attempt to take Kasr Al Kebir in Morocco in 1578. The news of the loss of 25,000 Portuguese troops in that action reached Francis Drake, who saw in this an opportunity to raid Cape Verde in the same year. Drake had already looted the islands with John Hawkins in earlier years, and both he and fellow Englishman John Lovell would launch a series of raids there through the rest of the century. Second, the horrible defeat in Morocco, pirate attacks in the Atlantic, and a great famine in Cape Verde all added to a domestic crisis in Portugal. These calamities caused such deep anxiety that Portugal's ruling class asked the Portuguese cardinal to assume the throne as King Henrique. The two years of his ill-fated regime, however, only led to the utter collapse of Portugal and to sixty years of rule by the Spanish Hapsburgs, under Kings Phillip II, III, and IV.

Aside from one short-lived revolt on Fogo against the Spanish king, Cape Verdeans carried on with their lives through this period—but not in peace and tranquility. English corsair raids in the islands, for example, persisted in 1582 and 1585. Drake's systematic looting of Praia, Santa Catarina (with a population of 2,500), and Ribeira Grande (population of 1,500) in November 1585 was especially harsh and humiliating. As a result, the first appointed *capitão-geral*, Duarte Lobo da Gama, tried to improve island defenses in 1587. A round of administrative reforms included the 1588 export of the *capitania* system of royal governors to Cacheu on the coast, but the *capitão* of Cacheu was still subordinate to the governor of Cape Verde.

Since the Portuguese were ruled by the Spanish Crown during this period, the news of Francis Drake's stunning and clever defeat of the Spanish Armada may have been welcome news to the pretenders to the Crown. However, for the victims of Drake's Cape Verdean raids and some 14,000 Cape Verdean slaves, this world event made little difference. Sadly, slavery, droughts, famines, and continuing English and Dutch raids in 1598 and subsequent years had become the norm.

Feudalism and Slavery

It is almost impossible to separate the slave labor system in Cape Verde from its feudal economic relations. The slave plantation system rested upon the feudal grants, administration, and legitimacy that was bestowed by the Portuguese Crown upon its local representatives. Each feudal *capitania* or *donatário* ("land grant") was administered to yield a personal profit to the individual *capitão* as well as a direct profit to the Crown. To accomplish this, each *capitão* was allowed a high degree of local authority. With the king far away in Portugal, these individuals were infamous for their abusive rule; Lisbon was hardly concerned with the welfare or human rights of slaves, so the *capitão* was rarely subject to inspection. From the earliest times, the *donatário* plantations were farmed by slave labor, and very often, the exploitative land use led to serious ecological degradation by overgrazing, deforestation, minimal water conservation, and abusive cultivation.

Paralleling the slave economy was the feudal social structure in the islands. Most elements of fifteenth-century Cape Verdean society were modeled after and imported directly from Portuguese feudal society. The highest local authority was the *capitãos;* next in line were the *fidalgos,* or noblemen, who were served by *cavaleiro-fidalgos,* or noble knights, and the *almoxarifes,* who worked as royal stewards and tax collectors. In the lower strata were council servants, petty officers, and manservants.

Portuguese feudal society also included *degredados* ("convicts"), *exterminados* ("forced exiles"), and simply exiles charged with civil or political crimes. Many of these people were exiled to Cape Verde for long terms, a practice that persisted until the twentieth century. Others received royal pardons to become settlers in Cape Verde or on the adjacent coast. There, some were termed *lançados,* a word derived from the Portuguese verb meaning "to throw out" (*lansar*) and related to their status as outcasts or fugitives in Luso-African coastal commerce. Many of the *lançados* were of Jewish origin, and a substantial number of these *degredados* settled in Santo Antão after 1548. In the 1550s and 1560s, many *degredados* were used as rowers in the galleys sent overseas. (In 1620, the Portuguese introduced a policy of sending *degredados* and prostitutes to Cape Verde as part of a "eugenic" effort designed to increase the European gene pool within the islands' burgeoning *mestiço* population—i.e., people of mixed-race backgrounds—but their numbers were too small to have a lasting effect or importance.[23]) At the bottom of Cape Verde's feudal society were the African slaves.

Feudalism also left its traces in the form of large, privately owned tracts of land for agricultural production, or *morgados,* which were transmitted under the principle of primogeniture. As with the *donatários,* injustices committed by the proprietary lords of the *morgados* were well-known. The *morgado* and *capela* ("church-owned") systems of feudal ownership were instituted when the early royal trading companies were closed. However, the *morgado* or latifundia system lingered on even though officially abolished in 1863 and further weakened by land reforms in 1876. Indeed, land ownership in Cape Verde today is still remarkably unequal.

The Slave Trade

Slavery must be put into context—not to justify it but to establish that it was a normal practice for all European, Arab, and African ruling classes in this period, as it had been among virtually all ancient or medieval state societies. The Moors who crossed into the Iberian Peninsula in A.D. 711 brought their slaves and also enslaved Europeans, and the Portuguese and Spaniards had no hesitation in doing likewise.

In the first well-known instance of the Portuguese capture of slaves from the African continent, one may see many dimensions of the slavery experience. Going ashore in southern Morocco or coastal Mauritania en route to Portugal in 1441, Antão Gonçalves attacked a group of local residents. In the ensuing struggle, some Africans fled, others were killed, and at least one Portuguese lost his life. Other Africans were forced onto ships to be taken to Portugal, where some were subsequently ransomed and returned in this inglorious business.

From a modern perspective, there can be no justification for this institutionalized human brutality and degradation. The "beneficiaries" were mainly a small class of royals and merchants, not just in Europe but in Africa as well; the glorious empires of Ghana, Mali, and Songhai, for example, were solidly built on systems of domestic and export slavery. But the slaves, in one way or another, all were prisoners of war or victims of personal greed, poverty, injustice, and brutality.

From the fifteenth to the nineteenth centuries, somewhere between fifteen and twenty-five million Africans were sent to work in the New World. How many died in acts of resistance on African soil or in the "middle passage" across the Atlantic will never be known with precision. Some estimate that for every slave landed in the Americas, at least one other died in Africa, and another 15 to 20 percent died in the crossing. One source states that from 1701 to 1810, English ships alone carried about two million slaves, and the French and Portuguese transported well over 600,000 each.[24]

Although slavery had a long history before the fifteenth century, the Atlantic slave trade system was marked by a substantial increase in scale. Data from Peru and Mexico show that in the first half of the sixteenth century, 74 to 88 percent of the slaves were Africans taken from Senegambia and Guinea-Bissau.[25] Table 2.1 underscores this point. The large number of Wolof can be explained by the high level of regional warfare in Senegambia at the time; later, the Fula people became common victims. More slaves were from Guinea-Bissau because of the military expansion of the Mandinka Kingdom of Gabu against the weaker, coastal Senegambian people.

With their strategic presence on the coast, Cape Verdeans were able to structure a three-part slave system in the islands. Under this system, import-export traders sold *escravos de commercio* ("trade slaves"), slave plantation operators used the labor of *escravos de trabalho* ("work slaves"), and wealthy families used slaves for domestic work. Within Cape Verdean society, slaves were further classified as: (1) *escravos bocais* or *novos* ("African-born, 'stupid' or raw slaves"); (2) *escravos naturais* ("Cape Verdean–born slaves"), and (3) *escravos de confissão* or *ladinos* ("baptized or 'civilized' slaves").[26] Cape Verdeans made other distinctions on the basis of African ethnicity. For instance, Fula girls and young women were favored as domestic servants and concubines, and the Wolof were valued as spinners of cotton. In addition, "free" slaves could work on the coast as *grumete* ("bodyguards" or "local militia"), as *tangomãos* ("translators" or "negotiators"), or as *linguas* ("translators") of the diverse Senegambian languages. The slaves who were imported to Cape Verde would be dispersed or concentrated depending upon market conditions and agricultural needs.

Slaves were not, however, the exclusive focus of economic interest in fifteenth-century Cape Verde. Traders from the islands sailed to the coast to sell colored

TABLE 2.1   Ethnic Origins of African Slaves in the New World, 1526–1550

| | Annual Average Export | |
	Number	Percentage
Senegambians	499	37.6
Wolof	271	20.4
Fula	4	.3
Tekrur	4	.3
Serer	110	8.3
Mandinka	110	8.3
Guinea-Bissau	543	40.8
Cassanga	23	1.7
Banhun	60	4.5
Beafada	249	18.7
Brame	211	15.9
Other places	288	21.6

SOURCE: Adapted from Philip D. Curtin, *The Atlantic Slave Trade: A Census* (Madison: University of Wisconsin Press, 1969), p. 100.

cloth and scarves, paper, salt, wine, bracelets, glass beads, utilitarian metalware (knives, pots, and pans), meat, hides, livestock, and horses. In the late fifteenth and early sixteenth centuries, Cape Verdean horses were highly valued by African nobility and cavalries—one horse was worth ten to fourteen hardy slaves—but further into the sixteenth century, their value slipped—a horse could be traded for only 6 or 7 slaves.[27] On their return voyage, the traders and smugglers carried cowhides, rice, grains, dyewoods, amber, iron, cotton, honey, beeswax, food supplies, ivory, gold, and, of course, slaves. Despite the risks of these voyages, the profits were high at each point of the trading cycle.

In the islands themselves, the limited scope of plantation agriculture meant that a labor force of 5,000 to 14,000 slaves for the entire archipelago was sufficient to handle domestic work; construction labor; the harvesting of sugar, cotton, and coffee; dock work; and salt and puzzolane mining operations. By the early sixteenth century, if not before, slaves also collected plant dyes, indigo, orchil, and urzella in the islands. These crops were usually exported under a private commercial charter issued by the Crown, but they were also important as dyes in the production of the *pano* cloths that Cape Verdeans used to trade for more slaves.

Portugal was the first European nation to initiate slavery in Africa, and it was the last to abolish it. And clearly, in one way or another, slavery was central to Cape Verde's social institutions and its economy. Even the decision to relocate the Cape Verdean capital from Ribeira Grande to the better protected city of Praia in 1652 was motivated, in part, by the desire to allow more slave ships to enter the harbor in greater security. Although this meant that the old slave entrepôt of Ribeira Grande would fall into ruin, eventually becoming known simply as Cidade Velha ("the Old City"), the shift in capitals brought improved security for

TABLE 2.2   Sixteenth- and Seventeenth-Century Slave Ships to Cape Verde

	Number of Ships Recorded	Average Number of Slaves per Ship	Average or Total Number of Slaves Shipped per Year
1513	7	55	382
1514	14	97	1,354
1515	16	88	1,404
1528	14	107	1,491
1601–1640			400
1641–1670			225
1671–1770			175

SOURCES: T. Bentley Duncan, *Atlantic Islands* (Chicago: University of Chicago Press, 1972), pp. 200–201 and 210; Luís de Albuquerque and Maria Emília Madeira Santos, coordinators, *Historia Geral de Cabo Verde*, vol. 1 (Lisbon: Centro de Estudos de História e Cartografia Antiga, Instituto de Investigação Científica Tropica, 1991), pp. 264–267, 294, and 296.

the slave trade. It also made life safer for those who collected royal taxes on slaves and other goods—the main sources of Crown revenue from the islands and the coast.

In the late fifteenth and early sixteenth centuries, a maximum of about 1,000 slaves were exported to the Atlantic islands and Europe each year. The data in Table 2.2 illustrate the scale of slave commerce between the Guinea coast and São Tiago, where the regional Crown monopoly was based. Profits were derived not only by the slave traders operating under the authority of the monopoly but also through the taxation of imported slaves and of the goods and services they produced.

The volume of the slave trade was not, however, constant: In some years during the early 1600s, only 400 to 500 slaves were exported out of Cape Verde and its coastal lands; in other years during the seventeenth century, there may have been as many as 6,000, if figures from all the slaving *companhias* ("companies") and smugglers are added together. Varying numbers of slaves were kept in the islands; others were quickly reexported to New World markets. How many slaves were smuggled as illegal contraband will never be fully known.

No one could anticipate the still greater regional upsurge in slaving from the middle to late sixteenth century into the seventeenth century. During this period, the total export of slaves from the Upper Guinea coast often reached some 5,000 a year. Perhaps one-third of these were sent to the Cape Verde Islands, but most did not stay there; instead, they were reexported, as suggested by Philip Curtin's data on slaves shipped from the region to the Americas. Other statistics provided by Curtin for the period 1551–1640 in Cape Verde show that 26,670 slaves were exported in this eighty-nine-year period, or an average of 299 slaves per year. But Cape Verdean rule also extended to the coast, where 65,400 more slaves were loaded (for an additional 734 per year). The combined total of 1,033 slaves exported annually is consistent with the early sixteenth-century portion of the data in Tables 2.2 and 2.3.

TABLE 2.3   Number of Spanish Slave Ships Departing Cape Verde and Guinea, 1551–1640

	Cape Verde and Guinea	Lower Guinea Coast
1551–1570	64	0
1571–1590	66	33
1591–1610	264	300
1611–1625	48	225
1626–1640	6	216

SOURCE: Adapted from Philip D. Curtin, *The Atlantic Slave Trade: A Census* (Madison: University of Wisconsin Press, 1969), p. 104.

These data reveal the overwhelming dominance of Senegambia and Guinea as sources for slaves in the 1500s and early 1600s. As the seventeenth century progressed, a greater overall portion of slaves originated in Angola, São Tomé, the Gold Coast (Ghana), Whydah (Dahomey), and the Slave Coast (Nigeria). By the end of that century, the portion of slaves from Senegambia and Guinea had fallen to 6 percent of the total according to slave population data from México or 18 percent in a small database from French Guiana.[28]

One result of slavery was a racial admixture, which can be seen in a 1582 São Tiago census. Jean Boulegue has listed a population of 600 whites and mulattos, 400 free blacks, and 5,000 slaves in Ribeira Grande, and George Brooks states that the population of Praia included 1,000 slaves and 200 residents. The interior plantation areas had 5,000 slaves and 1,000 residents; neighboring Fogo had 2,000 slaves and 300 residents. António Carreira remarks that only a mere 12.7 percent of the entire population of São Tiago and Fogo were free.[29]

Because of this level of slaving activity along the Guinea coast, the Portuguese Crown sought to reassert its control. The king awarded a six-year trade monopoly to António de Barros Bezerra in May 1675 in the name of the Companhia do Cacheu e Rios de Guiné, which was based in Bissau. The monopoly was extended until 1706, when it finally failed. One reason for its failure was the deep opposition expressed by local *lançados,* who resented this intervention in their commerce. At the time, the demand for slaves was so great that slave smugglers could not resist efforts to bypass the Crown tariffs, thereby undermining hopes for limitless profits for "legal" Portuguese commerce. It was not long before Bissau fell into neglect, and in the sixteenth and seventeenth centuries, Portugal saw a further erosion of its coastal bases due to English attacks. By this point, Portugal was mounting a holding action at best. Dutch attacks in the 1620s and 1630s resulted in Portugal's loss of possessions in the Caribbean, at Al Mina, and at Arguin. Trying another approach, the Portuguese signed a peace treaty with England in 1635.

The hard-pressed Portuguese in Cape Verde eliminated the corrupt system of private tax collection in 1656 and instead appointed a tax-collecting officer who was directly responsible to the Crown. To respond to the virtual anarchy in the slave trade, the Portuguese governor of Cape Verde elevated the coastal town of Bissau to the status of a captaincy-general in 1692. It was hoped that Bissau would link Portuguese merchants at Cacheu to the north and Bolama to the south. By 1696, the small town at Bissau held a fort, church, and hospital and controlled trade to the interior on the relatively long Geba and Corubal Rivers.

Effectively, however, the trade remained largely in the hands of sometimes renegade *lançados* and their *grumetes*. About a dozen settlers from Cape Verde were assigned to Bissau each year in the early eighteenth century; later, this number rose to forty per year, but most settlers were discouraged by a high deathrate from tropical diseases and frequent attacks on their ports and forts by neighboring Africans.

Taking advantage of Portugal's weaknesses, the French corsair *Jacques Cassard* launched a heavy attack against Ribeira Grande and Praia in May 1712, which caused much property loss. The French also cut deeply into the Portuguese slave trade, and by 1723, they were sailing some 200 slave brigantines from the Guinea coast in a typical year. The English also pressured the Portuguese more heavily in the early 1700s, exploring further and occupying the Gambia River in their search for peanuts, wax, horns, ivory, gold, hides, honey, and slaves.

Following their early-seventeenth-century expulsion of Dutch and French rivals in northern Brazil, the Portuguese again turned to Crown-backed slave trading companies to import African labor for agriculture and mining in Brazil. The depression in Portugal's economy from the 1670s to the 1690s caused all these companies to fail, but from 1685 to 1689, the Portuguese granted trade rights to a French *feitor* based in Bissau to allow the shipment of 2,800 slaves per year. The Crown also chartered the Companhia das Ilhas do Cabo Verde e Guiné in 1690; its more extensive trade monopoly reached even Calabar in modern Nigeria. This firm exported African products and about 4,000 slaves annually until it failed in 1706.[30] By the mid-1700s, some 20,000 slaves were arriving in Brazil each year, and approximately two million were exported between 1700 and 1820 to grow cotton and mine gold in the New World.[31]

Other nationalities began to appear in the Cape Verde Islands and on the Guinea coast in the late seventeenth century. These included English-American merchants who were now sailing from New England as often as from the British Isles. To circumvent English rule, the commercially ambitious New England traders often turned to smuggling slaves and rum in their struggle for economic freedom, a struggle that led, of course, to the American Revolution in 1776.

With the largest proportion of Cape Verdean Americans still concentrated in New England, it is notable that as early as the seventeenth century, this region led in the trade and transport of slaves. For example, from 1725 to 1807 Rhode Island was continously involved as "the principal American carrier."[32] From 1709 to 1807, a minimum of 106,544 slaves were carried in 934 known Rhode Island slave voyages.[33] The tie between southeastern New England and Cape Verde can also be seen in Newport, where some of the prominent slave traders were Portuguese Jews (such as Aaron Lopes, his father-in-law Jacob Rivera, and Mose Levy) who relied on the connections with their *lançado* counterparts.[34]

In the eighteenth century, most Rhode Island slavers found their cargos either on the Guinea coast or at a stop in Cape Verde.[35] Meanwhile, taxes levied in Newport on West African slave imports were so substantial in the first decades of the century that they funded large-scale public works, such as street construction and repair.[36] The population of slaves in Rhode Island reached 11.6 percent by 1756, the largest proportion of slaves in the north.[37] From 1698 to 1708, 103 ships were built in Rhode Island, with the majority of these used in the West African Triangle trade. This commerce spawned a diversity of subsidiary maritime and agricultural activities in Rhode Island. Above all, there was rum production: About 28 rum stills operated in Rhode Island in the eighteenth century, and almost 11 million gallons of rum (or 1,800 hogsheads annually) were sent to Africa for the barter of still more slaves.[38]

The Brazil–Cape Verde Connection

The "enlightened despotism" of the new Portuguese prime minister under King José I (1750–1777) brought still greater change to the vast colonial empire.[39] As prime minister, the marquis of Pombal, Sebastião José de Carvalho e Melo brought a new age of modernization, secularism, and free trade that linked Brazil, Cape Verde, and Guinea. In the wake of the attempted assassination of King José in 1758, the marquis reduced some feudal privileges and greatly centralized a more secular state, under his Laws of Good Reason. A kingdom police authority was established in 1760, and a royal treasury was begun in 1761. In addition, a rigorously censored royal printing press began operating in 1768, and a new university system was founded. Slavery was formally abolished—but only in Portugal. In Cape Verde, some feudal *donatários* were sold, slavery was intensified, and the administration's authority and power were expanded. The administrative center was also relocated from Ribeira Grande to Praia to be more responsive to Portugal's colonial needs on both sides of the Atlantic.[40]

When the marquis of Pombal rose in power in 1750, he was clearly bent on formally ending the Inquisition and feudalism and bringing Portugal into the modern age. With respect to Cape Verde and its adjoining Guinea, the marquis organized a new Crown-backed trading monopoly, the Companhia Geral do Grão Pará e Maranhão, (based in Brazil but legalized in Lisbon), which was designed to achieve the economic development of two northern, coastal Brazilian states by importing slaves from Cape Verde. Some of the company's eighteenth-century records are still located in Praia.

In 1752, under the approval of the Overseas Council, the Brazilian *capitanias* were given a monopoly in Cape Verde and the remaining coastal areas of Guinea for the trade in slaves, orchil, and *panos*.[41] The royal *Companhia Geral*, operating under the marquis, dominated the Cape Verdean economy for a quarter century. The extent of its involvement in Cape Verde is made clear in records showing that 28,167 slaves were shipped from 1756 to 1778, that 2,284 tons of orchil were exported from 1759 to 1774, and that 133,265 Cape Verdean *panos* were shipped mainly from the islands of Fogo and São Tiago to the coast between 1757 and 1782.[42]

Brazil's economic development was greatly enhanced by the *companhia*, especially in the production of rice, cotton, potatoes, sugar, cacao, hides, wood, and gold. The growth of U.S. industrialism and the American Revolution added to the demand for such agricultural products, which were produced largely by slaves routed through Cape Verde. By 1759, the *companhia* controlled some forty-one sailing vessels to transport slaves from West Africa and ship its diverse products to North America and Portugal for further processing and sale.

Notably, during the time of the marquis of Pombal, Cape Verde became a preferred entrepôt for slave traders, notwithstanding the inflated prices for slaves there. By stopping in the Cape Verde Islands, the slave buyers and sellers had a somewhat shorter Atlantic voyage, with less coastal cruising. Collecting a coastal slave cargo required frequent or delayed port calls, which entailed a greater exposure to tropical diseases and more opportunities for slave revolts and mutinies. The newly captured slaves were still *pretos bocais* (i.e., newly arrived "stupid black" slaves): Their spirit of rebellion was not yet oppressed, unlike the "seasoned" *ladinos* who more readily accepted their lowly position in the social hierarchy.

Initially, the *companhia* had a twenty-year lease on the Bolama-based slave trade in Guinea-Bissau, with provisions for extension, and its regional base was in Cape Verde. The large scale of its operations, brutal treatment of slaves, great amounts of wealth generated, and distant supervision by the king inevitably led to abuses and corruption. The *companhia* ended in 1778, a year after the marquis fell from power. It was succeeded by a new entity named the Sociedade Exclusiva do Comércio de Cabo Verde, which revived the slave trade until it too failed, in 1786.

During the American Revolution, particularly from 1778 to 1779, American corsairs attacked English targets in West Africa, and the Portuguese expressed a degree of sympathy for the American cause. However, by the early 1800s, England, France, and other European nations were beginning to end the slave trade for various moral and economic reasons—hardly a positive development for the slave traders of Guinea and Cape Verde (see Table 2.3). The French revolutionary fervor had helped to justify France's attack on Brava Island in 1798 in an attempt to dislodge the Portuguese influence there and on the coast. And America and the European nations that were pioneering in industrial mass production—using such devices as the cotton gin and mechanical loom, as well as wage labor and "legitimate" trade—were entering the long process that steadily undermined the economic structure of slavery.

If the supply of industrial raw materials and the mass markets were to grow, the perpetual coastal warfare required to generate slaves had to be restricted. Regional peace was necessary to the sale of manufactured goods. Moreover, uncompensated slaves were excluded from the cash and market economy, which capitalists wished to expand by transforming barter exchange to a monetized system.

Examination of the 1856 Cape Verde slave registers show that Senegambians, particularly those from Guinea-Bissau, continued to make up the largest single share of the slaves there (see Table 2.4). One exception was the Mandinka, who made up only 8.3 percent of the slaves in the 1526–1550 period, when the Mandinka state of Gabu was actively raiding for slaves. But by 1856, jihads of the Islamic Fula caused the portion of Mandinka to rise to 22.6 percent.

The 1856 data also show how the slave system functioned within the islands. Owning slaves was not the lot for most Cape Verdeans: Only a few hundred of the wealthier and landed families, absentee landowners, and nobility had sufficient means to afford such unsalaried servants and laborers. And beyond any wealth they might generate for their owners, slaves were also something of a social marker, indicating status or luxury. Indeed, an effort to understand slavery strictly on economic terms will overlook its complex, institutionalized nature. Of those who owned slaves, about a third had only one or two to perform domestic chores. (Since half or more of the entire slave population was female, this was still a very great number.) If one includes all slaves held in Cape Verde at this time, the average slave staff was three or four.

Although some gangs of slaves did toil in the fields and mines, rarely in Cape Verde did a single proprietor hold twenty or thirty slaves. In fact, the largest island plantation was the only place where forty or sixty slaves worked on a single farm. The colonial state held slaves for labor on public works and in construction, and the Catholic Church owned slaves for cultivating *capela* lands and maintaining church buildings. Many high church officials were also known to have fathered dozens of children with their slave concubines.

Social relations within the Cape Verdean slave system ranged from outright oppression and brutality, with almost no independence of action tolerated, to a comparatively benevolent paternalism. Freed slaves or runaways, termed *badius*, were generally viewed with indifference in the remote hills as long as they kept to themselves and pursued self-sufficient agriculture. The rapid creation of a Crioulo population of free children, born to slave mothers, led to increasingly subtle but complex interpersonal relations, which linger on in modern Cape Verde's society.

The 1856 data describe Cape Verdean slavery in its closing phases. The slave labor force was still rather large then, but African replacements had begun to decline. Most slaves at this time had been born into their status, and many were be-

TABLE 2.4   Ethnic Origins of Africans in the Slave Trade, 1856

Ethnic Group or Place of Origin	Number	Percentage
Mandinka (Bambara)	33	22.6

Senegambians
   outside Guinea-Bissau (Salum, Gorée, Costa da
   Mina, Jalof, Gambia)
   inside Guinea-Bissau (Balantas, Bissagos, Beafadas,
   Felupes, Papels, Brames, Bololas, Manjacos, etc.)
	9
	
	84
		6.1
		
		57.5

Fula (Toro)	12	8.2
Cape Verde Islands	3	2.0
Miscellaneous	5	3.4

Gender: males, 87; females, 51; unspecified, 6, N = 144

SOURCE: Calculated from data in the 1856 Registry of Slaves, Cape Verde National Historical Archives, Praia, Cape Verde.

ing manumitted. Individual records detail the slave's characteristics, occupation, ethnic origin, migration, ownership, and taxable value. At this time, increasing numbers of slaves fled to the interior.

The data in Table 2.5 reveal that Fogo and São Tiago—the islands with the largest plantations—not only had the greatest overall slave populations but also the most slaves per owner. The relative prominence of Sal in numbers of slaves per proprietor is due to its heavy demand for labor in salt production; this island had few other export commodities. Brava had the third greatest number of slaves overall, but also the lowest ratio of slaves to proprietors. This suggests that the majority of the slaves of Brava were in domestic service rather than agricultural or salt production. When the 1856 data on slaves are broken down by sex, it is clear that the overall slave population of the archipelago had a greater number of females (see Table 2.6). This implies a somewhat heavier reliance on female domestic servants rather than male plantation workers. The relatively small mean number of 3.49 slaves per owner demonstrates the fairly small scale of slavery in the islands. However, the overall number of slave owners reminds us of its extensiveness.

The officially recognized slave population for 1856 was 5,180, which was probably fairly typical for the later years. By contrast, sixteenth-century census put the slave population of Cape Verde at 13,700. This much higher figure was typical in the earlier centuries, but after the creation of a Crioulo peasantry, the number of slave laborers declined.

The age profile of the 1856 slave population can be constructed from a more limited database of 1,519 individuals whose ages were recorded (see Table 2.7). The two largest age groups, 10 years or younger, and 20 to 30 years, were probably Cape Verdean–born slaves for the most part, and the older group likely included more African-born slaves.

TABLE 2.5   Number of Slaves in Cape Verde with Known Origins, 1856

	From Same Cape Verde Island	From Other Cape Verde Islands	From Elsewhere in Africa	Totals	Number of Slaves per Owner
São Tiago	902	54	238	1,194	4.41
Fogo	720	5	54	779	4.37
Sal	60	66	33	159	4.28
Boa Vista	66	14	48	128	3.35
São Nicolau	109	19	31	159	2.54
São Antão	136	33	21	190	2.46
São Vicente	4	21	7	31	2.28
Brava	144	47	39	230	1.95

SOURCE: Calculated from data in the 1856 Registry of Slaves, Cape Verde National Historical Archives, Praia, Cape Verde, Books 327–337.

Since slaves were taxed as imports, exports, and private property, the authorities took great care in measuring their value. The most valuable were young men with job skills; the least valued were the unskilled elderly. The 1856 data show that the highest prices were paid for slaves between 20 and 40 years of age; ranging from 115 to 200 escudos (see Table 2.8). Prices for slaves between 10 and 15 years of age ranged from 65 to 100 escudos, and those over 70 might sell for as little as 20 to 35 escudos.

Documents on a few legal cases involving disputes between slave and master still survive. They show that "justice" almost always worked against the slave. There are no data to indicate how frequently the public whipping post still standing in the plaza at Ribeira Grande was used, but it is hard to imagine that such a large, rather ornate, and sturdily fashioned public structure was simply symbolic. Presumably, the daily labor routine and the overriding institutions and values of the slave system provided sufficient oppression for all to "know their place" and regularly accept the "appropriate" behavioral norms.

As the nineteenth century drew to a close, virtually all slaves were manumitted, or they simply fled into the interior. Their descendants became crioulized sharecroppers, tenant farmers, contract laborers, sailors, whalers, and, when possible and necessary, permanent emigrants. Over time, merchants had discovered that

TABLE 2.6   Inventory of Registered Slaves by Gender and Owners, 1856

	Number
Male slaves	2,300
Female slaves	2,442
Total number of slaves	4,742
Slave owners	1,358
Average number of slaves per owner	3.49

SOURCE: Calculated from data in the 1856 Registry of Slaves, Cape Verde National Historical Archives, Praia, Cape Verde.

TABLE 2.7   Age Profile of the 1856 Slave Population

	Males	Females	Both
Over 70 years	4	4	8
60–70	17	6	23
50–60	38	23	61
40–50	78	54	132
30–40	114	108	222
20–30	172	184	362
10–20	162	187	349
10 or younger	174	188	362
Totals	771	748	1,519

SOURCE: Calculated from data in the 1856 Registry of Slaves, Cape Verde National Historical Archives, Praia, Cape Verde.

slavery was costly in numerous ways. For example, slaves had to be maintained even during seasons when the demand for agricultural labor was low; some slavers found that hiring "free" labor at very cheap prices was far more economical in the long run, for their labor costs could simply be passed on to the consumer. In addition, the racist ideologies and brutal practices of slavery stimulated resistance and slave revolts that were sometimes costly to put down. Yet another cost was incurred when privately owned slaves were executed or maimed.

Elsewhere in the eighteenth and nineteenth centuries, related events steadily gained momentum and ultimately converged to force the obsolete system of slavery to be discarded at last. The abolitionist movement grew out of moral and ethical concerns raised during the Renaissance and the social revolutions in America, France, and Haiti. In the new United States, the Continental Congress passed an ordinance in 1783 forbidding slavery in the Northwest Territories, and the New England states, the early leaders in shipping slaves, also began abolishing slavery in the 1770s and 1780s.

Yet in 1788, of the 202 vessels that entered the port of Praia, 74 were registered in the United States, and other U.S. vessels called at Sal and Maio.[43] It is not clear how many of these were dealing in slaves, but private Rhode Island slave shippers were certainly among them. As an indicator, data from Charleston, South Carolina, indicate that 202 slave ships entered that port between 1804 and 1807, 59 of them owned by Rhode Islanders.[44]

Nonetheless, the abolitionist movement was gaining momentum. The slaveholding state of Virginia passed a resolution in 1800 that proposed sending slaves back to Africa, and in 1807, the United States formally prohibited the slave trade. By 1811, even U.S. President Thomas Jefferson, a slaveholder himself, proposed sending free blacks back to Africa. And Spain soon joined the movement, promoting a compromise position to end slavery north of the equator after 1817.

In the dynamism of those times, the first U.S. consul to Cape Verde was formally accepted by the Portuguese governor of the islands, in Praia in 1818. Per-

TABLE 2.8   Slave Price Ranges by Age

	Price (in 1856 escudos, Praia)
10–15 years	65–100$ 000
15–20	100–140$ 000
20–40	115–200$ 000
40–50	90–140$ 000
50–60	70–90$ 000
60–70	40–70$ 000
Over 70	20–35$ 000

SOURCE: Calculated from data in the 1856 Registry of Slaves, Cape Verde National Historical Archives, Praia, Cape Verde.

haps, in the wake of the War of 1812, it was hoped this consul, allied with wealthy Cape Verdean merchants such as Manuel Martins, would help improve the competition with British trade. Formally, this consular office was supposed to observe and register foreign and U.S. vessels, transmit diplomatic news, and serve the needs of the endless numbers of U.S. seamen stranded in the islands. The first U.S. consul, Samuel Hodges of Stoughton, Massachusetts, provided a rich and revealing history of early-nineteenth-century Cape Verde in his collected letters. Consul Hodges's letters to U.S. Secretary of State John Quincy Adams described some of the circumstances he faced.

On 22 October 1819, he wrote: "The slave trade is now carried on to an unprecedented degree,—and most of the Vessels that touch here from Havanna, bound to the coast of Africa, have on board an American, who reports himself as a passenger; but who is the real Captain of Supercargo." On 4 February 1820, he reported that he had found the register of a Baltimore sloop after its captain, David Newell, was murdered in Boa Vista, where he had fraudulently obtained the ship "with the view of compelling [a Captain Brown] to sell the sloop to be employed in the slave trade, in which he succeeded."

On 25 February 1820, Hodges wrote to Adams:

At a personal conference with His Excellency the Governor General of these islands last evening, he desired me to make known to the American Government, that in consequence of the Patriot Privateers who are often about these Islands, invariably hoisting American colours and plundering Portuguese Vessels thus disguised as Americans, and in several instances have fired shot into the harbors, particularly Praya, that he should treat as *Ships of War* and other suspicious Vessels under *American colours as Pirates.*

The importance of Cape Verde to U.S. regional commerce in the early nineteenth century cannot be overstated. Nor should America's role as an economic lifeline to Cape Verde be overlooked. When the United States was emerging as a maritime power, it had no serious claims to African ports or territories, and it therefore needed friendly ports of call in which to sell its growing line of products. At the same time, Americans were keen to buy ivory, ginger, peppers, beeswax and honey, gum senegal, palm oil, gold and silver, hides and pelts, exotic birds and wildlife, camwood, plant dyes (such as orchil, indigo, and urzella), and dyewoods.[45] Moreover, U.S. captains would often sail from New England, particularly from Providence and New Bedford, to sail to the Cape Verde Islands to recruit additional crew members—men who were eager to leave their impoverished homes and work on sealing, whaling, and fishing boats. Whether in the fictional characters of *Moby Dick* or as longshoremen, mariners, and harpooners, Cape Verdeans were present for at least two centuries.

By 1816, the expanding needs of the United States led to the appointment of U.S. vice consuls in São Vicente and even tiny Brava. Three years later, the U.S. Congress ratified a law to return slaves captured at sea back to Africa via Liberia, as the French were doing in Libreville in Gabon and the British were doing at Freetown in Sierra Leone. Notably, however, the Portuguese never had an equivalent repatriation haven for freed slaves. By 1833, the British had expanded the prohibition on slaving to include their overseas colonies. With the major powers now favoring abolition, the momentum was too strong for the process to be halted. But the Portuguese government and slave traders in Cape Verde and the coast were remarkably reluctant to follow suit.

The slave trade in Guinea declined somewhat in the 1820s and 1830s, but it certainly continued, as is shown in a remarkable diary kept by a Captain Conneau during his slaving experiences in West Africa from 1819 through the 1840s. He revealed that during his stops in Cape Verde, he slyly changed his ships' flags from American to Portuguese or Spanish to avoid the English antislave cruisers. Even in these late years of the trade in "blackbirds" (a widely used, colloquial term for slaves at the time), Conneau often dealt with Portuguese-speaking mulattoes and Jewish merchants in Guinea and Sierra Leone.[46]

The strong Cape Verdean presence on the coast at this time was exemplified in the person of Colonel Honório Pereira Barreto (1813–1859), the first Cape Verdean–born governor of Portuguese Guinea. He had been appointed as the superintendent of the Portuguese fort at Cacheu in 1834 and was the governor of Cacheu and Bissau in 1837. Barreto actively defended the Portuguese colonial and economic interests against the intrusions of the French and British. Clearly, Cape Verdeans were not only functioning informally in the Guinean economy at this point; they had also become part of the official administration.

During the Barreto administration, much of the long-standing Anglo-Portuguese conflict involving the fortified slave trading centers at Bolama and in the Bissagos Islands was located in today's Guinea-Bissau. Having been expelled earlier, the Portuguese returned to Bolama in 1828 to fortify the town and to restore their control. In 1835, a Bissau-based Portuguese merchant named Caetano José Nosolini was allowed by Governor Barreto to establish a large plantation in the neighboring Bissagos Islands, using 300 slaves from the mainland. The British protested and in 1837 sent the naval briganteen *The Brisk* to cut down the Portu-

Honório Barreto, first Cape Verdean governor of Guinea-Bissau (Photo by author)

guese flag and hoist the Union Jack. In turn, Governor Barreto issued numerous protests to the British in the late 1830s and early 1840s, especially after a British attack on Nosolini's plantation resulted in the freeing of all his slaves. The conflict was clearly destabilizing: From 30 November to 5 December 1842, a *grumete* rebellion raged in Bissau until it was put down by Governor Barreto. In this case and others, most Cape Verdeans seemed to identify with the colonial system and with slave trading and ownership, but Guineans or more "African-oriented" Cape Verdeans saw colonialism as part of their problem rather than a means of salvation. The role of Barreto is still hotly debated in discussions of the cultural identity of Cape Verdeans. Despite the legislation aimed at bringing the slave trade to a conclusion, Barreto and Nosolini actually allowed it to linger.

However, as the "legitmate trade" in commodities grew in the 1840s and 1850s, the slave trade was increasingly undermined. The 1843 agreement signed between Britain and Portugal on Boa Vista, calling for the abolition of slavery, was another step in this direction, but it was also an implicit admission of how little had been accomplished in the preceding years.[47]

Trade between West Africa and the United States stayed strong through the 1850s, especially that involving hides, copal, wax, ivory, and salt. Ironically, however, even as the nation was about to begin a protracted civil war against the slave-holding South, the slave trade persisted. According to one British report, 74 out of

170 slaving expeditions between 1859 and 1862 originated in New York, and another 43 came from other U.S. ports; this was far more than from Cuban or European ports.[48] And the New England towns of Boston, New Bedford, Portland, and Salem lagged only somewhat behind New York in slave shipping.[49] But despite this brief upsurge, the final collapse of the slave trade was at hand.

The Final Collapse of Slavery in Cape Verde

That a new era of enlightenment was being born was symbolized by the advent of the first commercial printing operation in Cape Verde in 1842. A few years later, in the 1850s, Brava began an early secondary school, which attracted students from throughout the archipelago and from Guinea-Bissau. In 1866, the influential seminary in São Nicolau was opened.

Under the Treaty of Washington, ratified in August 1842, the U.S. Navy was authorized to establish an African Squadron to be based in the Cape Verde Islands from 1843 to 1859. The squadron was charged with curtailing the trade in African slaves by using a fleet of sailing cruisers. The U.S. antislavery policy allowed suspected ships to be boarded and their slaves seized. Supposedly, the squadron functioned jointly with British seamen under similar orders, but communication between the two groups was poor.

This phase of the abolition effort had its origins in the earlier 1815 Anglo-Portuguese Treaty of Vienna and the 1819 Anglo-American Treaty. But even in the 1840s and 1850s, the slave trading interests within the United States and Portugal consistently sabotaged the treaties. Furthermore, these nations would not agree to mutual inspection of each other's vessels.

In fact, mutual inspection had been proposed by James DeWolfe, a U.S. senator and major slave trader from Bristol, Rhode Island. The compromised nature of this relationship between commerce and politics is underscored by the fact that DeWolfe was also related by marriage to Matthew Perry, the first commander of the U.S. Africa Squadron in Cape Verde.[50] Moreover, the secretary of the U.S. Navy in 1843 was Abel B. Upshur—a Southerner who strongly supported slave ownership. Upshur assigned only four or five poorly equipped ships, carrying eighty guns, for the Africa Squadron. The squadron's annual budget of $250,000 was lower than that of any foreign sailing squadron. Upshur insisted on a conservative policy that placed the highest priority on protecting U.S. lives, commerce, and ships, thereby limiting the possible effectiveness of the squadron's captains. Thus, given the deep structural bias toward slave trading, it is not surprising that the Africa Squadron was largely symbolic and ineffective.

Clearly, the squadron's task was complicated by the fact that its ships were harbored in the Cape Verde Islands, where slave ownership was common. Some of the cruisers, such as the *Preble, Perry,* and *Jamestown,* were based in São Tiago; others were at São Vicente. At times, the U.S. sailors approached a slave ship flying

Small Catholic church built in 1855, Sal Island (Photo by author)

the Portuguese flag, knowing full well that the "innocent passenger" aboard was an American who owned the vessel. Americans intending to load slaves would simply wait until the Africa Squadron cruisers had departed the area, or they would fly the Portuguese flag, taking advantage of the protocol that allowed sailors on U.S. cruisers to board U.S. flagships only.

While Captain William Perry was commander of the Africa Squadron, from 1843 to 1845, only one slaver was reported captured, and this ship was later freed by a New Orleans court. But on 5 November 1844, cruisers of the Africa Squadron were called from Cape Verde to intervene in Bissau to protect U.S. interests there. Remarkably, the U.S. agent in Bissau at the time was none other than the slave plantation operator Caetano José Nosolini.[51] Clearly, the antislavery mission of the Africa Squadron was fundamentally compromised when the interests of a major slave owner were to be protected. Such complex relationships were common in the region during this period.

Over its sixteen years of operation, only nineteen slavers were actually brought to trial. Among those cases that went to trial, four of the accused were released and the others only had to pay small fines or serve light jail terms. When the squadron was disbanded in 1859, its ships carried a total of 113 guns. But the inflated prices for slaves, given their relative scarcity, still made smuggling irresistably profitable to some. It was not until 1869 that Portugal ordered an immediate end to slavery in all remaining parts of it empire.

Meanwhile, for more than thirty years, the Bolama conflict simmered. Various acts of violence occurred, and ownership of the island of Bolama shifted back and forth between England and Portugal. The death of Cape Verdean Governor Barreto in 1859 left the local Guinea-Bissau administration weak, but the Portuguese persisted in rejecting the British claim that they, not the Portuguese, "owned" Bolama. In frustration, the Anglo-Portuguese dispute over Bolama was sent to U.S. President Ulysses S. Grant for arbitration. Grant ruled in favor of Portugal and the British withdrew in January 1869. (Until very recently, there was a statue of President Grant in Bolama, commemorating this favorable ruling.) To improve their restored administration, the Cape Verdean authorities then gave Bolama and Bissau the status of *comunas,* or urban units of local colonial administration (making them two of only four *comunas* in Guinea-Bissau), so they could intensify efforts to "pacify" and colonize the local population. When the administration of Guinea-Bissau was fully separated from Cape Verde for the first time in 1879, the capital at Geba was transferred to Bolama and later to Bissau.

Cape Verde: The Colonial Inheritance

The conflict over Bolama was soon dwarfed by the great conference of colonial powers in Berlin from 1884 to 1885. Representatives from Portugal, France, England, Spain, Italy, Belgium, and Germany, as well as U.S. observers, met to establish the territorial divisions of the entire African continent. The dominant European powers were determined to bring a new day to Africa, even though no African representative was on hand.[52]

The result was a European scramble for territory on which they could renew or stake their claims if they could demonstrate effective control. As in the Portuguese case, the European presence in Africa had historically been limited to offshore islands, riverbanks, and coastal enclaves for the most part. Little could these masterful empire builders imagine that less than a century later, Portugal would consist only of its mainland territory and the Azores and Madeira archipelagos.

Now, armed with modern firearms and great expectations of wealth to be had for the taking, the European powers eyed Africa hungrily. The rush to Africa's interior would soon be under way. If African peoples resisted, they would be crushed in "pacification" missions and "punitive" campaigns. The European forces had Gatling guns and steam-powered ships and trains at their disposal, with which they could enforce policies that were often genocidal in practice. Moreover, where the climate or natural resources were especially favorable, European settlers would begin to arrive in greater numbers, complicating African politics and history for a century to come.

The Berlin Congress was dominated by France and England, but claims to African territory were also made by the host nation, Germany, as well as by Portugal, Italy, Spain, and Belgium. Portugal's claim to Cape Verde remained intact, but its presence on the Upper Guinea coast was reduced to the trade forts at Bolama, Bissau, and Cacheu and to a few interior posts. Ultimately, the basic configuration of modern Africa's national boundaries largely resulted from decisions made at the Berlin Congress, with various small, local adjustments made throughout the colonial and postcolonial eras.

As a sequel to the Berlin Congress, another meeting was held in Brussels in 1889–1890. The Brussels agenda focused on antislavery measures, showing there was still unfinished business on this vital issue. The Brussels conference banned the importation of arms and liquors in a zone between 20°N and 22°S of the equator. The conferees urgently wanted this importation to stop so that Africa's territories, resources, and people (and their labor) would be secured for legitimate trade and colonial ambitions.

For the Cape Verdean peasantry, these events probably meant rather little. Poverty and colonial rule by Portugal, which had characterized the entire known history of the islands, continued under the *parceiro* ("sharecropping") and *rendeiro* ("tenant-farming") systems as they replaced the slave plantations. Slave labor was supplanted with *contratados* ("contract labor"), *brigadas de estrada* ("road work gangs"), and *frentes de trabalho* ("unskilled labor force"), which persisted until the last days of colonialism in 1975. So, too, did intolerable labor conditions—pitiful pay, harsh treatment, poor health, and early death for thousands. With the amount of arable land averaging just 0.3 acres (0.12 ha) per person and agricultural yields representing as little as 10 percent of consumption, the economic situation was bleak indeed.

The late nineteenth and early twentieth centuries did bring an increase in coal- and oil-bunkering activities, after major shipping companies began using steam power in the mid-1800s. As a consequence, the large deepwater port at Mindelo grew from a minor village to a *vila* ("town"), finally attaining the status of *cidade* ("city") in 1879.[53] The Cape Verdean connection to the world also improved in 1870 when a major British trans-Atlantic telegraph cable reached Mindelo. Mindelo was said to be the world's fourth largest coaling depot after Port Said, Malta, and Singapore, but the opening of the Suez Canal later diminished its strategic role. Even at present, however, the port at Mindelo handles more foreign and domestic commerce than does the capital at São Tiago.

In 1859, 167 vessels stopped at Mindelo, and in 1898, the harbor was visited by 1,503 vessels.[54] After the Great Depression, shipping at Mindelo fell back to 1,039 vessels in 1938. The confused situation in the Atlantic during World War II brought the numbers even lower; a mere 214 vessels docked at Mindelo in 1941.[55]

However, with high expenditures for imported rice, flour, and manufactured goods and with few local exports, Cape Verde continued to have a small-scale and colonial economy. The legal presence of slavery was a thing of the past, but recurrent cycles of drought, famine, and mass starvation in the islands left the population vulnerable to exploition and primed for emigration. Cape Verde would have an unfavorable balance of trade for decades. From 1951 to 1971, for example, imports increased in value eleven times, but exports increased only threefold.

In Guinea, the first three or four decades of the twentieth century saw almost continuous revolt and resistance by the Papels, Fulas, Balantas, and Bissagos peoples. In Cape Verde, resistance also occurred, despite the centuries of colonial rule. As growing numbers of Cape Verdeans became educated, much of this resistance was expressed in cultural or literary forms. For instance, Cape Verdean intellectuals delivered a profound political message in their *Claridade* ("clarity") movement for literary self-expression and *Crioulo* self-identity.

The twentieth century opened with the assassination of Portugal's king and crown prince in 1908 and the popular overthrow of the Portuguese Bragança monarchy in 1910. The spirit of revolutionary optimism grew with the birth of the Republican Portuguese government in 1911. As other antimonarchist and secular revolutionaries in this century promised to end global tyranny once and for all, some in the Cape Verde Islands thought that they, too, might achieve progressive and democratic reforms through agitation. At the same time, socialist parties and the Soviet "workers' state" promised their followers a final triumph over the exploitation of man by man. All these events and movements encouraged the workers, peasants, and colonially oppressed people of Cape Verde, who were beginning to consider self-determination and pan-African unity.

Around the world, movements and parties in solidarity with these themes continued to gain confidence. Just as confident in their mission were the colonial architects who intended to "up-lift backward Africa," where there were many "souls to be saved." This pressing mission was seen as the "white man's burden."

The African dream was cut short with the rise of António Salazar, who directed Portugal's "new state" fascism and launched a military coup d'état on 28 May 1926. Under his leadership (he became prime minister in 1932), severe limitations were imposed on civil liberties, backed by a very repressive internal police system known as the Polícia Internacional e de Defesa do Estado(PIDE).[56] These police were particularly fierce in trying to crush the small Portuguese Communist Party, which began to organize against the fascism of Salazar and later Marcello José Caetano, and to agitate for the return of democracy. Antistate actions were especially attractive to the few "assimilated" students from Africa who were equally interested in expanding their rights—rights that were doubly limited by both fascism and colonialism. This brought intellectuals from Lusophone Africa into a radical nationalism that received critical intellectual input from the Portuguese Communist Party and its members working underground. In Portugal's overseas provinces, the same authoritarian dictatorship was found, but the measures used in colonial repression were less obvious to the world and even more intimidating.

Between 1885 and 1956 in Guinea-Bissau, the Portuguese repeatedly used military force to crush mutinies, collect myriad taxes, and silence anticolonial opposition. (One antifascist revolt by deported politicians in Bissau did last a month in 1931, but it, too, was put down.) In 1933, the Colonial Act formalized Portugal's colonial relations with Africa through constitutional provisions.

In the Cape Verde Islands, the desertlike climate, aggravated by frequent drought, accomplished much the same purpose as colonial repression—that is, the severe ecological pressures kept the population vulnerable and dependent. As if colonialists had conspired with the climate, adverse natural conditions were only aggravated by the lack of water conservation, the soil erosion, and the overgrazing so typical under colonial rule.

Oppression in colonial Cape Verdean prisons was also widespread, and there was always room for dissidents from the islands or from Portugal and its far-flung colonies. Thus, even though Cape Verde had a separate administration, it still shared a common experience of oppression with Africa. The situation was even more complicated because a number of Cape Verdeans played integral parts as mid-level colonial administrators.

Meanwhile, the United States and Western Europe galvanized themselves against the budding socialist and anticolonial movements. African nationalism was viewed as secondary to the battle for the "containment of Communism." Militant Africans were dismissed as the dupes of Moscow or, later, Peking and Havana. Only when a more aggressive war of fascist nationalism was started by Germany, Italy, and Japan could the western capitalist nations agree to align with the

Soviet Union to defeat the greater enemy, Nazism. Before and during World War II, African conscripts had gained military training and combat experience to defend their colonial "mother" countries. Fighting on many fronts throughout the world, they saw and participated in the struggle for other people's national liberation. Later, seeking their own independence, Africans observed that the most serious opponents of the colonialism that oppressed them were the socialist nations, and they began to follow the dictum "the enemy of my enemy is my friend." Although the roots of African nationalism must also be traced to pan-Africanism, "back-to-Africa" movements, and an inherent search for free and independent expression, the great ideological cleavage of the twentieth century undoubtedly gave this nationalism added force and purpose.

Shortly after the conclusion of World War II, the socialist world encompassed most states of Eastern and Central Europe, as well as the gigantic People's Republic of China. The ideological struggle between socialism and capitalism was on, and protagonists on both sides mobilized their proxy powers, carried out subversion, and orchestrated coups and assassinations.

In the twentieth century, the political unity between Cape Verde and Africa was suspended by colonialism and reconfigured from 1956 to 1974 by the mobilization for national liberation. In the process, the long ties between Cape Verde and Guinea-Bissau were renewed, the critical leadership role of Cape Verdeans was revived, and the Cape Verdean consciousness began to shift from Portuguese to African—or at least Crioulo. The tug-of-war between the forces of nationalism, socialism, and capitalism made for a century filled with events and transformations of world-shaking importance: new political alignments, dramatic population growth, technological innovation, and fundamental changes in communication and transportation on a rapidly shrinking planet. In this context of global tumult, it is not surprising that five centuries of Portuguese colonial rule in Cape Verde would finally conclude.

Life had always been a struggle for residents in Cape Verde, whether they were fighting hunger, famine, or the environment. But for those engaged in the political struggle, it was even harder. The more radical they became, the more fierce was the repression of the Portuguese state police organ—the PIDE—which broadened its powers of arrest, detention, brutality, assassination, and exile. The ancient pattern of sending *degredados* to Cape Verde was resumed: The fearsome "work camp" at Chão Bom (which means "good earth"), constructed in 1949 near Tarrafal, São Tiago, was soon filled with dissidents from Portugal and all of its colonies. As early as 1957, PIDE operatives were sent to Bissau to assist with intelligence, counterinsurgency, and the arrest of nationalists. In the following years, many cases of brutality and torture were widely reported, especially from Chão Bom.[57] Another contingent of 105 PIDE agents arrived in Cape Verde in 1971 to infiltrate and break up the underground operations of the PAIGC in the islands.

By the early 1970s, the PIDE had gained such widespread notoriety that its leaders felt compelled to change its name to the Direcção Geral de Segurança (DGS).

On 18 March 1949, the Western European nations and the United States formed the large military alliance known as the North Atlantic Treaty Organization (NATO) to defend the interests of the capitalist world. Portugal joined in the same year. Officially, areas to the south of the equator were out of NATO jurisdiction, but Portugal's membership permitted NATO to contribute very significant military and economic aid to Portugal. NATO's promise to defend freedom and democracy seemed rather empty when fascist and colonial Portugal joined the fold, but in those days, the Cold War was very hot.

On 14 May 1955, the Eastern European nations responded with the opposing Warsaw Pact, to defend the interests of socialism. Every local struggle, whether in South Africa, Cuba, or Vietnam, was viewed by the United States and Western Europe through the prism of the Cold War.[58] Third World issues assumed international importance based upon the political alliances of the nations involved, more than the merits of the leaders, the causes, or the hardships of the people. African perspectives about racism, apartheid, colonialism, and neocolonialism were generally heard—and ignored. And in Portuguese colonial Africa efforts at reform, such as the exposé and revolt by Henrique Galvão, were crushed.[59]

The NATO military aid directly helped Portugal acquire the munitions and training needed for all their counterinsurgency wars in their African colonies. Before 1958, Portugal spent between 3 and 4 percent of its gross national product (GNP) on the military, an amount similar to the expenditures of other Western European nations. But by 1964, Portugal's "national defense" requirements had reached 8 percent of the GNP, and in 1965, more than half of the state revenues went to the military. Portugal was supported mainly by West Germany and the United States, via loans and grants and their purchases of colonial products. U.S. aid to Portugal through NATO was measured in hundreds of millions of dollars. Between 1949 and 1968, the U.S. military aid to Portugal officially reached $349 million, but this did not include costs incurred under other bilateral agreements that eased Portugal's own hard-pressed economy. Toward the end of the Guinea-Bissau war, the United States arranged financial assistance to Portugal totaling well over $400 million. The vast portion of Portugal's NATO-committed forces were actually in Africa and using NATO equipment, especially heavy artillery, armored vehicles, and aircraft, not to mention the U.S.-trained Portuguese counterinsurgency specialists who fought in Guinea-Bissau. All figured importantly in Portugal's prosecution of its wars in Africa from 1961 to 1974.[60]

The dominant colonial powers, England and France, still weak from their narrow World War II victories, saw that radical nationalism was beginning to challenge their outdated colonial policies. Africans across the continent were taking up placards, petitions, and sometimes arms to seek self-determination. By 1950, the Third Pan-African Congress was held in London, and representatives from the Portuguese colonies were present in the form of the *Liga Africana* (African League). The Front for National Liberation in Algeria began a long and bloody conflict against the French, which ran from 1954 to 1962 and reached the streets of Paris itself. The English tried to paint a savage picture of the Mau Mau revolt in Kenya (1951–1962), but both sides really knew that nationalism was at the heart of this uprising. Meanwhile, Ethiopia and Liberia were already sovereign, and Egypt was the next to rid itself of a puppet king serving British interests. Libya, the Sudan, Ghana, and Nigeria were soon to follow. Clearly, the pace of national independence was quickened, with the very problematic exceptions of European settler rule in Rhodesia and South Africa—and the Portuguese colonies.

Reasonable people assumed that fascist, anticommunist, and colonial Portugal would soon get the message as well. But for the people in the Cape Verde Islands, the misery continued—more drought, famine, poverty, exile, and forced emigration to hard labor in the plantations of São Tomé and Príncipe. Embarrassed by this situation and buffeted by formal complaints, the Portuguese ducked the issue of colonialism in Cape Verde with a 1951 change in nomenclature: The "colony" became an "overseas province."

3

SOCIETY AND
CULTURE

I N A SMALL, isolated nation such as Cape Verde, one might expect to find a degree of simplicity and homogeneity in the population, at least by conventional measures. But in fact, in the evolution of its demographic structure, its composition by race and class, and the development of its *Crioulo* society, the Cape Verde archipelago is remarkably complex and diverse.

The Demography of Cape Verde

The islands have experienced great fluctuations in population over time, especially in the past century. During most of the earlier years, the islands were sparsely populated, and repeated episodes of emigration and death by famine depleted the population in the past. But in recent decades, the population has surged to new levels, as indicated in Table 3.1.

The figures in the table chart the *overall* population growth of the archipelago; it would be wrong to conclude that each island has experienced parallel patterns of growth. From the latest data for each island, it is clear that Boa Vista and Brava have experienced relative demographic stagnation. By contrast, Sal, São Tiago, and São Vicente have shown remarkable growth in their populations more recently. In the last two cases, the largest increase has been in the main cities, Praia and Mindelo. For the smaller Sal, rapid growth has been based on expanded tourist and airport services. In Fogo, Maio, Santo Antão, and São Nicolau, the population has shown some increase, but there have also been notable fluctuations (see Table 3.2).

47

TABLE 3.1   Population of Cape Verde, Census Years 1550–1990

	Number of People		*Number of People*
1550	15,708	1910	142,552
1580	9,940	1920	159,672
1650	13,980	1927	148,300
1720	23,130	1930	146,299
1730	38,000	1936	162,055
1800	56,050	1939	174,000
1810	51,480	1940	181,286
1832	60,000	1950	148,331
1861	89,310	1960	199,902
1864	97,009	1970	270,999
1871	76,053	1984	326,212
1878	99,317	1985	333,128
1882	103,000	1986	338,560
1890	127,390	1987	347,060
1900	147,424	1990	336,798

SOURCES: Compiled from data in T. Bentley Duncan, *Atlantic Islands* (Chicago: University of Chicago Press, 1972), pp. 255–257, and Direcção-Geral de Estatística, Cape Verde censuses and projections.

Sex Ratios

Within the overall population of Cape Verde, the proportion of females has almost always exceeded that of males in recent decades. This is a result of the persistent pattern of male migration away from the islands for employment purposes and a function of the differential in life expectancy, which favors women. In Cape Verdean census data from 1936 to 1990, the lowest proportion of females was 52.1 percent (1990); the highest was 54.7 percent (1950). Contrary to this strong general trend, the islands of Santo Antão, Sal, and Boa Vista had slightly greater male populations in 1990. Overall, the proportion of females in the 1990 population ranged from 48.5 percent in Sal to 53.6 percent in Maio.

Life Expectancy, Mortality, Fertility, and Natural Increase

At independence in 1975, the Cape Verdean life expectancy for males was only 48.3 years; for females, it was just 51.7 years. By 1989, this had improved substantially: The mean number of years lived rose to 57 for males and 61 for females. This is not as high as in the United States, but it is more appropriate to compare these statistics with those of neighboring West Africa. In Guinea-Bissau in 1989, for example, life expectancy for males was a low 43 years, and for females, it was 47 years.

The length of life may also be expressed in the crude death rate (CDR), which was 7.72 per 1,000 in 1987, a decline from earlier years. For African nations, this CDR is quite low. The infant death rate (IDR) was still quite high at 54.6 per 1,000

TABLE 3.2   Population of Individual Cape Verde Islands, 1580–1990

	Boa Vista	Brava	Fogo	Maio	Sal	Santo Antão	São Tiago	São Nicolau	São Vicente
1580	50	100	1,200	50	0	400	8,000	140	0
1650	150	400	2,500	120	10	1,000	9,500	300	0
1720	1,000	1,200	5,000	250	30	3,000	12,000	650	0
1800	2,200	3,000	8,000	700	50	12,000	26,000	4,000	100
1900	2,600	9,200	17,600	1,900	500	29,900	64,900	12,000	8,800
1927	2,495	6,819	22,596	?	672	25,936	57,554[a]	14,519	17,709
1930	2,454	6,383	21,563	?	764	23,973	63,154	10,573	14,639
1940	2,653	8,510	22,914	?	1,142	35,930	77,192	14,827	15,867
1950	2,903	7,902	17,520	1,879	1,813	27,947	58,893	10,316	19,158
1960	3,309	8,646	25,457	2,680	2,626	34,598	88,587	13,894	21,361
1970	3,463	7,888	29,692	3,466	5,505	47,200	128,782	16,308	34,500
1980	3,397	6,984	31,115	4,098	7,500	43,198	145,957	13,572	41,792
1990	3,452	6,975	33,902	4,964	7,715	43,845	171,433	13,557	51,277

[a]This figure includes Maio.

SOURCES: Compiled from data in T. Bentley Duncan, *Atlantic Slave Trade* (Chicago: University of Chicago Press, 1972), pp. 254–257, and Direcção-Geral de Estatística, Cape Verde censuses.

in 1987, but this was the best rate compared to other West African nations. The IDR was 108.6 per 1,000 in 1975 and 64.3 in 1982, proof that the improvements in health delivery systems since independence have been dramatic. Nonetheless, the rather high IDR is certainly a major factor in keeping the overall life expectancy at its present level.

In addition, it must be stressed that the population of Cape Verde is quite young, with 31 percent of the people between the ages of 4 and 14 years. The general population had a birth rate of 37.25 per 1,000 persons in 1987, but this was down from 38.33 in 1984, perhaps reflecting an increased use of birth control. When the birth and death rates are taken together, there was a natural increase of 29.53 per 1,000 in 1987. Statistics indicate, then, that this young and dynamic population can be expected to show substantial sustained growth in the future. Judging from the past, however, this growth might be reduced by significant out-migration by workers seeking employment or by ecological refugees.

Urbanization

Although there are numerous villages and towns throughout the archipelago, only in two cities—Mindelo in the Barlavento Islands and Praia in the Sotavento Islands—is any substantial urbanization found. Both of these cities have generally been gaining in size during recent years, but Mindelo has fallen a bit due to a weak shipping economy and resultant losses in employment. The data in Table 3.3 detail the growth of these cities between 1983 and 1990.

Another perspective on Cape Verdean urbanization is derived from the 1990 population statistics for the archipelago, showing that 32.33 percent of the people resided in primary urban places, which include Praia and Mindelo, and their suburbs. Meanwhile, another 12.46 percent of the population lived in *conselho* ("council") capitals or other secondary urban places, and 1.83 percent lived in semiurban settlements (the small towns and villages). But despite the rapid process of Cape Verdean urbanization, 53.39 percent of the people were still living in rural areas in 1990, areas that are poorly served by utilities, transportation, and communication facilities.

Class and Social Structure

The social structure of Cape Verde should be understood, in part, in terms of its historical evolution. The previous chapter described the earliest feudal relations, the slave system, and colonial society. Though these epochs are over, it is very clear that the modern social strata and today's cultural and racial categories have evolved from these earlier relationships. Under both feudalism and colonialism, Cape Verde experienced a racial stratification that was simultaneously blunt and

TABLE 3.3   Population of Two Urban Centers in Cape Verde, 1983–1990

	1983	1987	1990
Praia	44,718	55,258	61,797
Mindelo	42,171	48,381	47,080

SOURCES: The 1983 and 1987 data are from Direcção-Geral de Estatística, *Boletim Anual de Estatística* (Cape Verde: Ministry of Planning and Cooperation, 1989), p. 6. The 1990 data are from Ministério do Plano e da Cooperação, *Resultados Provisorios do Recenseamento Geral, Outubro,* p. 11.

subtle. Those in the top ruling positions—the feudal *capitãos,* the absentee land-lords of the *donatarios,* the *fidalgo* nobility, the *feitor* and *lançado* merchants, and the foreign representatives—were almost universally *brancos* ("whites"). Whether the *brancos* were European Portuguese or Italians appointed by the king or European *degredados,* they were always viewed as well above the lowest rank of the Cape Verdean social structure—a position reserved for the *escravos.* Virtually all slaves were of African origin, coming from such diverse groups as the lighter-skinned Moorish and Fulani Muslims, the Wolof and Mandinka, and the animist Senegambians along the coast. Given the extreme diversity of the population, the social strata of Cape Verde were profoundly racist in their configuration.

Much less clear were (and are) the floating distinctions of phenotype within the majority population of *Crioulos* or *mestiços.* Although there are many racial and ethnic admixtures in Portuguese society itself, the *Crioulos* and *mestiços* thought of themselves as "pure" Portuguese. But though the vast majority of Cape Verdean people have a *Crioulo* culture, the colonial taxonomy typically viewed *Crioulos* as a residual group that can be conceptualized by socioeconomic context and diverse phenotypes. In the *Crioulo* social strata, one finds sophisticated functionaries, civil servants, and professionals, as well as *contratados* and *rendeiros;* among the "peasant" *badius,* there are many *rebelados* ("religious revivalists").

Under the repressive relations of slavery, feudalism, colonialism, and Portuguese fascism, the foreign or local rulers required—or at least benefited from—a Cape Verdean population that was internally divided by "race," and so, in practice, it was. Yet much has been made by scholars of Angola, Brazil, Mozambique, and Cape Verde about the great racial experiments, racial democracy, racial accommodation within the church, and Lusotropicalism of the Portuguese.[1] These perspectives notwithstanding, I would simply stress that although Cape Verde's colonial experience was unequivocally marked by racism, social inequity, and racial stratification, any effort to impose an American, South African, or European model of racial hierarchy onto Cape Verdean society will surely fail.

The class structure of Cape Verde is rather complex in its specialized occupations but simple in that it is overwhelmingly geared toward agricultural production. Essentially, one may apply the term *peasant* in describing the relations of production in Cape Verde, for there is a dominance of agriculture and a cultural heritage of the feudal-like values of Portugal. In Cape Verde, the forms of land ownership known as *morgados* (a feudal land ownership system for large-scale agricultural production, usually done by slaves, *capelas, capitanias,* and royal land grants) were dominant for most of the islands' history. The farmers grew subsistence crops for themselves if rains were sufficient; if not, they worked on other irrigated lands as wage laborers or sharecroppers. Bananas, sugarcane, and coffee have long been some of the more important (but still limited) cash crops.

The working class proper was and is rather small, centered around the light industries that process agricultural and animal products. In addition, this sector includes workers in the small industries that catch and process fish products for domestic consumption or export. Cape Verdean wage earners also work in the public and private transport of passengers and cargo, and a rather significant group of maritime laborers work in bunkering, on fishing and cargo ship crews, and as stevedores—jobs that have provided an escape route for thousands of Cape Verdeans to the port cities of the world. Many others work in service sector positions, as drivers, repairmen, mechanics, street vendors, secretarial and clerical worrkers, and domestic servants. There are some artisans involved with weaving, pottery-making, painting, and music, but such activities are usually pursued to supplement other work.

Another group of workers earning very low wages in the public sector were those serving on the *brigadas de estrada.* These road brigades were predominantly composed of women and children, and even in the twentieth century, a considerable amount of construction and porterage was done by women and children. This occurred for several reasons: (1) Labor costs were kept very low, (2) the interior terrain was not accessible by wheeled vehicles, and (3) much of the male working class had emigrated to Europe or North America. Indeed, there is essentially an absentee working class among Cape Verdeans since males working overseas play a vital role in the economy through the remittances they send home. There are also staggering numbers of unemployed, who constitute one-third to one-half of the potential working force. Though physically present, they are absent in terms of contributing to production; they also keep the wages of all workers at a perpetually low level.

The depressed Cape Verdean economy has given rise to a small group of lumpen or a declassé strata of petty criminals and prostitutes, although the government has sought to reduce their numbers with innovative social programs since independence. But given the poverty of the islands, it is remarkable that the levels of crime and violent behavior are actually quite low, especially in comparison with the United States.

Cape Verde's military during colonial times was largely composed of Portuguese conscripts. Officers were typically European Portuguese, although field troops and some crack commando units were made up of Africans and Cape Verdeans. Just after independence, troops in Cape Verde joined the People's Revolutionary Armed Forces (FARP), which had defeated the Portuguese colonial army in the forests of Guinea. Presently, Cape Verde's small armed forces are made up of Cape Verdean volunteers.

Those in the mercantile strata in Cape Verde are usually from the islands, as the *lançados* had been in centuries past. The more prosperous members of society—shop owners, owners or operators of rental services, travel agents, hotel operators, and bankers—form the upper strata of Cape Verdean society at present, as they did during the late days of colonialism. High-ranking civil servants and government officials are also associated with the upper classes. In the mid-1970s, when the Portuguese colonial authorities departed, the top positions in Cape Verdean society were vacated, to be assumed by new leaders having the socialist orientation of the PAIGC/PAICV. A sharp but short political struggle between the battle-hardened guerrilla fighters and the relatively weak petite bourgeoisie took place in 1975. Members of the weaker group welcomed the end of colonialism, but they were not able to organize an effective opposition to the PAIGC/PAICV until 1990.

Race and Racism in Cape Verde

To appreciate the racial composition of Cape Verde, it is first necessary to examine the racist categories that so often allowed the Portuguese to see difference rather than unity. That there are variations in human appearances goes without question, but given the diverse origins and long-term mixtures of Cape Verdean people, virtually any system of racial classification will fail. In *Race, Language, and Culture,* pioneering anthropologist Franz Boas insisted on the separation of these very different human variables.[2] Naturally, these three aspects of society, as well as class, can overlap in important ways, but they must be kept intellectually and analytically distinct. Even when there is a correlation, great methodological care must be taken to determine any causal association between race and class or culture.

Such theoretical points must be considered in studying the archaic racial classification that was developed and elaborated in Cape Verde during the nineteenth century. The three-part schema of Negroid, Caucasoid, and Mongoloid long ago proved to hopelessly inadequate in describing even supposedly "homogeneous" populations, not to mention Cape Verde, where merging and blending has long been a central theme. The three popular phenotypic characteristics—skin color, hair texture, and nose shape—may be handy ways to recognize individuals, but on examination of much less obvious genetic characteristics such as blood type, resistance to specific diseases, or internal anatomical structures, one quickly discovers the very poor fit between these characteristics and the three characteristics that are stereotypically considered so essential in racial typologies. Above all, it should not be forgotten that most racial systems reflect social and power relations. In turn, these are overlaid upon physical characteristics that themselves have a complex genetic basis.

In Cape Verdean history, absolute power rested with the external kings, presidents, and their appointees and representatives in the islands. Until 1975, power always lay outside the islands and virtually always in the hands of the Portuguese or a few other Europeans resident in the islands. Given their lighter complexions relative to the majority, these rulers and their agents and allies were termed *brancos* in Portuguese. The Moorish, Jewish, and Mediterranean diversity that is also found in Portugal's own racial inheritance is typically overlooked, and the term *brancos* is used, in practice, to refer to those of apparent European origin and in positions of power. In the fifteenth century, when the initial settlement of the islands was taking place, there were simply two large groups: (1) the *brancos*, the rulers, *capitãos*, administrators, noblemen, and top officers, settlers, and their wives and children, in addition to some exiled Portuguese criminals, and (2) the *pretos* ("blacks"), who initially were almost all slaves, with some exceptions for those who played special roles in slave raids and trade, in translating, in enforcement of the slave system, and in military service.

This simple, bipolar system may have lasted as little as nine months before it began to be ambiguous. It was a common practice for slavemasters to have sexual relations with their slaves, especially when so many Portuguese masters did not bring their wives into their new colonial possession. When children were born, masters could accept them as their own but thereby weaken the slave system or dismiss their paternity and keep the slave system alive. Every successive birth and generation and manumitted status only made this more complex—and "racial purity" is already a very dubious scientific concept.

The Cape Verdean "racial" composition is illustrated in Table 3.4. These data show the rapid emergence of the majority *Crioulo* or *mestiço* from the earliest days to the present.

The 1550 data show that the *branco* population was a very tiny minority from the start, and from the earliest decades of Cape Verdean history, the *mestiço* population very quickly grew to be the sustained majority. Actually, the fluctuations in the "racial" composition in the 1930–1940 period have little to do with actual changes in the population itself; rather, they relate to the observations of the colonial enumerator and judgments made about subjective "racial" categories into which people were assigned. According to Cape Verdean "racial" taxonomy, *brancos* can include *Madeirenses, lançados, colonas, Judeus, degredados,* or other Europeans. *Crioulo* folk taxonomy uses the slightly perjorative term *Nyambob* to refer to whites; this is derived from the Mandinka word, *Tubob* for the same group. *Mestiços* are also known as *mulattos,* or *mistos,* and *pretos* are those of apparent African cultural or racial origin, such as Balantas, Beafadas, Bijagos, Brames, Banyun, Felupes, Jalofas, Fulas, Felupes, Mandinkas, Manjacos, Serer, or Susu.

TABLE 3.4   Percentage of "Racial" Composition of Cape Verde

	"White"	"Mestiço"	"Black"
1550	1.96	69.61	28.38
1900	3.19	62.47	34.34
1930	3.98	59.80	36.27
1936	3.89	75.23	20.86
1940	3.19	62.47	34.34
1950	2.06	69.09	28.84

SOURCE: The data are given in or calculated from Cape Verde censuses; after independence, the "race" category was dropped; Instituto Nacional de Estatística, *Anuário de Estatística II*, Provincias Ultramarinas (Lisbon, 1971).

Ethnic identity was often preserved in slave shipping manifests and on slave tax registers, in linguistic patterns, and in some aspects of material culture. Generally, the Portuguese made little or no effort to preserve African culture; indeed, advocates of the systems of slavery and colonialism waged a continual ethnocidal offensive against African names, languages, music, and religious practices. When slaves boarded the slave ships, they were prisoners of war, but during the few days of sailing before going ashore in Cape Verde, they had already begun the process of becoming *ladino:* The slave registers almost always listed Latin-based names for the slaves, who were frequently baptized and introduced to Catholicism as they disembarked from the ships.

Although Portuguese, Spaniards, and Italians were generally considered *brancos,* Portuguese Jews were sometimes categorized with other "oriental" peoples. An awareness of Jewish roots in Cape Verdean society still persists, as already discussed, but it is rather quietly recognized as another additive to *Crioulo* culture. Many well-known families are aware of specific members in the families with a Jewish heritage. If identifiable at all, Cape Verdeans perceive Jews as a "racial" group similar to the Arabs or Moors, that is, Muslims from the Maghreb (Algeria, Morocco, Mauritania, and Tunisia) who were either despised, avoided, or enslaved. The appearance of Moorish people seemed to fall outside both the *brancos* and *pretos* groupings, so the term *Moreno* emerged to describe either Moors or Jews. In some cases, such individuals had actually been convicted of crimes or enslaved and brought to the islands. Others, with some sort of intermediary image between *branco* and *preto* were once noted as having a *Moreno* ("Moorish") appearance, but such descriptions are no longer heard in Cape Verde, and the reference has become obsolete.

In 1856 slave records at the Cape Verdean National Historical Archive, observations were sometimes made about African ethnic origins and various physical features deemed of significance. Color was most often reported simply as *preto(a)* ("black"), but there are many who are recognized as *preto fula* or simply *fula* colored, with a suggestion that an individual had a somewhat lighter complexion

*Hebrew headstone in Varzea
Cemetery, São Tiago Island
(Photo by author)*

typical of the interior Fula people. In the Portuguese language, color references
were to brown, light tan, dark tan. If this were not sufficient, the system of racial
taxonomy could then turn to types of noses which might be flat, or very flat, while
faces were: *arab fula* (like a Berber or Moor), or *rosto comprido* (long-faced), or
rosto redondo (round-faced), *feiçaõs corretos* (correct features). Stature might be
noted as regular, medium, strong, tall, or smallish. Other notable features were
also reported such as crippled, limping, one handed, pock-marked, and thin-
necked.[3]

As the *mestiço* population emerged, there was an intensified interest in the subtle taxonomy of hair types including the *cabeca seca* (dry or wiry headed), the *cabo
crespo* (frizzy hair), and *cabo encrespado* (curly hair).[4] In short, for Cape Verdean
people, every variety was possible. The minute differences listed here are not
meant to be exhaustive or scientific but only illustrative of the kinds of distinctions that were deemed important. For South Africa or the United States, "race"
categories tend to be much more sharply divided, and if an individual exhibited
even one "African" characteristic, it was enough to be prompt social and legal

measures of isolation and restriction found in racist societies. For Cape Verde, the complex terminology and the clearly unequal access to power are sufficient proof of a racist system as well, but it was not identical to other models of racial hierarchies that had their own de facto and de jure structures and regulations.

Once the majority population of *Crioulos* or *mestiços* was established, other factors were added to the equation. Higher levels of wealth, power, educational status, and class position began to "lighten" a person's "racial" classification, while poverty, uncouth behavior, and illiteracy "darkened" it. The vast majority of Cape Verdeans are somewhere in the middle.

In studies of Brazil and Lusophone African countries, some have easily counted a score of racial terms, and others making finer distinctions have recognized more than a hundred subtle differences. In addition to the stereotypes of "white" and "black," some people were termed *bermedjo* ("red") as well as the vast middle ground of *mestiços, mulatoes,* and *mistos.*

The well-known work on racial categories in Brazil by Wagley also found that wealth and class may actually transcend race and "lighten" peoples' appearances. Indeed, Charles Wagley notes that there is a racial category in Brazil termed *cabo verde* that refers to those who are lighter than *pretos* but still very dark; a *cabo verde* is ironically considered as "a black white man" who is black but has "good hair."[5]

With such complex variations, it is apparent that *Crioulo* is not only an authentic linguistic and cultural category but a "racial" category as well. Despite the need to separate race, language, and culture as a general anthropological principle, the paradoxical situation in Cape Verde is that all three factors are interlocked in practice. The failure to be comfortably accommodated within a static European or American racioethnic framework is not a problem for Cape Verdeans. However, when the majority of this population only exists in a residual or mixed group, then something is clearly wrong with the categories themselves. In sum, just as Cape Verde is the product of specific historical conditions, it has also evolved its very own, sometimes enigmatic logic of racial classification.

Race and Racism: Victims and Victimizers

Cape Verdeans certainly recognize and operate within a broad array of racial categories. One result of this was the division of their own communities to the advantage of colonialism. Even in the postcolonial situation, such consciousness has helped to maintain some degree of socioeconomic stratification. Nonetheless, in hopes of attaining the colonial status of *assimilado* or repelled by the negative colonial images of Africanity, some segments of the Cape Verdean community have not come to terms with their own position, vis-à-vis European racism. Similarly, some Cape Verdeans also reject to some degree the social and political African roots of their society—roots that have, by any measure, contributed much more to the Cape Verdean genetic inheritance than did any European roots.

Cape Verdeans commonly were strategic intermediaries in the colonial system, serving as local administrators and functionaries in all parts of the Luso-African world. On the one hand, Cape Verde was itself an exploited Portuguese colony, where the mechanisms of divide-and-rule were firmly in place. This often meant that the legitimacy of the Cape Verdean identity and cultural self-expression was denied. On the other hand, relative to other Luso-African colonies, Cape Verde was considerably better off, and residents had little incentive to identify with other Africans whose economies, health conditions, and educational systems were often substantially worse. Five hundred years of colonialism in the archipelago led many to accept that there would simply never be any other alternative. Thus, in complex and contradictory ways, Cape Verdeans, especially those in top positions of colonial administration, were trapped in a system in which they were simultaneously subordinated and elevated. Historically, Cape Verdeans had been both slaves and slavers; consequently, they were both victims and victimizers in the colonial structure.

As a function of poverty, drought, famine, disease, and limited opportunities, Cape Verde has long been a nation of emigrants. Whether as colonial administrators, *lançados, grumetes, ladinos, escravos, contratados,* or labor migrants, Cape Verdeans have long been on the move. A sense of Cape Verdean cultural identity has kept this diaspora unified to a degree, but race, class, and educational differences have also pulled in opposing directions.

Circular, permanent, and temporary contract emigration has been a significant feature in the lives of Cape Verdeans for many years. This emigration history, spanning several centuries, has resulted in the development of diaspora enclaves of Cape Verdeans and their descendants across the globe. Substantial numbers of Cape Verdeans are found in Europe, Africa, and South America. However, the largest Cape Verdean diaspora community is located in southeastern New England. Other Cape Verdean populations exist in the urban areas of the Middle Atlantic states and in the port cities of California and Hawaii. Conservative estimates indicate that some 50,000 people of Cape Verdean ancestry and self-identity are living in the United States today. If second- or third-generation Cape Verdeans with at least one parent of Cape Verdean descent are included, the number may be as great as 250,000. Clearly, the number depends largely on matters of definition of ancestry and identity, which is problematic.

Other countries with sizable Cape Verdean immigrant communities are Portugal and Spain (40,000), Angola (35,000), Senegal (22,000–25,000), France (10,000–15,000), the Netherlands (8,000–10,000), São Tomé and Príncipe (8,000), and Italy (8,000–10,000). Other concentrations are found in Brazil, Uruguay, and Argentina.

As already suggested, emigration to the United States and elsewhere has always been a crucial socioeconomic strategy for Cape Verdeans. Emigration has helped them cope with the disastrous effects of drought; it has also reduced island unemployment, lowered population growth rates, and provided an essential source of income through the remittances the emigrant workers send to those who remain at home. In the first wave of Cape Verdean–U.S. immigration during the late nineteenth and early twentieth centuries, the newcomers benefited from the opportunities they found in the United States, and their savings could mean the difference between survival and starvation for their loved ones at home. The influx of U.S. dollars into the islands also aided the Cape Verdean economy as a whole. Many merchants depended on U.S. capital to start businesses and to stock their stores, and with the help of remittances from the United States, some sharecroppers were able to buy the land on which they worked. Today in Cape Verde, remittances account for almost 50 percent of the gross domestic product (GDP).

The economic and social benefits of large-scale emigration from Cape Verde have probably outweighed the drawbacks of losing productive members of the population to other countries. The postcolonial governments have not actively encouraged emigration, but they have attempted to ensure that emigration will serve the welfare of the Cape Verdeans, who count on the remittances and U.S. social security payments that are channeled back into the domestic economy. The governmental commitment to this issue is real: There are representatives in the Cape Verdean Peoples National Assembly for diasporic *Crioulos* and in government offices whose sole function is to serve the needs of emigrants. It is estimated that between 1970 and 1980, the net emigration corresponded to 15 percent of the population.

Cape Verdean emigration to the United States burgeoned with the packet trade on sailing and steamer ships between the late nineteenth and mid-twentieth centuries. The expansion of steamship service to major Atlantic ports in the late nineteenth century brought an end to most sailing ships, but on smaller and less lucrative routes, the schooners kept on sailing far into the twentieth century. One such ship—the 112-foot (34-m) schooner *Ernestina*—was presented as a gift and symbol of cooperation from the government of the Cape Verde Islands to the United States and is now on the National Historic Register.

Amazingly, the *Ernestina* is still afloat. Because of its great symbolic heritage, the schooner carries both *mantenas* ("greetings to continue contact") across the Atlantic as well as the very *saudade* ("soul") of *Crioulo* culture, which combines a nostalgic longing for the old country and a deep appreciation of the hardships in the islands. As the last surviving sailing ship to take free and independent immigrants from Africa across the Atlantic, the *Ernestina* has both great practical and great emotional significance for Cape Verdeans.[6]

Other Social Groups in Cape Verdean and Guinean Society

Other social groups within *Crioulo* society, such as the *assimilados* and the *badius*, merit further analysis. The *assimilados* were formally recognized in the Colonial Act of 1930, just prior to the onset of Antonio Salazar's rule. While Salazar was minister of the colonies, the status of *assimilado* was assigned to those residents in the Portuguese colonies whose literacy, education, financial position, or other attainments entitled them to fuller rights as Portuguese citizens. Generally, *assimilado* status was applied more often in the Lusophone colonies on the African continent rather than in the islands. But since the relationship between Cape Verde and the continent is so deep, functionally integrated, and legally overlapping, it is useful to examine the *assimilados* more closely: Their status relates to basic issues of race, racism, political standing, and cultural identity in the region.

Assimilado status was distinct from the classification of *indigena* ("native"), which was also described in the Colonial Act of 1930. *Indigena* status was applied to the vast majority of Africans, making them wards of the state who were denied basic civil rights (including the right to vote), relegated to the lowest paying jobs and inferior schools, and subject to a head tax, restricted movement, and more severe and arbitrary punishment within the criminal justice system.

Even as late as May 1954, as expressed in the Portuguese Native Statutes, the official attitude was that "individuals of the Negro race or their descendants who were born or habitually reside in the said Provinces and who do not yet possess the learning and the social and individual habits presupposed for the integral application of the public and private law of Portuguese citizens are considered to be 'natives.'"[7]

Under such circumstances, Africans were increasingly subject to all means of racial prejudice as Portuguese colonialism penetrated ever deeper into the interior of Africa.[8] Cape Verdeans, however, were encouraged to think that they had a greater cultural similarity to the Portuguese, and they clearly had little to gain by associating or identifying with Africans; they were implicitly considered to be *assimilados* and therefore were at least second-class citizens of colonial Portugal. Because this entitled them to somewhat greater access to Portuguese state schooling, they tended to be better educated than other peoples of Lusophone Africa, and they could serve the Portuguese as public administrators throughout the other colonies. However, in reality, the political and economic position of Cape Verdeans in colonial times was closer to that of the African *indigenas* in terms of discriminatory policies, limited civil rights, and inequality of opportunity.

The enduring institutions of Portuguese colonialism depended upon dividing some better-off Cape Verdeans from both the poorer *badius* and peasants exiled in the mountainous interiors and the African *indigenas* in the forests of Guinea. To strengthen the system of divide-and-rule, the Portuguese introduced the cultural and political concept of the *assimilado*. The status of *assimilado* was then to be granted residents in African colonies who wanted recognition, empowerment, and social mobility. Those of European birth, no matter how high or low the station, acquired this status as a birth right. But Africans or native Cape Verdeans who hoped to become *assimilados* had to possess education and property and display unquestioned obedience to a state that negated at least some aspects of their roots and cultural history. Some were willing to pay this price, but others struggled for a new cultural identity and legitimacy. Foremost among those who resisted the cultural and political implications of *assimilado* status was Amilcar Cabral, who suggested that even "class suicide" might be required and that "if imperialist domination has the vital need to practice cultural oppression, national liberation is necessarily an act of culture."[9] In Chapter 4, some of the implications of Cabral's practice and philosophy will be examined in relation to contemporary Cape Verde.

Badius

The Portuguese colonial system of education allowed or even encouraged Cape Verdeans to believe that Africa and Africans had no significant history. In response, the postindependence Cape Verdean government attempted to recover this history. With the African roots of Cape Verde so profound and yet ironically denied, the new radical nationalists rediscovered the virtues of the lifeways of the *badius*, which preserved their Africanity and demonstrated their freedom. Oppressed by hard lives in the impoverished environment and economy of the São Tiago interior but free to be themselves, the *badius* came to represent a romantic symbol of the twentieth-century struggle for Cape Verdean legitimacy, authenticity, and even national independence. The Portuguese contempt for the life and customs of the *badius* only enhanced this. Even the musical forms of the *badius* were actively suppressed. The PAIGC and others who advocated twentieth-century Cape Verdean nationalism and the "re-Africanization" of the *Crioulos* believed that if the *badius* were so opposed by colonials, they must represent something positive for those waging modern struggles. Thus, in the independence period, the *badius* and their ethnomusicology became a topic for legitimate research.[10]

Within the general social category of *badius*, two groups—the *contratados* and the *rebelados*—warrant additional identification and recognition.

The *rebelados* exist primarily within the *badiu* populations in remote and inaccessible regions of São Tiago. In a spontaneous and syncretic movement of religious revival, perhaps as early as the 1940s but at least by the early 1960s, these peasants rose up in culturoreligious rebellion against the attempts of the Portuguese Catholic Church and the colonial administration to control their religious practices. Since the Catholic Church was so closely associated with the colonial and fascist state, the *rebelado* movement inevitably took on political overtones. More specifically, the *rebelados* rejected the authority of priests, preferring to perform their own traditional baptisms, weddings, and other rituals. Followers worked the land communally, refused to deal with money, and forbade the killing of living creatures. When the *rebelados* refused to allow their homes to be fumigated during a government antimalaria campaign, the colonial authorities began to see their movement as a threat; *rebelado* leaders were subsequently arrested, interrogated, and banished to other islands.

Many *contratados* also come from the *badiu* population, but are Cape Verdeans driven into emigration to escape poverty, famine, and drought. *Contratados* agree to sell their labor power for a proscribed period of time to a specific labor contractor. The contract system was used extensively in colonial Cape Verde to reduce the population pressure in times of drought and famine, to generate remittances to be sent back to the islands, and to meet agricultural labor needs.

Finally, the class structure of Cape Verde includes the *brigadas de estrada*, or road crews made up of marginally employed women, unemployed men, and children. These crews supply the enormous amount of labor used in building the endless Cape Verdean cobblestone roads and related public works. To this group might be added the women and children working in domestic service as launderers, cleaners, and cooks. Women and children also dominate the public food markets. Many women also work in the informal sector street markets, selling cloth, clothes, footwear, and processed foods. In Islamic societies in Africa, women are rarely present in the public economy, but market women in non-Islamic coastal West Africa are famed both for their numbers and for their influence. The women have been joined recently by men from Ghana, Nigeria, Senegal, and elsewhere in West Africa who work as street vendors, selling a variety of nonfood merchandise.

About 24.8 percent of the resident working population over ten years of age is involved in primary production, such as agriculture, fishing, and mineral extraction. With another 19.8 percent working in undefined activities and 18.6 percent in construction, a total of 63.2 percent of this population is involved in rather vulnerable primary or construction activities.[11]

Drought and Famine

The recurring cycles of Sahelian drought in Africa and in the Cape Verde archipelago have caused a major demographic transformation in the population. On many occasions, Cape Verdean famines have cut the population by 10 to 40 percent. Statistics from 1747 to 1970 show that there have been 58 years of famine and over 250,000 related deaths in some 12 drought periods.[12] The drought of 1832, for example, was associated with a severe famine in which 10 percent of the population died. In 1854–1856, it is estimated that about 25 percent of the population perished, reducing the number of islanders from over 120,000 to less than 100,000. During the famines and droughts in 1902–1903 and 1941–1943, perhaps 20,000 people died and another 20,000 became *contratados*. Other drought periods were seen in the late 1970s and the mid-1980s. These drought cycles have also caused massive economic disruption through losses in crops and livestock. With the unpredictability of agricultural employment forcing thousands of men to leave Cape Verde and seek cash employment elsewhere, the islands have become disproportionately populated with elderly, children, and women.

Colonial rulers and European labor markets benefited from cheap Cape Verdean labor and had little inclination to invest the funds needed for meaningful economic or resource development in the islands. After independence, the PAICV leadership began water conservation, reforestation, and deep-well drilling and built desalinization plants and soil erosion control and catchment dams to reduce the disastrous social effects of drought.

Probably the most common destination for Cape Verdean *contratados* were the so-called Cacão Islands of São Tomé and Príncipe. First discovered in 1471, these islands, far away in the Gulf of Guinea, were initially administered from Lisbon and Cape Verde. The Portuguese set up a plantation economy there, using slaves drawn primarily from Angola, Cape Verde, and other areas along the coast. Typical contracts ran for two years, and *contratados* would try to return to their homelands before accepting new contracts.

In addition to the Cape Verdean laborers , who were always in the minority in São Tomé and Príncipe, the labor force also included prisoners taken during punitive "pacification" measures in Guinea-Bissau or Angola. Almost always, the labor crews had white overseers, although Cape Verdeans sometimes would be allowed to work independently. High levels of disease and mortality were common, and the work schedule of sixty-two hours per week was brutal and debilitating in this tropical climate. Often, conditions on these coffee and cacão-producing islands were so poor and the means of recruitment so coercive that the labor migrations to São Tomé and Príncipe differed little from the system of slavery that preceded it.

With Portugal's official abolition of slavery in 1869 and Brazil's in 1888, the contract labor system evolved to replace slavery, continuing essentially until independence. Forced emigration to "the south," as the *Crioulos* termed São Tomé and Príncipe, was a desperate and despised alternative to famine. The laborers worked exhausting hours and were routinely tortured, beaten, and put in chains. Recruitment for this labor was finally prohibited in the Barlavento Islands, so that the bulk of the workers were *badius* from São Tiago and Fogo, the two islands that had been dominant in the slave plantation era in Cape Verde.[13]

In the first decades of the twentieth century, drought and poverty also led to emigration to the United States. Many Cape Verdean people, especially from Fogo and Brava, booked passage on the packet ships, hoping to survive the Atlantic crossing. This trans-Atlantic movement continued steadily until the more restrictive immigration laws of 1921 and 1924 were enforced in the United States; the Portuguese government also imposed obstacles to this westward emigration. What followed was a long period of dormancy that contributed heavily to the demise of the packet trade itself.[14]

Prominent among this first generation of Cape Verdean settlers in the United States were several attorneys, such as Alfred Gomes, George Leighton, and Roy Teixeira. These men directly contributed to the definition of the Cape Verdean–American community, especially by providing legal counsel to many packet ship captains and owners concerning the intricacies of immigration law.

Irregular recordkeeping, clandestine departures and arrivals, and extensive return migration make it difficult to determine the exact number of Cape Verdean–American immigrants. However, recent research indicates that between 35,000 and 40,000 Cape Verdeans arrived in the United States during the years 1820 to 1976. Since the independence of Cape Verde in 1975, emigration from the archipelago to the United States has increased again, with an annual average of 913.6 persons arriving between 1975 and 1980.[15]

Many Cape Verdeans went to southeastern New England and Cape Cod to work in the cranberry and blueberry industries for which that region is famous. From the end of the nineteenth century to the present, the wild cranberry, native to Cape Cod, has been an important agricultural crop, requiring a seasonal workforce of Cape Verdean harvesters. The early immigrants found their work and housing conditions were somewhat better than those of the *contratados* in São Tomé, and soon work in the cranberry bogs became one of the major sources of income and mobility for the new arrivals. In fact, they could earn enough during a good season to take them through the cold winter months and have a surplus to send back to the Cape Verde Islands or, in some cases, to make the return trip themselves. The money would also be used to bring other family members to the United States in the links of chain migration. Approximately one-quarter of the immigrants arriving from Cape Verde during the period of mass migration, 1900 to 1920, listed Plymouth County in the heart of the cranberry district as their intended destination. Cranberry pickers came primarily from Fogo, the island that most closely resembled the cranberry region in terms of its agricultural economy. But though the economic success of the cranberry industries became almost completely dependent upon the labor of Cape Verdean immigrants, very few Cape Verdeans themselves became owners of these productive bogs.[16]

Maritime Trades

With close ties to the sea, another escape route for Cape Verdeans was in the maritime trades. Cape Verdeans were famed as harpooners, whalers, ship crewmen,

Hunting for sea turtles off the Cape Verde Islands in the sixteenth century (Reproduced from Peter Sammartino, Columbus, Italy Italy Magazine, *Rome, 1988, p. 33)*

sealers, and, to a lesser extent, fishermen.[17] In the neighborhoods where they settled, they usually dominated the longshoring industries as well. As whaling ended in the early twentieth century, their role in the labor movement in New England increased. This is well documented in the history of the Coal Trimmers Local, founded in 1922, and the Rhode Island Longshoremen's Union, Local 1329, founded in 1933. In both cases, the chief organizer was the Cape Verdean leader Manuel Q. Ledo. The local National Maritime Union, composed almost exclusively of Cape Verdeans, also followed some years later.[18]

Religion in Cape Verde

Even though Cape Verdeans endured numerous hardships caused by the recurrent famines and droughts, harsh labor conditions, and emigration to foreign lands, they could always find solace in their religious traditions. Overwhelmingly, the institutionalized religion of Cape Verde is Catholicism, and religious life in all the larger towns of the islands is dominated by Catholic churches. Many of these

Church group photo, ca. 1930, Brava Island (Waltraud Berger Coli Collection)

trace their roots directly back to the early Diocese of Guinea and Cape Verde, which operated both in the islands and on the adjacent Guinea coast. As of 1982, 297,304 people (98 percent of the total population) were considered to be of the Roman Catholic faith.

Roughly 2 percent of the population in 1982 belonged to Protestant sects, including the Church of the Nazarene, the Sabbatarian, and the Mormon faiths. Most converts to these religions are returned emigrants from the United States, and some of the converts were drawn to the evangelical groups due to disillusionment with the compromises of the Catholic Church under colonialism.

In more recent years, there were persistent t ensions between the PAIGC/PAICV and the Catholic Church; in fact, such tensions were probably a factor in the PAIGC/PAICV electoral defeat in 1991. Today, Protestantism is certainly expanding in the islands, and a number of small new churches can be found in some of the larger towns.[19] Missionizing or conversion efforts are conducted by small groups such as the Ba'hai and the Mormons, and though there is no organized Jewish presence, the Jewish community has played an important role in the evolution of Cape Verdean society. To a small degree, African syncretic beliefs and practices are also present. Some African street merchants have recently imported Islam, albeit in an unorganized fashion, and certainly, Islam was once imported to Cape Verde by many Mandinka, Fula, and Wolof slaves. But from the time of the Inquisition, any formal expression of Islam was very strongly suppressed and essentially extinguished.

In the next section, I will attempt to articulate the ways in which social, economic, ethnic, racial, and religious groups helped to shape the *Crioulo* culture that ultimately emerged.

The Origins of *Crioulo* Culture

European Roots

Many of the very first European settlers in Cape Verde soon died there or returned to Portugal, but by the end of the fifteenth century and into the early sixteenth century, more came to replace them. Of this small group of Europeans, most were Portuguese. Many were from the Lisbon area, but a notable number came from the Algarve region of southern Portugal. This was strategically close to the ancient sea-trading town of Cadiz, which first launched Phoenician exploration into the Atlantic. Portuguese-speaking people from the Madeira and Azores Islands also went to Cape Verde, seeking new lands and new opportunities. Following the Inquisition, substantial numbers of Portuguese Jews (known as New Christians after their forced conversion) were added to this mixture. Most of the Europeans were functionaries of the state or church; others were military officers, *fidalgos,* and state and private merchants. The Crown enticed the earliest settlers with promises of free trade, even for slaves, on the coast. The promises were kept—but only for a very few years.

In a census of 1513, after more than a half century of settlement, Ribeira Grande officially had a grand total of 162 residents, including 58 "whites," 12 priests, and 16 "free blacks"; the rest were soldiers, *degredados,* and landlords. The *degredados,* or those convicted of criminal or political crimes in Portugal, would play an important role in the early settlement and economy of the islands. Some had been sentenced to life in the islands, but others stayed after being pardoned, having little incentive or inclination to return to Portugal. The early population at this point also included about 13,000 slaves, but as "nonpeople," they were usually recorded as property rather than citizens.

Those of Italian (i.e., Genoan and Venetian) extraction were also among the first inhabitants of Cape Verde. Members of the da Noli family from Genoa were some of the discoverers and first *capitãos* of the southern *donatário* of São Tiago. In addition to the Italian and Jewish residents in the "white" population, a few Lebanese Christians, Moroccan Jews, and even Chinese also settled in the islands. The inventory of Europeans who left their traces in names and genes must also include the pirate attackers, passing sailors, and maritime merchants from Spain, France, England, Holland, Brazil, and America. Some of these came in a spirit of open aggression, with the goal of looting and raping the resources, slaves, and women; others were more friendly. The poverty on the islands also forced a few women into prostitution to help sustain their families. Cape Verdeans, especially the men, are a traveling people, and there is a long tradition of women having to rely on their own hard work to get by. Timothy Finan and Helen Henderson suggest that the effects of poverty and male out-migration linger on in the now-institutionalized female-headed households of Cape Verdean society.[20]

African Roots

The majority of the sixteenth- and seventeenth-century Cape Verdeans came from Africa. With the Portuguese controlling the vast coast from Arguin in Mauritania to the Cape of Good Hope in South Africa in the fifteenth century, the African roots of Cape Verde are found throughout this broad region. The majority of slaves in Cape Verde came from the "Guinea Rivers" region, from the area Cap Vert in Senegal to Sierra Leone that is also known as the Upper Guinea coast. But as the centuries wore on, the Portuguese position on the coast was steadily eroded by Dutch, English, and French interlopers who had their own economic and military interests. And as Portugal's coastal domain was restricted, so was the area in which the Portuguese could gather slaves. Therefore, Portuguese slaving in the seventeenth and eighteenth centuries was largely confined to an area that approximates today's Senegambia and Guinea-Bissau. In the old slave warehouse at Gorée, adjacent to modern Dakar, the tourist guides still speak of the *sinhares,* or *mestiço* madames, who descended from Luso-African slave traders; they are famed for their wealth, seductive charms, and business skills in dealing with foreigners seeking African slaves.

According to the slave registers from 1526 to 1550 (see Table 2.1), the majority of slaves were from the peoples of Senegambia (particularly the Wolof, then at war with the Fula), and Guinea-Bissau (especially the Beafada), trapped between the coast and the Mande kingdom of Gabu. Even in the slave registers for 1856, most slaves still were being taken from the peoples on the Upper Guinea coast.[21] These registers list such coastal Senegambians as the Bagas, Baiotes, Balantas, Banhuns, Beafadas, Bololas, Brames, Cassangas, Cobianas, Diolas, Felupes, Manjacos, Nalus, Papels, Qissis, Susus, and Tandas, as well as the offshore Bissagos and some inland peoples, such as the Mandinkas and Bambaras. These rice-farming and fishing people were well organized for the practice of local democracy at the village level but not for sustained resistance against slave raiders—be they Europeans from the coast or Africans from the interior—who exploited their weakness. In fact, these people were victimized by the raiders in greater numbers and for a longer period of time than any other group in the region. From their villages, they were taken to Banjul, Bissau, Cacheu, Farim, Gorée, Joal, Portudal (Porto do 'Ali, now known as Mbour), or other trading centers to await shipment to the Cape Verde Islands or directly to the New World.

Historians at the Customs House Archives in Praia have managed to preserve one rather complete collection of slave records for 1856 for the entire archipelago, as well as 1867 records for São Tiago. Only to the extent that other records exist in Portugal will the African ethnic roots of the Cape Verdean people be more clearly known. In most cases, these origins have been utterly obliterated, and even when more precise identification is available, typically only the coast of Africa or the trading town where the slaves were purchased is noted. Although the vast majority of slaves came from Portuguese Guinea, especially in this late period, a tiny number also came from Cabinda and Angola, another thousand miles away.

In later centuries, as African societies such as the Mandinka, Fula, Sine, Salum, Serer, and Wolof became more centrally organized under chiefs and leaders of some importance, their people's names appeared less frequently on the slave rosters. But their fate also depended upon their fortune in military combat. In the endless raiding and warfare, some members of these ethnic groups fell captive or were sentenced to slavery to pay a debt or settle a criminal charge. If such was their fate, they were also among those transported from the Portuguese coastal *baracoons* ("coastal slave warehouse," or "stockades"). The *lançado* traders on the coast were not too particular when it came to African ethnography.

Most slaves were soon baptized, thereby attaining the new status of *ladino*. Once these slaves converted, it was said, their "souls" were destined to "be saved" following their lives of toil without compensation. The *ladinos* were given Latin first names, and sometimes they were also assigned the surname of their owner. Speaking the languages of Africa was actively discouraged in Cape Verde, even if one was fortunate enough to find a member of the same language group in the ethnic mosaic of Cape Verdean slave communities. Crioulo, a hybrid language of commerce and multiculturalism, was born of necessity in the first decades of the settler and slave era.

Remarkably, despite the general practice of ethnocide relative to African culture, important features of African heritage and traditions have persisted. Most obvious of all are the racial phenotypes that are dominant in the islands, revealing the African roots, but there are other manifestations as well. For example, although Islam, the religion of many slaves (especially those of Wolof, Fula, and Mande origin), was very actively repressed in the islands, some African beliefs relating to animism still survive, such as the notions of spirit possession and the evil eye. Moreover, some Mande words linger on in *Crioulo,* even though the overwhelming psycholinguistic structure of the language is derived from Portuguese.

The traditional forms of African weaving on a narrow band loom carry forward in the cloth *panos* that are still made as a national handicraft. They also symbolize Cape Verde's culture. *Panos* were once made from cotton produced by Cape Verde slaves, and the cloths were woven by slaves. They were used in dress, as currency to buy slaves, and in carrying both children, bundled on the back, and head loads. The custom of human porterage is unquestionably African in origin, as is the use of the heavy wooden *pilão* ("mortar and pestle") for grinding corn and husking rice.

Old World crops and foods of Africa such as rice, bananas, papayas, melons, millet, and peppers are still harvested as well. The very popular game of *ouri(n),* played widely in Cape Verde today, is of ancient origin; indeed, it was played several thousand years before Christ in the ancient Middle East. Similarly, certain musical traditions—especially the percussive polyrhythms of the *batuko* dancers or the modern *finaçon,* a tropical music genre, and *funana,* a music and dance form—have almost nothing to do with an Iberian past. The lyrics of the Cape Verdean *mornas* are sung as a painful lament about the hardships of life in the islands—another cultural feature that is uniquely Cape Verdean, although comparable to the Portuguese *fados* in their folk tradition.

The Crioulo *Cultural Synthesis*

The mother tongue of the Cape Verdean people is based heavily upon Portuguese syntax and lexicon and enriched with an African phonetic system and with loan words from both stocks. On the West African coast, there is also an English-based Creole and pidgin, as well as dialectical, patois French languages. Although the official language in the Cape Verde Islands is Portuguese, Crioulo is the usual language of expression. It is considered most suitable for sharing intimacy and feelings and for expressing the *saudade* of the archipelago. Varying from one island to another, Crioulo is the vehicle of everyday communication in Cape Verde for individuals at all levels of society. It is also a defining linguistic feature of the Cape

Verdean cultural identity that has been transmitted to the United States and other parts of the world. In this way, the term *Crioulo* is used not only for the Creolized language but also for identifying the distinctive and dynamic culture—including the complete array of folklore, customs, cuisine, music, and literature of this people.

As noted earlier, it was only in the earliest part of Cape Verdean history that the bulk of society was composed of slaves. For most of its history, Cape Verde has been a *Crioulo* society. Data for the mid-19th century—provided by the late, great historian of Cape Verde, António Carreira—reveals that only a minority of the population actually held slaves, and in a group of 549 slave owners from São Tiago (where slavery was the most significant), the average owner held only 4.4 slaves. On the neighboring island of Maio, there were 3.4 slaves per owner, and only 17 out of the 549 slave proprietors on São Tiago had 20 slaves or more. One of these had 64, and another had 50, but these are most exceptional cases.[22]

So, although one may speak of Cape Verde as a slave society in terms of the central role slavery played in the export and agricultural economy and in the wealth it generated, it must be emphasized that throughout most of its half millennium of history, slaves were a minority of the total population. Often, slaves escaped to the interior to become *badius*; through manumission, other slaves and their descendants became free. Nor was slavery equally important for each island. Similarly, only a minority of economically powerful landowners (usually serving the interest of the Crown) or merchants serving royal commerce were heavily committed to this business. Thus, the relative proportion of slaves in the society fell from a (brief) majority to a rather stable 5 to 10 percent—the level maintained in the eighteenth and nineteenth centuries, until the institution of slavery was, at long last, curbed.

It was not uncommon for colonial officials, slave masters, landlords, and even clergy to take their sexual pleasures with their slaves. (One bishop spent considerable effort to arrange surprise raids on his priests' nightly trysts—but with little lasting effect.) Finan and Henderson have coined the term *informal polygyny* to apply to this practice, which was linked with the generalized economic deprivation in the islands, especially for women.[23] The relationships produced offspring, thereby regenerating the labor force without requiring additional expenditures for purchasing slaves. Nineteenth-century records show that there were some steady new slave arrivals from the coast even in this late period. Nonetheless, the majority of the slaves officially registered for tax purposes in each island also originated from that same island. Of the 1,194 slaves sold within São Tiago in 1856, for example, 902 were from that island. Taken as a whole, even while the Africa Squadron was based in São Tiago, the Portuguese ruling Cape Verde legally imported at least 417 slaves from Africa in 1856 (see Table 3.5).

The attitudes and practices of racial oppression, economic exploitation, sexual access, and intraisland movement continued into the twentieth century. One re-

TABLE 3.5 Cape Verdean Interisland Slave Commerce, 1856

Island of slave's residence	Slave's Place of Origin										Import Total
	Brava	Boa Vista	Fogo	Sal	Santo Antão	São Nicolau	São Tiago	São Vicente	Maio	Africa	
Brava	144	1	44	0	0	0	1	0	1	39	86
Boa Vista	1	66	6	2	2	1	2	0	0	48	62
Fogo	0	0	178	0	0	0	0	0	0	0	0
Sal	7	33	14	60	9	1	2	0	0	33	99
Santo Antão	2	14	7	5	136	3	2	0	0	21	54
São Nicolau	2	2	4	0	0	109	10	0	1	31	50
São Tiago	2	9	39	0	0	0	902	0	4	238	292
São Vicente	0	6	1	3	6	1	4	4	0	7	28
Export Total	14	65	115	10	17	6	21	0	6	417	NA

NOTE: Data for Maio are unavailable, but the slave population on Maio was probably lower than that on Boa Vista.
SOURCE: Calculated from data in the 1856 Registry of Slaves, Cape Verde National Historical Archives, Praia, Cape Verde.

sult was that only a minority of the women giving birth were formally married. When slaves were sold arbitrarily or as a punishment, their partners often vanished. And even among freed slaves, *badius,* or sharecroppers, life was sufficiently precarious that permanent unions were hard to sustain. A deeply entrenched value system in which males were supreme also fostered informal unions. In fact, given the prevalence of "informal polygyny," males sometimes had forty children or more.

In this way the *donatários,* the *fidalgos,* the ranking military officers, the colonial functionaries, the large-scale merchants and shippers, and the bishops and priests all held political, economic, and sexual power over the inhabitants of their *capitanias.* As such, they were station masters on the biological track to *Crioulo* synthesis.

Cape Verde's external power relations may be explored in the context of this upper stratum, which one might call the *capitão* model. All the privileged members of Cape Verdean society were able to keep their rank and position by virtue of their relations to the secure, external power base represented by the kings and presidents of Portugal. They could rest assured that revolt or rebellion would be rare, and they would only have to await reinforcements from other islands or the coast or perhaps from Portugal before their positions would be defended or restored. The persistent threat of external force was sufficient to keep the colonial administrative structure in place for five centuries. The key here is that it was an external power base, with its own economic interests, that gave the ruling classes in Cape Verde their self-confidence and security.

Also useful in exploring the history of power relations in Cape Verde is the *lançado* model derived from the coastal traders and their island counterparts. The *lançados* of the sixteenth and seventeenth centuries were tolerated because they benefited the commercial interests of the Portuguese Crown—or at least, so the Crown thought. Having been subject to Portuguese pogroms and anti-Semitism, the *lançados* were not so keen to be economically loyal. Also associated with the Luso-African *tangomãos* in their role as intermediary translators of African languages, the *lançados* had a love-hate relationship with the Lisbon authorities. Always suspicious of the *lançados'* economic freedom and success, the Portuguese regularly sought new controls and measures to ensure the payment of taxes and tariffs. Yet if the *lançados* had not had a measure of freedom in their work, the flow of slaves, gold, hides, ivory, honey, and wax would have begun to trickle, and they would have looked for customers on merchant ships on other nations. In reality, however, the *lançados* were only tolerated, and any economic advances they made were likely resisted by the *capitãos.* Nonetheless, although their power seldom rested upon royal favor or patronage, the *lançados* were at the economic crossroads of the slave export economy that was central to wealth and power in Cape Verde. Much of the islands' history can be seen as a tug-of-war between those with ties to the formal powers in Lisbon and those with the practical, commercial links to the coast.

The *lançados* were seldom slave owners, except for the brief period during which the slaves were transferred from the coast to the archipelago. But they were the shippers and traders. Needing a lingua franca in the coastal commerce that was the focus of their lives, they created the context for the evolution of the Crioulo language. Their strength lay in their strategic position and their grassroots links, which kept them secure on the coast without much more than a bodyguard of *grumete* mercenaries to protect their *baracoons,* warehouses, presidios, and coastal settlements. Not only did they pioneer in Crioulizing the Portuguese language, they also spread Crioulo from their coastal *baracoons* and *feitorias* toward the interior via their Dyula (Mandinka) slave trading allies. They were only restrained by other Europeans also penetrating the interior from their own coastal bases.

At almost any point in Cape Verdean history, there was a tension between the interests of the state (whether feudal or republican) or the *capitão* representatives, on the one hand, and the interests of the intercoastal merchants, represented by the *lançados* who were the gatekeepers of commerce at the point of production, on the other. The Cape Verdean majority existed between these two groups, ever more Crioulized and ever more powerless. Also caught in the middle were the Senegambian slaves, who were victimized and exploited by all.

The Case of the Badius

Having already explored the social position of the *badius,* I will now consider their cultural role in *Crioulo* society. As the etymology of their name suggests, the *badius* of Cape Verde are wanderers and runaways. Essentially, they form the core of the peasant population in the interior of São Tiago and are descended, in most cases, from runaway slaves. They have retained a certain degree of African-based cultural distinctiveness in their customs, folklore, religious practices, and dialect of Crioulo: Living in remote regions and maintaining a social distance from the rest of the population during the years of colonial rule, the *badius* were less assimilated to Portuguese culture than the rest of the Cape Verdean population. They were viewed as the primary representatives of an African heritage, and, as such, they have historically been denigrated by colonial authorities and looked down upon by other Cape Verdeans. The few known instances of slave and peasant rebellion in Cape Verde tended to occur in the *badiu* populations, giving them a certain notoriety in popular mythology that has engendered both disdain and admiration. Perhaps because of the threat they once posed to the colonial authorities by resisting assimilation, the *badius* were more likely to be recruited for contract labor, and they were the backbone of the system of forced emigration to the cacão plantations on the islands of São Tomé and Príncipe.

Badiu folk culture is intimately linked with the spiritual nostalgia, soul, or *saudade* of Cape Verde. In turn, the essence of *saudade* is partially embodied in the *badius's* popular musical traditions—the main area in which their Africanity was tolerated during the centuries of slavery and colonialism. The ethnomusicology of the *badius* includes several basic forms, such as *batuko, finaçon, funana, cola-cola,* and *tabanca.* Specialists in African popular music and ethnomusicology—among them Peter Manuel, Susan Hurley Glowa, Katherine Hagedorn, and Gei Zantzinger—have added considerably to the study of the form and function of this rich integration of *Crioulo* music, the *badiu* subculture, and the wider Cape Verdean society.

Crioulo Cultural Markers

The term *batuko,* applied to one form of music and dance among the *badius* of São Tiago, is derived from the Portuguese verb meaning "to beat." The beats coordinate the collective involvement in this musical tradition. The *batuko* was and is performed exclusively by women, generally at night. Throughout the archipelago, Bibinha Cabral was famous as a *batuko* singer, and her work has been recorded on disk, described in books, and featured in Zantzinger's film *Songs of the Badius.* As a lead singer, she improvised lyrics about political, secular, sexual, and other topical themes. Several women, arranged around her in a rough circle, sang choral responses and executed rhythms by clapping hands and beating on cloth pads held between their legs. One or more women danced vigorously inside the circle, each wearing a shawl or *pano* around the upper thighs. *Batuko* and the related *finaçon* employ polyrhythmic beating, call-and-response, and gender segregation, which demonstrate its African or Moorish derivation.

Batuko often incurred the disapproval of the Catholic Church for its sexually provocative dance style; at the same time, colonial rulers intermittently repressed this genre for its obliquely militant texts, and the middle classes or *assimilados* tended to disparage it as vulgar. The Portuguese authorities went so far as to ban the *badius* dancing in the *batuko* style, which was projected as "too African" and "too primitive." Some *badius* in the twentieth century responded by "outrageously" reinterpreting the meaning of Catholicism as the *rebelado* movement emerged. This merged Catholicism with a folk and personal spiritualism that the bishops and priests found repugnant.

During the war of national liberation and after independence, the PAICV promoted and celebrated *batuko* to empower and legitimize the *badius* population; this was part of an effort to build new alliances and discard the colonialist and racist oppression of these people. As Amilcar Cabral stated,

> The experience of colonial domination shows that, in an attempt to perpetuate exploitation, the colonizer not only creates a whole system of repression of the cultural life of the colonized people but also provokes and develops the cultural alienation of a part of the population, either by supposed assimilation of indigenous persons, or by

the creation of a social gulf between the aboriginal elites and the masses of the people.[24]

In the spirit of "re-Africanizing" Cape Verdeans, the PAICV promoted both the serious study of *batuko* through research on oral traditions and the recording of this music by popular modern musical groups, such as "Bulimundo." It remains to be seen what the official attitude of the MpD government will be in light of its delegitimization of the PAICV and its African orientation.

Funana is another musical and dance genre associated with the *badius* of São Tiago. According to Peter Manuel, *funana* typically includes a vocalist who

> improvises verses in a fast quadratic rhythm, while playing a simple chordal ostinato on the the concertina-like *gaita*. Another musician provides rhythmic accompaniment on the *ferrinho*, a strip of metal which is scraped, like a rasp, with a small peg. Others present may sing loose choral responses to the lead vocalist's lines. The harmonic pattern usually consists of a simple alternation between two adjacent chords.[25]

Funana accompanies informal and sometime erotic couple dancing, similar to Caribbean dances such as the merengue. Like *batuko*, *funana* has seen a popular revival since independence, and it is now featured in a number of records, tapes, and the music of modern dance bands. An example of this musical form is found in the work of Carlos "Cachass" Martins, the "King of Funana" who was born on the east coast of São Tiago in 1951. He and Nórberto Tavares are considered to be pioneers in the *funana* revival, which liberated the African musical traditions in Cape Verde from years of colonial cultural oppression. It is said that "Cachass" brought *funana* "to the plateau," meaning that his style was so popular and widespread that even the "high society" plateau area of Praia could not help but recognize it.

Manuel has identified the *finaçon* as another women's musical and lyrical form common to the *badius* of São Tiago.[26] In this instance, one or two vocalists improvise topical verses, while other women join in by beating on cushions held between their legs, producing polyrhythmic patterns corresponding to those used in *batuko*. The verses, covering a broad range of subjects, are rendered in an intense, highly rhythmic, but at most semimelodic style. *Finaçon* is sometimes performed in competitive song "duels," provoking gaiety and laughter.

The Cape Verdean *coladeira* has traditionally involved an open-air procession dance, accompanied by drums and whistles, performed at the festivals of São João and São Pedro, especially on the islands of São Vicente and Santo Antão.[27] Alternatively, it has utilized one caller in a group of women who performs improvised topical verses in a lively call-and-response style during certain festivals, accompanied by male drummers. At present, the term more commonly denotes a popular dance song in fast duple meter, sung with alternating verse and chorus. This modern *coladeira* emerged in the 1960s. It appears to have been influenced by Carib-

Mountain home, Santo Antão Island (Photo by Waltraud Berger Coli)

bean and Afro-American dance music, by the *morna,* and perhaps by the processional *coladeira.* The genre is popular throughout the archipelago and in Cape Verdean emigrant communities. *Coladeira* may be played by an ensemble using traditional instruments, such as those associated with the *morna,* or by a modern dance band with a drum set and amplified stringed and keyboard instruments. The appeal of the *coladeira* lies in its fast, danceable rhythm; its harmonies and lyrics lack the sophistication of the *morna. Coladeira* texts are generally simple, topical, lighthearted, and often satirical or humorous, and the music accompanies couple dancing or, more traditionally, line dancing.

The musical form known as *tabanca* is derived from the *Crioulo* word meaning "village."[28] *Tabanca* committees were formed by the PAIGC in villages throughout the liberated zones of Guinea-Bissau during the nationalist struggle; they served to link the party with the peasantry. In Cape Verde, the term *tabanca* refers to aspects of the musical and folk life of the rural *badius.* Cape Verdeans also use the term to refer to a processional dance performed at certain festivals on São Tiago, especially during the feast of São João. During this dance, the participants walk in loose formation throughout the town, singing, clapping, and dancing to the accompaniment of drums, conches, and whistles.

Last but certainly not least in the musical markers of *Crioulo* culture is the *morna*, which is the most popular poetic and musical genre of Cape Verde. It is regarded as one of the most characteristic and quintessential expressions of national culture.[29] The appeal of the *mornas* extends to all classes and all islands. *Morna* may denote an instrumental song or an independent poem, but most typically, it refers to a poem consisting of a series of quatrains, set to music. The *morna* is normally sung in medium-tempo quadratic meter by a solo vocalist, accompanied by stringed instruments such as the violin (*rabeca*), the guitarlike *violão*, the viola, and the *cavaquinho*, a small guitar. A variety of formal structures may be used; most typically, a melodic line is sung and repeated, followed by another phrase that is also repeated, resulting in an "aabb" pattern; this pattern may be repeated three or four times, occasionally incorporating an instrumental solo. The origin of the *morna* is obscure, although it appears to have first emerged in Boa Vista in the mid-nineteenth century, possibly influenced by the Portuguese and Brazilian *modinha*. In its vocal style, instrumentation, and use of harmony, the *morna* is predominantly European rather than African in character. *Morna* texts, generally in *Crioulo*, often reflect considerable sophistication. They are topical and frequently express sadness, nostalgia, longing for loved ones, and other serious, romantic, or philosophical subjects.

Since independence, these musical genres, partially derived from *badiu* society, have quite literally "reached the plateau." As such, they are now broadly accepted as an authentic *Crioulo* cultural tradition. The Cape Verdean musical forms—the *batuko, tabanca, funana, finaçon, coladeira,* and *mornas*—have been joined with other musical and dance traditions from Europe, such as the *mazurkas* and *valzas*.

Another important, distinguishing facet of *Crioulo* culture has evolved from its literary traditions.[30] These may be traced back to 1894, with the publication of the first literary annual, *Almanach Luso-Africano,* in Ribeira Grande, São Nicolau; the first book of poetry, Pedro Cardoso's *Caboverdeanas,* was published in Praia in 1915. Generally speaking, the early writers followed Portuguese literary conventions and were not directly focused on cultural matters relating to Cape Verde.[31]

These early works were followed by a literary movement known as *Claridade*. The literary journal for which this movement is named has long ceased publication, but in its short history, it came to symbolize and legitimate the uniqueness of *Crioulo* culture. Some members of the *Claridade* movement laid the literary foundation for what finally became the political movement for independence. To a remarkable degree, the struggle for national liberation was expressed in the metaphors of poetry.[32]

The *Claridade* movement was founded in 1936 by a group of Cape Verdean intellectuals and writers, including Baltasar Lopes, Jorge Barbosa, and Manuel Lopes. The primary purposes of the journal they published were to explore the sources of *Crioulo* culture, to develop an original Cape Verdean literature, and to seek freer cultural expression. *Claridade* was partially inspired by the contemporary Portuguese literary magazine *Presença*. In addition, a group of Brazilian writers of the same period were also breaking away from the classical Portuguese forms in order to create a modern regionalistic fiction. With the contributions of such Cape Verdean social commentators as Felix Monteiro and sociologist João Lopes, *Claridade* soon became more than a literary review: It encompassed a socioeconomic analysis of the archipelago as well. Though *Claridade* was published only sporadically, it is a significant benchmark in the evolution of a distinctive *Crioulo* cultural and literary tradition. The most recognized writers from the *Claridoso*'s tradition interacted around discussions of their works published in their journal and around the small seminary of São José, where the *Claridade* were concentrated.

Others associated with this "classical school" include the writers José Lopes, Januário Leite, Pedro Cardoso, and Eugénio Tavares. Most of them wrote in Portuguese, but Tavares and Cardoso were exceptions to this rule; they began the practice of writing in the Crioulo language, addressing the *Crioulo* experience and culture as well as the socioeconomic conditions of the archipelago. From the late 1930s came the first Cape Verdean novels, an anthology of Cape Verdean short stories, and a wealth of essays on *Crioulo* culture and language.

It is impossible to discuss *Claridade* without noting Baltasar Lopes da Silva (23 April 1907–28 May 1989), one of the most celebrated Cape Verdean writers.[33] He is the author of *Chiquinho,* the pivotal novel of Cape Verde that was first published in 1947. Lopes was born in the village of Ribeira Brava on the island of São Nicolau, and he earned degrees from the Faculties of Law and Letters at the University of Lisbon. After spending several years teaching in Portugal, Lopes returned to Cape Verde in the 1930s to work at the Liceu Gil Eannes on the island of São Vicente, where he was the director for many years before retiring in 1972. As one of the founding members of *Claridade,* Lopes became a leading figure in the development of modern Cape Verdean literature. He was a poet, a short story writer and an essayist, as well as a novelist, writing his poetry under the pseudonym Osvaldo Alcantara. With the 1957 publication of the monograph *O Dialecto Crioulo de Cabo Verde,* Lopes spearheaded the movement to legitimize Crioulo as a viable and autonomous language. In 1960, Lopes edited the pioneering anthology of Cape Verdean stories, *Antologia da Ficção Caboverdiana Contemporânea,* which included six of his own works. Although offered a prestigious faculty position at the University of Lisbon in the 1940s, Lopes decided to live, write, and die in his native Cape Verde, where he is buried.

Another noted poet and cofounder of *Claridade* was Jorge Barbosa (1902–1971).[34] His first collection of poetry, *Arquipelago* (published even before the *Claridade* journal), synthesized ideas and topics that received additional attention in the *Claridade* movement. Born in Praia, Barbosa received little formal schooling, yet he occupies a special place in the history of Cape Verdean literature as the first poet to make a definitive break with the earlier "classical" tradition. He is especially famed for his poem "Lost Islands." Barbosa died in Lisbon while receiving medical treatment but because he was an opponent of colonialism, his remains were not returned to Cape Verde until after independence. His impressive tomb in Varzea Cemetery in Praia bears an apt inscription: "Great Respect from the Cape Verdean People to the Poet of the Archipelago."

Any list of the literary greats of Cape Verde must also include José Lopes (1871–1962), who was a very productive poet laureate of the classical period.[35] Lopes was born in São Nicolau, one of seven children. At ten, he became an orphan, and for a time, he attended the São José seminary, which produced so many literary leaders. But by fifteen, family responsibilities forced him to leave school. From that time on, Lopes was self-educated, mastering Latin, French, and English well enough to write verse in those languages. He became a schoolteacher and produced, over the years, several weighty volumes of poetry.

Manuel Lopes (1907–   ), also a distinguished poet and writer of prose fiction, was another founder of *Claridade*.[36] Lopes was born on Santo Antão and educated at the University of Coimbra in Portugal. He returned to Cape Verde to work for Western Telegraph on São Vicente, a position that enabled him to travel to the Açores and Portugal. His writing focused on the uniqueness of the Cape Verdean experience, adding much to the literary wealth of the archipelago. He was the recipient of several distinguished literary awards, and his works have been translated into a number of different languages. His second novel, *Flagelados do Vente Leste* ("Victims of the East Wind"), was dramatized in the first Cape Verdean–produced feature-length motion picture. The film carried the same title and was shot on Lopes's native island of Santo Antão.

Cape Verde's musical and literary heritage was also enriched by Eugénio de Paula Tavares (5 November 1867–1930), who is known for his evocative renditions of Cape Verdean *mornas*, that combine poetry, song, and dance to evoke the very *saudade* of the archipelago.[37] The nostalgic tone in his *mornas* could bring audiences to tears, and his impact on later generations of *morna* players is great. A native of Brava and self-educated, Tavares worked for most of his life as a civil servant. Writing almost exclusively in Crioulo, he played a critical role in maintaining the viability of Crioulo as the language of the people. In his verse, Tavares often drew upon folkloric sources. He has become a legendary figure in the archipelago, particularly in Brava, where rich stories of his life and loves have become part of the popular culture. To this day in Brava, Tavares's classic *Hora di Bai* ("The Hour to Leave") is the *morna* that is, by custom, the last sung, signifying not only the close of an evening's music but also the endless departures from the land of emigrants. Tavares is also known for his contributions to such publications as *Luso-Africano* and *Cartas Cabo-Verdianas*, which added substantially to the islands' heritage and the consciousness of Cape Verdean culture and its problems.

Most of these writers had to exercise great caution during colonial times, for the authorities were quick to detect any spirit of protest or cultural independence. As an example, the work of Ovidio Martins was confiscated by the PIDE, which perceived it as too strong an expression of anticolonialism and a Cape Verdean yearning for cultural freedom. Martins, born in São Vicente in 1928, was especially known for his works *Caminhada* and *Tchutchinha,* published in 1962; both were collections of poems in Portuguese and Crioulo.[38]

In the years since 1975, with colonial restraints gone, the *Claridosos* and their disciples can be celebrated openly. *Funana* and *finaçon* are heard on the radio, which also broadcasts discussions of hotly debated topics on culture and politics. New poems, novels, and films are being produced at a great rate in the islands and in their global diaspora. Cape Verdean folklore has also been substantially expanded, with the oral tradition of *Nho Lobo* (Mr. "Clever" Wolf) folktales now being reevaluated and closely studied.[39] Other folkloric traditions in the islands include the *mastro* ceremony in which a facsimile of a sailing ship mast is raised to celebrate a saint's day, such as those of São João or Santo Antão.[40] The mast is covered with candies and fruits that are retrieved by eager children at an appointed moment.

Cape Verdean culture has also produced specialties in cuisine. The more important foods include chicken dishes, such as *djagacida* or *jag, catchupa* or *matchupa* (a corn and bean stew), *papa de milho* or *xerem* (corn porridge), *camoca* (a farina sweet), *cuscuz* (farina), *gufong, fong,* or *funguin* (corn bread, sometimes with sugarcane syrup), and *conj* (chicken soup). In addition, there are numerous Cape Verdean ways to prepare fish of many species, sea turtles, and pork.[41]

Handicrafts include the gaming boards called *ouri, wari, uril,* or *urim* which are often handsomely carved in mahogany. This rather complex "seek-and-capture" game is played elsewhere in West Africa (where it is known as *mancala* or by many other names), which clearly shows the continuity that existed in African cultures as long as there was no threat to the colonial institutions. This game is virtually Cape Verde's national sport and is played widely and with great enthusiasm. There are also artisans producing carved pipes, ship models, and carved cow horns, coconuts, and turtle shells, as well as pottery. Musical instruments of African origin, such as the *berimbau, tambor, pandeiro,* and *catreba,* are also found in the islands.[42] And many women are well known for their crocheting and embroidery work. It is also said that each island can be distinguished by the varying techniques used in tying womens' headscarves. Although not a part of material culture, there are numerous children's games played throughout the islands that help the young become socialized in the *Crioulo* culture; these include: *bfongue, climintinha, cruntchinha, cuisão, elgurinha, landôm, páca, rabáta, reanáta,* and *tunguinha.*[43]

Special mention must also be made of the Cape Verdean *pano,* a unique form of untailored Cape Verdean textile that has been produced for centuries.[44] *Panos* are woven from cotton fiber grown in the islands and made on a narrow loom. Six strips are sewn together to make a wider cloth that is typically dyed with very dark blue indigo, also grown in Cape Verde. The weaving technique used in making *panos* is of Mande origin, transmitted to Cape Verde through its trade with Africa. In fact, some slaves were imported to Cape Verde just to become weavers of *panos.*

The blue dye used on *panos* is from the urzella and indigo plants, which were exported as cash crops from the Cape Verde Islands. *Panos* are worn exclusively by women as a shawl or waist sash, part of the traditional costume used in folk dancing. They are also wadded in a tight ball and beaten by the women to accompany the *batuko* dance chants. Mothers also use *panos* to carry their infants on their hips in a typically African manner.

As exports, the value of the dyed *panos* was increased with more intricate designs in the weaving and more skillful sewing. Fogo was famed for its deep indigo *panos pretos,* and São Tiago had a great reputation for the volume and quality of its *pano* production. When there was a relative scarcity of iron bars for exchange in the slave trade, the *panos* were sometimes used as currency; in the sixteenth century, they were widely employed in barter exchange, just as rafia cloths were used in the Congo. By 1680, two high-quality *panos* had a standardized value equal to one standard iron bar.

When some individual Cape Verdeans became successful and independent in the slave trade, the Portuguese Crown issued the Decree of January 23, 1687, which proclaimed that the sale of locally made *panos* to foreigners was punishable, even by death. Indeed, even those selling raw cotton privately could face the same penalty. By 1721, the Portuguese still held that the trade in *panos* was illegal and punishable by severe penalties. This reiteration of the 1687 edict was made to reassert the Crown monopoly and to keep Cape Verdean merchants from trading privately. In recent years, the small scale production of *panos* has restored this textile as a symbol of Cape Verdean identity and folk tradition, carried on strongly by the *badius* in particular. *Panos* are still valued, but they have largely been replaced by cheap, machinemade textiles.

In myriad ways, Cape Verdeans have managed to preserve and enhance important features of their unique culture. The *badius,* for example, have protected African customs, beliefs, and material culture throughout their search for freedom in the remote interior region. In times of pirate attack, famine, and drought, these refugee descendants of slaves were economically marooned in their hideaways. Yet this gave them a measure of freedom from social oppression, although they suffered the ravages of ecological degradation and cultural humiliation. Even African household architecture is preserved by the *badius,* in their round *funcas* made of Cape Verdean basalt and thatch roofs rather than the "proper," Portuguese-style tile.

Women in Cape Verde

Stephanie Urdang, an observer of the movement for national and women's liberation in Cape Verde and Guinea-Bissau, noted that the women in both lands suffered from the triple oppression of colonialism, racism, and male supremacy.[45]

Measured by a wide variety of social indicators, Cape Verdean women suffer a notable degree of gender discrimination—in their relatively higher level of illiteracy, lower pay, and diminishing numbers in upper social, political, and educational positions. Generally, there is a paucity of prominent Cape Verdean women writers, although Vera Duarte, Yolanda Morazzo, Orlanda Amarilis, and Maria Nunes stand as important exceptions.[46]

In contrast, women are very prominent in heavy labor: working on road brigades and public works projects, pounding food grains, and carrying heavy water containers over long distances and to high elevations. Cases involving the physical and psychological abuse of wives are common in the homes but rarely heard in the courts. The vulnerability of women is worsened by the high levels of male migration and "informal polygyny," which often leave women with few resources to provide for themselves and their children. The substantially lower level of women's formal participation in the political process also weakens their overall power, which itself has been shaped by the broad presence of a machismo ideology. Nevertheless, women's organizations have addressed these problems in their programs; their plans for action seek to increase female involvement and representation and focus on issues of family planning, abortion, health, and education. To advance the position of women, the Democratic Union of Women (UDEMU) was formed in 1961 in Conakry as an organization supporting the anticolonial movement led by the PAIGC.[47]

Like the PAIGC, UDEMU sought to represent both Cape Verde and Guinea-Bissau. It also advocated its own concerns; however, women's issues were usually viewed as secondary to the urgency of the war for national liberation that raged at the time. UDEMU was active in bringing about women's representation in village committees during the war and concerned with various family and social issues, such as the opposition to polygyny and bridewealth payments in Guinea-Bissau, greater access to divorce, and legislation encouraging greater paternal responsibility. Currently, both Cape Verde and Guinea-Bissau recognize International Women's Day.

Although there are no formal barriers to their political participation in Cape Verde, women are not equally represented in the political parties or legislative bodies. Toward the end of the war, UDEMU was replaced by the Women's Commission, which continued the links with women's organizations in other nations.[48] The year after the 1980 coup d'état in Guinea-Bissau, the separate Organization of Women of Cape Verde (OMCV) was formed when the Cape Verdean branch of the PAIGC changed its name to the PAICV; the first congress of the OMCV was held in 1990. Paula Fortes, the present secretary-general of the OMCV, has held seminars and conferences on issues such as family planning, AIDS, housing, nutrition, and the household economy. In the most recent Cape Verdean elections for the Peoples National Assembly, only ten of the seventy-nine seats went to women: This may compare favorably with the number of elected women legislators in some other nations, but it is obviously far from parity.

Despite these hardships and discrimination, a number of women have played important leadership roles, especially during the period of PAIGC/PAICV rule (1975–1991) when Cape Verde and Guinea-Bissau were politically unified. Moreover, many women who gained prominence in Guinea have been widely recognized in Cape Verde,[49] including Maria Boal, the director of the Pilot School and Friendship Institute, and Ernestina "Titina" Silla, a martyr of the PAIGC who is often portrayed as an exemplary, self-sacrificing heroine. The war years also brought Carmen Pereira (1937–) into prominence in the PAIGC as the political commissioner for the entire South Front. She was the only woman in the twenty-four-member Executive Committee of the Struggle (CEL) and the head of the Woman's Commission. In addition, Pereira was the second vice president of the Peoples National Assembly and one of the fifteen members of the PAIGC's Council of State.[50]

The case of Sofia Pomba Guerra also deserves some note here. Guerra was neither Cape Verdean nor Guinean but a Portuguese pharmacist who worked in Bissau in the early years of the PAIGC. Because of her support for the Portuguese Communist Party, she had been exiled from Portugal. In Bissau, she became influential in the ideological development of the PAIGC's program and strategy.[51]

In Cape Verde, Dulce Almada Duarte, a sociologist by training, was a very early and active member of the PAIGC. In June 1962, she gained prominence by addressing the UN Committee on Decolonization, then meeting in Rabat. Ireneu Gomes was trained in Brazil as a physician and psychologist and pioneered in these fields in Cape Verde. She is also a women's rights activist and a longtime member of the PAIGC, in which she served as minister of health and social affairs.

Thus far in the MpD administration, one can see a continuing commitment to the women's movement and women's issues. Prominent in the new generation of leaders is Maria Deolinda Delgado Monteiro. She is an elected member of the Peoples National Assembly, occupying an MpD seat, and perhaps more importantly, she is the general director of Empresa Pública de Abastecimento (EMPA), the huge parastatal trading company that deals in basic commodities, foodstuffs, and building materials for the entire archipelago. As such, she is directly in charge of a staff of 1,000 and oversees the major shipping, storage, and distribution networks. This places her squarely in the middle of the major MpD policy of privatizing the Cape Verdean economy while continuing to provide for the subsistence and supply needs of the wider population.

Finally, there is Bibinha Cabral, who is known to all Cape Verdeans for her *batuko* songs and popular music. Bibinha is certainly not a woman's liberationist in the normal sense, but her indomitable *badiu* spirit has come to represent a fundamental rejection of both male domination and colonialism; thereby, she also symbolizes the relative empowerment of women. Clearly, the struggle for women's rights in Cape Verde has begun. But there is still a long way to travel.

Cultural Conclusions

The twentieth century has witnessed many great political movements. While the socialist and capitalist nations clashed in the global Cold War, the Third World nations were struggling with their movements of anticolonialism and national liberation. Given the extent and power of these global movements, it was inevitable that the famous "winds of change" would finally buffet the Cape Verde Islands. For those of African origin and self-identity, these movements were telescoped with the rise of the great spokesmen of nationalism, socialism, and pan-Africanism such as George Padmore, W.E.B. DuBois, Kwame Nkrumah, Sekou Touré, Leopold S. Senghor, Julius Nyerere, Jomo Kenyatta, C.L.R. James, and Nelson Mandela.

In Cape Verde, the new breed of questioning intellectuals noted that their own society was only projected as a residual or hybrid culture of the Portuguese. Colonialists allowed it no self-generating legitimacy or authenticity and, at best, viewed it as a bastard society to be used by the colonizers for cheap labor and in colonial commerce. Even Crioulo, the unique form of Cape Verdean language, was projected merely as "poorly spoken Portuguese," rather than accepted on its own sociolinguistic terms. These new thinkers believed that a people with no effectively expressed awareness of their history, culture, and language would never be destined to rule themselves and have their fate in their own hands. This turning point is well described by Dulce Almada Duarte:

> The facts, however, proved that Cabral's perception of the deep roots of Cape Verdean culture being located in Africa was exact and that only the policies of assimilation and alienation practiced by the Portuguese colonialists had allowed this reality to be obscured. Had it been otherwise, it would have been impossible to obtain such a profound unity as that which came to exist, on the one hand, between the Cape Verdean popular masses—upon taking integral consciousness of their true cultural identity—and the popular masses of Guinea-Bissau; and, on the other, between these and the Cape Verdean petite bourgeoisie, which by consciously opting for the struggle of national liberation identified itself with the popular masses of Cape Verde and thus, following Cabral's well-known projection, showed itself willing to commit political suicide.[52]

The first active explorations in this search for a new consciousness would be found in literary movements that spoke about the Cape Verdean life experience. At first, this was done in Portuguese, then later, in the early written forms of Crioulo. By the early decades of this century, the movement crystallized in the *Claridade* literary journal. Symbolically, it spoke with clarity of a personal and, later, a national vision. But the seeds of democratic republicanism in Portugal in the early twentieth century were not to last. The "new state" of Portugal's fascist leadership was quick to eradicate the smallest threat to its authority. And a heavy

darkness fell on *Claridade* and its illuminating *Claridosos.* Desite this, the new nationalist *saudade* was expressed through sports teams, arts, food, folklore, historical research, and any other means that might be used to break Portugal's intellectual and cultural monopoly—a monopoly that had long stifled Cape Verdeans'
self-discovery and self-expression.

Chapter 4 addresses the struggle for independence in Cape Verde and Guinea-
Bissau, which began as a peaceful protest and appeal, only to end with a decade of
war.

4

RADICALS, SOLDIERS,
AND DEMOCRATS:
POLITICS IN
CAPE VERDE

I N PRE–WORLD WAR II times, Portugal was economically aligned with Western capitalism, but it had political affinities with German fascism and dictatorship in its desire to block radical socialism. At this point, the movement of anticolonial national liberation in Africa was only in its formative stage, and due to its colonial status, Cape Verde could be an observer—but little more.

The Struggle for Independence

After World War II, the Cold War struggle escalated as local-level conflicts around the world were typically viewed through the prism of the East-West dichotomy. England and France saw that the days of their colonial empires were drawing to a close, but the attitude of Portugal was markedly different. Indeed, the Portuguese opposed any movement expressing anticolonialist or nationalist sentiments in their African colonies. Thus, when the anticolonial movement blew the "winds of change" across Africa, it was inevitable that the peoples of Cape Verde and Lusophone Africa would be affected.

A small number of Cape Verdean intellectuals could not accept that most of Africa would be decolonized and that Cape Verde would remain as a colony. Despite efforts to keep them uninformed, a number of Luso-African *assimilados* began to study the writings of Karl Marx, Vladimir I. Lenin, W.E.B. DuBois, and C.L.R. James; gradually, they formulated a political strategy of pan-Africanism and national liberation. In the late 1940s and early 1950s, a few new leaders from Portuguese-speaking Africa began to appear, including Eduardo Mondlane, a sociologist and founder of the Frente de Libertação de Moçambique (FRELIMO); Agostinho Neto, a medical doctor and poet and the first president of the Movimento Popular de Libertação de Angola (MPLA); and Amilcar Cabral, the Cape Verdean agronomist born in Guinea-Bissau.[1] Often meeting in Lisbon or wherever chance brought them together, these three and others from Portuguese colonies met to discuss their plight. Once they recognized their common circumstances as colonial peoples, they began to transform this consciousness into the political and military work of national liberation. Their double objectives were to end both Portuguese fascism and colonialism. These goals often brought their radical nationalism into alliance with the Portuguese Communist Party and its underground members.

When the PAIGC was formed on 19 September 1956, the emerging nationalism of the leaders was fueled by their collective anger about—and frustration with— the colonial conditions they knew firsthand. But recalling the African adage that "it is the grass [the Africans] that is trampled when elephants [the Cold War rivals] fight," this was a time for great caution. To complicate matters further, the worldwide socialist movement became deeply divided over Soviet intervention in Hungary in 1956 and in Czechoslovakia in 1968, which deepened the ideological split in the movement and spawned independent Marxist and socialist parties in Western Europe.

The PAIGC cautiously moved closer to the Soviet Union because of its need for arms, but it maintained a nonaligned or independent political posture from the very beginning. It valued the support of the Portuguese or European Communist Parties, but it would try to stay clear of the warring "elephants"—whether in Washington, Moscow, or Peking. The embryonic PAIGC still had a great deal of experience to gain.

The group's leaders were influenced by the Portuguese Communist Party and other European Marxists and social democrats but were creative in applying their theories to local circumstances. After watching their neighbor Guinea-Conakry become independent of France in 1958, members of the PAIGC were both optimistic and impatient. They thought their struggle would be short and that a period of nationalist agitation, demonstrations, leafleting, petitions, and appeals to such international bodies as the United Nations would be sufficient to gain independence. But given the Portuguese intransigence, this early prediction was far from the mark.

When Amilcar Cabral, Luís Cabral, Aristides Pereira, Fernando Fortes, Julio de Almeida, Eliseu Turpin, and (probably) Rafael Barbosa had their historic meeting to form the party in Bissau, they could not anticipate what lay ahead.[2] However, from the very start, they agreed with the common goal of liberating and integrating *both* Portuguese Guinea and the Cape Verde Islands, just as most of the colonial history of these two lands had been linked. This policy would have complex effects and create alliances that last to the present day.

The Cabral brothers, for example, were the children of Cape Verdean parents, but they were actually born in Guinea. Cape Verdean *assimilados* were spread throughout top positions in the infrastructure of Portuguese Guinea. Beyond such ties, it was apparent that the territory of Guinea and its easily penetrable borders with Senegal and Guinea-Conakry would provide more freedom for guerrilla infiltration than could be achieved if the nationalist agitation were initiated in the islands: One false move in the islands could mean brutal internment in the Chão Bom prison of São Tiago. This decision to conduct the actual war only in Guinea-Bissau was also to have another important effect since the people of the Cape Verdean archipelago were never galvanized in the protracted military conflict in Guinea-Bissau.

The PAIGC was the organizational descendant of the Movement for the National Independence of Guinea (MING), founded in 1954 by Henri Labéry and Amilcar Cabral. The main difference between the MING and the PAIGC was that independence for the Cape Verde Islands was a goal of the PAIGC but not the MING. Also, there were more craftsmen and manual workers in the PAIGC than in the MING group. Labéry later went on to form the Front for the National Independence of Guinea (FLING), a small and very persistent rival of Cabral and the PAIGC.

In 1958, the PAIGC leaders helped to organize a series of protonationalist strikes with a membership base of only about fifty people. By 1959, Amilcar Cabral, under the nom de guerre of "Abel Djassi," was given political support by members of the British Communist Party. A forerunner of the PAIGC had been formed in Dakar to launch the propaganda phase of the struggle, and from this early time, the goal of one party across two nations was clearly stated. More than mere nationalists, these militants were *internationalists,* and at a meeting in Tunis in January, the PAIGC and the MPLA were joined in a common African revolutionary front for nationalist independence.[3]

At this time, the first traces of the União das Populações das Ilhas de Cabo Verde (UPICV) movement were also seen.[4] The UPICV only sought independence for Cape Verde; it did not seek unity with the struggle in Guinea as the PAIGC did.

The secret membership of the PAIGC was actually composed of forty-some colonial functionaries, most of them of Cape Verdean extraction; in retrospect, these few civil servants with little military knowledge could not be expected to succeed. Following the established orthodoxy of Marxist organizing, Luís Cabral made an early and important effort to attract dockworkers in Bissau; so, too, did Abílio

Duarte in Mindelo, São Vicente. In these first years, Amilcar Cabral, the secretary-general of the PAIGC, was usually in Angola, working as a Portuguese-trained agronomist and hydrological engineer. However, the vigilant fascist police structure of Portugal had intelligence information about their activities, and when the Bissau workers at the Pijiguiti dockyards went on strike on 3 August 1959, the police were armed and ready.

To counter the PAIGC's nationalist demands linked with the strike, the Portuguese soldiers and armed settlers reacted with twenty minutes of gunfire, killing as many as fifty and wounding about a hundred. Subsequently, twenty-one people were convicted of subversion. This critical event gave the PAIGC reason to reflect, rethink, and plan ahead. For them, there were now martyrs and friends to avenge. For the Portuguese, there was the last remnant of their great empire to defend.

Luckily, the infant PAIGC organization had Aristides Pereira working in a strategic senior position in telecommunications, and Fernando Fortes held a comparable job in the postal service. Consequently, they were able to alert other clandestine members to prepare to flee and regroup in neighboring Guinea-Conakry, still in its first year of independence.

Amilcar Cabral returned to Bissau six weeks later to meet with the secret network on 19 September 1959 and make another pivotal set of decisions. First, the plan for a peaceful transition to independence would be abandoned because it would only put party members at risk of arrest, deportation, or death. The means of achieving freedom would, of necessity, now include armed struggle. Second, the theater of operations would shift from the towns to the countryside and to a reliance on rural farmers rather than urban workers. The main office of the PAIGC would be established in Conakry. Third, the resolve to reach total victory through the liberation and unification of *both* Cape Verde and Bissau was reaffirmed, justified by the blood shed by the martyred Pijiguiti dockworkers. As the PAIGC grew, it attracted additional port and transport workers, who later (in 1961) organized the National Union of Guinean Workers (UNTG).

Despite their painfully inadequate resources, PAIGC leaders decided the next step was to expand the group's office in neighboring Conakry. Earlier, Amilcar Cabral had met with Sekou Touré, the president of Guinea-Conakry, who agreed to host the PAIGC office in Conakry. But this put Touré at risk: The PAIGC presence in Conakry made his young and insecure government still more vulnerable.[5] Having made no major political achievements to that point, the nascent PAIGC also had to contend with other weaknesses and challenges to its leadership. Support was not forthcoming from Senegal at this time, which underscored the need for a secure external office in a more friendly state having common borders with Guinea-Bissau. This was to be a source of endless anxiety for both host—Conakry—and guest—the PAIGC. As the war progressed, two serious Portuguese military efforts to destroy the PAIGC occurred on Conakry's soil.

Critical to this formative period was the political organization and mobilization in the countryside of Guinea-Bissau. PAIGC leaders made a careful study of the political and military dimensions of the rural-based revolutions in Algeria, China, Cuba, and Vietnam in these years. Meanwhile, by 1961, the Portuguese intelligence and security organs had already experienced a widespread African insurrection—and its bloody suppression—in Angola, and on a smaller scale, the counterinsurgency approach in Guinea-Bissau was similar to what had been tried in Angola. The policy included arrests, extrajudicial executions, collective retribution, commando raids, psychological warfare, and other military measures.

These were to be critical years for both sides in the conflict. For the PAIGC to win, it had to survive; for the Portuguese to win, they had to root out the small enclaves of African resistance. Not wanting to jeopardize its organization, the PAIGC refrained from making military countermoves until all was ready. Yet with little PAIGC action on the battlefield between 1959 and 1963, their credibility as a viable movement was also at stake.

At this time, the literary works of Baltasar Lopes were published in the islands as a passive protest against colonial culture. But this was too mild an action for the PAIGC: From late 1960 through 1961, calling for a peaceful end to colonialism, the group circulated some 14,000 tracts, wrote open letters to the Portuguese people, and sent appeals to the United Nations.

However, deciding upon the option for armed struggle in 1961 was not the same as implementing it. April 1961 saw the Frente Revolucionária Africana para a Independência Nacional de Colónias Portuguesas (FRAIN) replaced by the Conference of Nationalist Organizations in the Portuguese Colonies (CONCP) in Casablanca, and the PAIGC played a leading role as this organization linked and expanded the struggle in Guinea and Cape Verde to those initiated in Angola in 1961 and in Mozambique in 1964.[6] In mid-July 1961, the parallel Movement for the Liberation of Guinea and Cape Verde (MLGCV) joined with the PAIGC briefly to become the United Front for the Liberation of Portuguese Guinea and the Cape Verde Islands (FULGPICV). Despite the awkward acronym, this alliance gave both groups added political experience in building united fronts, which would be useful in Cape Verde in the years to come.

The PAIGC appealed for support and understanding at U.S. embassies and even in the U.S. Congress. But worried about antagonizing Portugal, its anti-Communist NATO ally, the United States consistently turned a deaf ear to these pleas. Toward the end of 1961, the PAIGC moved closer to taking the concrete steps that would lead to direct armed action. As early as 1962, Amilcar Cabral became fond of saying that the PAIGC was a party of "soldiers for the United Nations." Now, he was preparing for war.

To block this move, the Portuguese secret police arrested an early PAIGC member, Rafael Barbosa, in March 1962—the month when the PAIGC made a small, abortive attack in Praia in the Cape Verde Islands. In June and July, the PAIGC responded again with small acts of sabotage inside Guinea-Bissau. This escalation soon put Bissau under martial law, with more than 2,000 suspected activists arrested, and the Portuguese military strength was quickly augmented, to a force of about 10,000 soldiers. Lessons learned in this period proved that the struggle would be hard, long, and costly. It would be a fight in which the winner would take all, and any compromise with rivals would be negotiated from a position of strength. For the PAIGC, these critical years of organizing—1959 to 1963—were carefully devoted to building a hierarchical structure of groups and sections united into thirteen zones and six regions so that all activities could be closely coordinated, yet self-sufficiency maintained.[7]

The War of National Liberation, 1963 to 1974

On 23 January 1963, the armed phase was initiated with the PAIGC's attack on the small Portuguese fort at Tite. The South Front was opened, and the guerrilla war began in earnest. Within the first year of military struggle, a substantial part of Guinea-Bissau south of the Corubal River was liberated. With attacks already under way in the south in early 1963, the PAIGC's People's Revolutionary Armed Forces could turn to the north later in the year to expand their theater of military action. In a meeting in Dakar on 21 July 1963, the idea of expanding the war to the Cape Verde Islands was raised.[8]

In November, Portugal's foreign minister, Alberto Nogueira, made a feeble effort to disguise the colonial status of Cape Verde and Guinea-Bissau. A special decree from Lisbon was issued, stating that these two territories had become "overseas provinces" and hence, an integral part of metropolitan Portugal. The PAIGC responded by consolidating its gains to such a degree that from 13 to 17 February 1964, the first party congress was held in the liberated zones in the southern front at Cassaca. There, Amilcar Cabral cautioned against overconfidence or "claiming easy victories."[9] During this congress, critical points of party policy were emphasized; leaders stressed that the FARP was always in the service of the party and that the PAIGC was a party of militants but not militarists. Furthermore, field commanders or "warlords" who had abused their armed power were removed, for fear of jeopardizing the ties of trust between the people and the party. Thus, the PAIGC had survived and expanded in these critical, challenging years.

Some of the notable actions taken at this congress were: (1) an enlargement of the Central Committee from thirty to sixty-five members; (2) the establishment of seven departments—armed forces, foreign affairs, cadre control, training and information, security, economy and finance, and mass organizations; and (3) the official recognition of the People's Revolutionary Armed Forces, the *Armazens do*

Povo (the "People's Stores"), and an expansion of medical and educational services. With these moves, the PAIGC was now venturing into state building and power consolidation, and divisions within the PAIGC were eliminated or repressed. There was now an infant armed force and bureaucracy in place, with all their strengths, weaknesses, and demands.

Typically, the PAIGC armed forces were involved in ambushes on Portuguese rivercraft, the destruction of transport and communications facilities, road mining operations, and harassing attacks at fortified Portuguese posts and administrative centers. By 1964, it would be fair to say that the Portuguese had lost effective control of about 15 percent of the territory they called their own. The PAIGC strategy began to draw the Portuguese into the classic dilemma of counterinsurgency forces: Should they disperse to pursue the enemy, but increase vulnerability, or should they concentrate their forces for security, while abandoning the countryside to the guerrillas?

Major military clashes and victories from 1964 to 1967 gave the initiative to the PAIGC, which could then sideline and bypass the rival nationalist group (FLING) in Guinea. The military advances also brought political gains at the Organization of African Unity, which, in 1967, gave its full support to the PAIGC. The OAU, the first modern pan-African organization, was itself only formed on 25 May 1963 by the then-independent African nations. The African Liberation Committee of the OAU helped to coordinate political and military support for the PAIGC and other movements, which gave these movements valuable experience in international relations.

With the PAIGC now on the offensive, the Portuguese military was clearly off balance, having failed to contain or adequately appraise its rival's strength. Precise Portuguese casualty figures are still classified, but at least several hundred Portuguese troops were killed or wounded by the PAIGC in 1963–1964. In turn, these casualties caused the Portuguese to call for an additional troop buildup, to between 12,000 and 14,000 soldiers. The PAIGC was not able to control the extreme coastal regions to the west, nor mount military actions in the east—a region of Fula peoples who had shown a basic opposition to the policies of the non-Muslim *Crioulo* leadership of the PAIGC.[10]

Before long, the PAIGC claimed that a third of the country was under its control. To maintain this control, the PAIGC then introduced a military structure that distinguished their local militia forces (FAL)—which had a defensive function— from the offensive *bi-grupos*—which constituted the embryo of the People's Revolutionary Armed Forces. As the war progressed, the liberated zones allowed for a further development of health and educational services and for a system of regulated exchange through a network of People's Stores.[11] Notably, even as the PAIGC destroyed the Portuguese colonial presence, during this phase of the war, it was actively building a new society and mobilizing the people.

In January 1964, a major test of strength unfolded on the coastal Como Island in a ten-week battle with Portuguese forces. Casualties were heavy on both sides, but the Portuguese lost the battle and as many as 700 soldiers. Even while both sides were diverted at Como, the PAIGC held its first congress in liberated territory at Cassaca.

New recruits and future leaders such as Silvino da Luz, Vasco Cabral, Francisco "Chico Tê" Mendes, and João Bernardo "Nino" Vieira were now very important figures within the movement. These early militants of the party carefully guarded their positions. In retrospect, it is clear that they did not recruit or train a successor generation of leaders. This deficiency was especially obvious in the Cape Verde Islands, which experienced neither war nor mass political socialization of local recruits to the PAIGC until *after* 1975. In Guinea, the wartime mobilization resulted in the creation of political training centers and instruction manuals that were as vital as the military weapons training. Within the liberated territory, many of these political priorities were set down in the fashion characteristic of Cabral—with patience, clear thinking, persuasion, service to the people, and deep commitment. Cabral was known for the creativity of his analyses and the simplicity of his explanation, not for divisiveness, ideological purity, or patronizing behavior (which he had observed in other revolutionary circles).

Cabral was not content with battlefield successes alone; he also maintained a parallel offensive in international arenas, building new alliances even as he sought the international isolation of Portugal. Ever since the U.N. Resolution 1514 denounced colonialism, there was real hope that the anticolonial struggle could be won with minimal bloodshed. The Portuguese diplomatic ploy of terming its African territories "overseas provinces," rather than colonies, did not fool the United Nations: It insisted that Cape Verde and the other Lusophone African territories were, in fact, colonies, and the direct implication of this finding was that Portugal, like France and England, should make immediate preparations for decolonization. The Portuguese answer was the Pijiguiti massacre in Guinea-Bissau and stepped-up police repression in Cape Verde. The PAIGC did not sit back and accept this response but turned to the People's Republic of China as early as 1960 for military support and training. Later, the PAIGC shifted away from China and toward the Soviet Union and Eastern Europe.

Another important facet of the PAIGC was its alliances to FRAIN, the CONCP, and the OAU, which internationalized the base of support for them all. The Organization of African Unity and its African Liberation Committee had a clear channel through which it could offer its political legitimization and modest military, health, and educational aid. Just as the Berlin Congress had demanded that the colonial powers demonstrate an effective military presence, the OAU stressed that it would only support the liberationists who were actually fielding combatants—who were militarily engaged with colonial troops. Given his group's steady progress, Amilcar Cabral was invited to present the PAIGC position at the United Nations in 1962. In the midst of their international offensive, he and other African liberators were granted a reception by the pope in 1964, which infuriated the rulers of the overwhelmingly Catholic nation of Portugal.

With a parallel armed struggle being waged in Mozambique by FRELIMO since 1964, a meeting of the Second Congress of the CONCP was held in 1965 in Dar Es Salaam, where FRELIMO had its offices. Such actions and alliances expressed a growing sense of resolve and solidarity. The independence of nearby Gambia in 1965 was another sign that the PAIGC was on a winning path.

By 1965, the military situation had stabilized, with the PAIGC and the Portuguese each holding about half the territory. To break this stalemate and resume the initiative, Pedro Pires was sent to Cuba in 1966 for more advanced military training. More serious military equipment from the Soviet Union and Eastern Europe, such as bazookas, large mortars, small cannons, and 75mm recoiless rifles, were added to the arsenal of small arms and mines. Most of all, the PAIGC forces had the support of the rural population, which supplied them with shelter, food, and water.

Matching these military developments, tighter internal party controls were achieved in 1967 with the restructuring of the original seven departments of the PAIGC's Central Committee. The seven were reduced to five: control, security, foreign relations, national reconstruction, and internal organization and orientation. The main result of this tightening of the party structure in the liberated zones in 1968 was the consolidation of the key decisionmaking positions in the party. Although the circumstances and needs justified the move—and it only led to more success—one may say in hindsight that it also began to reduce democratic access to the party's ruling circles.

With internal political problems resolved, comparative security in the "rear areas," numerous diplomatic successes, and stronger arms, the FARP units were decidedly ready to reengage the enemy. This determination was detailed in a major conference of international solidarity, held in Cuba in 1967, where Amilcar Cabral presented an address. The small PAIGC was always dependent on external political support, which it carefully cultivated from the Cape Verdean diaspora communities in Dakar, Rotterdam, and New England.[12] Support was also solicited from the neighboring governments of Senegal and Guinea-Conakry, the OAU, major backers in Eastern Europe, and the international socialist and anticolonial movements.[13]

The year 1968 was to be a major turning point for many political movements. In Czechoslovakia, the former Soviet Union put down a movement for democratic pluralism and liberalism, which deepened the Sino-Soviet split and divided the leftist organizations that had supported the PAIGC. Cleavages between pro-Soviet and anti-Soviet Marxist parties and groups were dangerous for the PAIGC, for it needed the political support of all Western European and U.S. socialists and especially the weapons from the Soviet Union and its allies. The PAIGC adopted an independent socialist position, but it continued to receive clandestine support from the pro-Soviet Communist Party of Portugal.

In the United States in the 1960s, a small but growing group of anticolonialists was already actively supporting the liberation movements in Portuguese and southern Africa. To some extent, leaders of the anticolonial movement tried to become incorporated within the powerful civil rights movement during these significant years. Yet the U.S. support of Portugal as an anti-Communist NATO ally meant that there was little coverage of anticolonial movements and the "obscure" war in Guinea-Bissau in the mass media. Leaders of the civil rights movement were always defensive about charges of "Communist influences," and they were hesitant to be too closely associated with the radical and armed liberation movements in Africa. This was especially true while the war in Vietnam was tearing the United States apart, as seen at the 1968 Democratic Convention and in military draft resistance.

For members of the PAIGC, there was little spare time to reflect; moreover, fresh battlefield reports from 1968 to 1970 gave them assurance that all was well. PAIGC forces attacked harder and more frequently; when they attacked the Bissalanca International Airport at Bissau on 19 February 1968, the Portuguese were truly shocked. In February 1969, the PAIGC continued fighting and managed to take a fixed objective—the Portuguese fortified town at Medina Boé in southern Guinea-Bissau.

Portugal responded with the 1969 book-bomb assassination of FRELIMO's president, Eduardo Mondlane, who had resigned his post as a professor at Syracuse University. Dr. Mondlane would later be memorialized on a Cape Verdean coin, and when Amilcar Cabral visited the United States in 1970, he delivered a tribute to Mondlane at Syracuse University. In his famous address, Cabral stressed that unless and until people are politically free, they are bound by mental constraints that deny cultural self-expression, self-fulfillment, and inherent legitimacy. The war of national liberation in Guinea-Bissau, he said, was truly an "act of culture." As Dulce Almada Duarte stated, "Cabral and his companions understood that the 're-Africanization of the spirit' had to be the first step taken along the road to national liberation and indeed, to the expression and legitimacy of Cape Verdean identity." Furthermore, she noted that

> elsewhere the popular masses did not experience the need to seek their roots in Africa because Africa was present in their daily social and cultural behavior. Only in the case of Cape Verde did the popular masses relegate to the unconscious much of what had been transmitted to them through the collective and imaginatory memory of their African ancestors by seeking to adapt themselves to the imperatives of the assimilation policy.[14]

Cabral was back in Rome on 1 July 1970 for a conference on international solidarity with the peoples of the Portuguese African colonies. On his trip, he stopped again at the Vatican, accompanied by Agostinho Neto of the MPLA and Marcelino

Dos Santos of FRELIMO, for another papal audience and to reassure his Catholic supporters. Gaullist France, still allied with Portugal through NATO, did not allow Cabral to visit there.

The combination of military and diplomatic defeats led the Catholic rulers of Portugal to attempt even more desperate acts. Throughout 1969 and 1970, they launched intensive bombing attacks, using burning white phosphorus and napalm provided by the United States carried in planes from Italy, as well as other weapons from France, Belgium, and South Africa. They also tried and failed to divide the PAIGC on the basis of ethnicity and race. Then, on 22 November 1970, the Portuguese responded in a typical colonial fashion by invading Conakry, not only to kill Cabral and destroy the PAIGC but also to overthrow the regime of Sekou Touré. Their intelligence was faulty, however, for Cabral was not even there. And given the stalwart defense of the PAIGC led by Vasco Cabral, the main objectives of the Portuguese raid were not achieved.

This abortive mission failed, just like the "reforms" introduced by the Portuguese military governor of Guinea, António de Spínola, in his "Better Guinea" program. Meanwhile, having their enemy on the run in 1971, the PAIGC armed forces launched even bolder attacks with rockets and light artillery against the main towns of Farim, Bafatá, and Bissau. Revisions of the Portuguese Constitution in 1971 and the Overseas Organic Law of 1972 gave still more formal autonomy to the "overseas provinces" of Guinea and Cape Verde, but the momentum of the PAIGC was now too strong for the Lisbon authorities. In the early 1970s, the worldwide antiwar movement against U.S. intervention in Vietnam had created a widespread revolutionary and anti-imperialist atmosphere in Europe and North America. Thus, it was an opportune time for the PAIGC underground operatives to launch a campaign of mass agitation, with nationalist slogans painted prominently on public walls in Cape Verde.

These events all helped, at least in the short term, to boost PAIGC vigilance and resolve, as well as to cut severely into Portugal's international legitimacy. In 1972, with three-fourths of the territory of Guinea-Bissau under PAIGC control, plans were made to declare the independence of this country. Always eager to transform military prowess into political capital, the PAIGC invited a unique mission from the United Nations to visit the liberated zones in April 1972; this mission was endorsed by the 27th session of the UN General Assembly later that year. After Amilcar Cabral visited the United Nations in October to ask for a General Assembly seat for Guinea-Bissau, the 848th session of the UN Decolonization Committee recognized the PAIGC as the only effective movement operating inside Guinea-Bissau. Cabral went on to make a special visit to the predominantly Afro-American Lincoln University in Lincoln, Pennsylvania. There, he intimated that Guinea-Bissau would soon be declared independent. Meanwhile, back in Cape Verde, the underground PAIGC movement managed to organize large anticolonial demonstrations in Praia on 21 September, despite the repression of

PIDE. These were all turned into major diplomatic triumphs for the PAIGC's effort to isolate and discredit Portuguese colonial rule.

Harder-hitting approaches were introduced in Guinean forests via new antiaircraft guns and small but very effective surface-to-air "Estrella" missiles from the Soviet Union. These weapons permitted the PAIGC to compete for the airspace over Guinea-Bissau, which had formerly been the exclusive domain of Portuguese helicopter gunships and fighter-bombers—and the source of the fearsome and deadly napalm and white phosphorus bombs.[15]

In August 1972, the first elections in the liberated zones were held for 273 regional commissioners, and elections for 99 representatives to the PAIGC's Peoples' National Assembly were planned for late 1973. For the Portuguese, matters were spinning further out of control; the PIDE/DGS police hoped that by broadening their powers, they could resist this spreading insurgency. It soon became clear that 1973 was going to be a watershed year in the political history of Cape Verde and Guinea-Bissau. And on 8 January 1973, the PAIGC published results of the vote to approve the decision to proclaim independence later in the year.

Amid these victories, the last thing the PAIGC expected was a great tragedy. Yet in the evening of 20 January 1973 in Conakry, Amilcar Cabral was shot to death by a disgruntled PAIGC member, as part of an intricate Portuguese-inspired plot to eliminate the PAIGC and protect colonial interests. The ill-conceived conspiracy included an attempt to organize PAIGC dissident elements, the FLING partisans, with logistic and intelligence support from the Portuguese. Apparently, the Portuguese had forgotten their bitter defeat of the 1970 attack on Conakry. The PAIGC had likewise forgotten the critical role of internal security and vigilance.

In retrospect, Cabral's assassination was pointless, for it did not divert the PAIGC from its objectives or diminish its momentum. Perhaps the tragedy could have been avoided if Cabral had had a bodyguard. In any case, many errors by the plotters, quick intervention by Sekou Touré, timely intelligence from the Soviet Union, the rescue of kidnapped Aristides Pereira, and the execution of the perpetrators soon restored the PAIGC's control. But there was a huge gap in its leadership ranks.

The loss of Amilcar Cabral was very deeply felt, but the organization he had carefully built over many years had such momentum that it went on to greater achievements, pushed by a resolve to avenge the loss of Cabral. The PAIGC response to Cabral's death was predictable, carefully measured, and focused on three "messages."

The first message was sent explosively, via the recently acquired SAM-7 missiles. The Portuguese control of the sky had not been effectively challenged before; with these weapons, the war was finally taken to the air. The memorial to the martyred Cabral was to be a military campaign dedicated to him, and the target was the Portuguese fortified *aldeamento* (a military camp and rural population relocation center) at Guiledge. This base was some 547 yards (500 m) on each side, surrounded with high barbed wire, minefields, and flood lights. Each corner held fortified positions for mortars and 155mm howitzers, as well as subterranean bunkers and a small airstrip. Throughout the spring of 1973, FARP small-arms and mortar units had pinned down the Portuguese defenders of Guiledge, but heavily armored columns and air supply and support kept the base functional. However, when SAM-7s were brought into the siege, they were able to bring down some twenty Portuguese aircraft. The Portuguese military situation soon deteriorated further, and a relief convoy was urgently needed. Anticipating this, FARP's military engineers had placed eighteen antitank mines in the escape route; when these were detonated, the relief convoy was destroyed—along with the remaining morale of the defending soldiers, who organized a full withdrawal from this strategic frontier base on 25 May 1973.[16]

The second message to the Portuguese was written from 18 to 22 July at the Second Congress of the PAIGC at Medina Boé. The Congress elected Aristides Pereira as the new secretary-general, and Luís Cabral became the deputy secretary-general. In addition, the Supreme Committee of the Struggle (CSL) was enlarged. The Permanent Commission of the Executive Committee was created, which included Pereira, Luís Cabral, Francisco Mendes, and João Vieira. Most important of all were some final touches in the proposed constitution, which would be prepared for the 23 to 24 September 1973 historic meeting of the First Peoples' National Assembly.

The assembly solemnly proclaimed the Declaration of State, adopted the constitution, and approved the executive structure of the state, including Luís Cabral as president of the fifteen-member Council of State, eight state commissioners (ministers), and eight sub-commissioners of state (deputy ministers). Immediately, scores of nations around the world recognized the new republic; by early October 1973, diplomatic recognition had been extended by sixty-one nations, even though Portuguese troops still occupied the major towns.

Elsewhere in Africa, especially in Mozambique, the liberation movements made comparable gains. It became increasingly clear that the end of Portuguese colonialism was near. For his failures, General António Spínola, the Portuguese governor of Guinea-Bissau, was relieved as commander of the war. By 2 November 1973, the United Nations General Assembly called on Portugal to cease all military activity in Guinea-Bissau: It could hardly do otherwise. Then, on 19 November 1973, Guinea-Bissau was admitted as the forty-second member of the OAU. On 29 March 1974, Abílio Duarte, the Executive Committee of the Struggle (CEL) member of the PAIGC, addressed the United Nations Committee on Independence to Colonial Countries to denounce Portuguese colonialism. He also reiterated that the PAIGC was ready for negotiation at any time but was also ready to fight for Cape Verde to establish unity between the islands and the mainland.[17]

Militarily defeated in Guinea-Bissau, isolated in Mozambique and Angola, and ostracized by the international community, the architects of African colonialism and Portuguese fascism had nowhere to turn. Young Portuguese officers, led by General Vasco dos Santos Gonçalves, were tired of the endless and humiliating wars in the colonies; finally, they determined that the Portuguese emperor had no clothes, and in the virtually bloodless coup d'état of 25 April 1974, they swept out the colonial and fascist Portuguese government of Prime Minister Caetano—the political descendant of the dictator António de Oliveira Salazar (1889–1970). The Armed Forces Movement (MFA), ushered in by symbolic red carnations stuck in the gun barrels of the Portuguese coup-makers, was very largely created by Africans wanting to be free. In the process, they also created a force so powerful that it even liberated the Portuguese people from their twin political burdens of colonialism and dictatorship.

Politics Under the PAIGC, 1975 to 1990

It is critical to understand that the circumstances in Guinea-Bissau in 1974–1975 were not mirrored in Cape Verde, where the colonial forces still operated and where the PAIGC militants were still imprisoned, underground, or under scrutiny. The long-suffering people now had the complex task of transforming the armed struggle on the adjacent coast to a political struggle in the islands. For the PAIGC and the MFA, the forces with the more radical and less compromising positions had won the day. For Cape Verde, the long-stated PAIGC goal of creating a unitary, anticolonial party and nation could now be achieved for both Guinea and the Cape Verde archipelago. The main political difference this time was that power relations flowed from the coast to the islands, not from Lisbon. The *Crioulo* and the African descendants of *lançados,* slaves, and *grumetes* were about to exercise full power in a new nation. The power descending from the *capitãos, fidalgos,* and foreign trading *companhias* was about to end.

Surprisingly, General Spínola, recently dismissed as the defeated military governor of Guinea-Bissau, became the new president of Portugal.[18] The MFA immediately took steps to restore democracy to Portugal, and it promised historic decolonization for Portuguese Africa. The old guard of colonialism and the agents of PIDE appeared to be retreating, but they were not yet defeated. Spínola went on the radio to say,

> Portugal today is living through a great hour of her history … the time has come to inform the Portuguese in Europe and overseas with regard to the formal declaration of the recognition for the people of the overseas territories of the right to their own destiny in their own hands.
>
> Portugal has a responsibility towards those nations whose people are waiting for a second mother country, in the same way as Brazil. We shall try to remain united, and even though the moment is one of nostalgia, it is also a moment of peace and progress on the part of all potentialities which have been consumed by 13 years of war without any finality.[19]

A whirlwind of pivotal events only intensified the revolutionary exuberance, and a huge crowd gathered on International Workers' Day, 1 May 1974, at the notorious Tarrafal prison camp in São Tiago as scores of long-incarcerated and brutalized political prisoners were released. Quickly, the PAIGC brought operatives into the islands to create a very broad united front for national independence.

The leader of the now-legal Portuguese Socialist Party, Mario Soares, met with Aristides Pereira on 15 May 1974, and negotiations for the full recognition of Guinean independence were under way. Meanwhile, in Cape Verde on 19 May, huge rallies were organized in Mindelo and in Praia, where Portuguese troops were ordered to fire on the demonstrators who sought to exchange the Portuguese flag for that of the PAIGC. Eight demonstrators and one policeman were injured, and at least one was killed.[20] In Lisbon, the junior officers of the MFA were deeply divided over this incident. And Vasco Gonçalves began to push António Spínola away from the MFA's decisionmaking circles.

The 2 June 1974 visit by UN Secretary-General Kurt Waldheim provided proof that Guinea-Bissau was about to be free, for such a ranking diplomat would not have intervened in this way if he had judged the situation still unresolved.[21] In this crisis atmosphere, the local Portuguese authorities in Cape Verde were no longer able to block a referendum four days later that recognized the PAIGC as the leading force for Cape Verdean decolonization. By this time, PAIGC flags had sprouted from trees, buildings, posts, and poles throughout the islands.

Still hoping to salvage a colonial Cape Verde, Portugal officially stated, on 27 July, that it was prepared to grant independence to Guinea-Bissau, and on 26 August 1974 in Algiers, the final details for the Portuguese withdrawal from Bissau were determined. The Algiers Accords were signed by Portuguese Foreign Minister Mario Soares and the vice defense minister of Guinea-Bissau, Pedro Pires, who would later become Cape Verde's first prime minister. Already, behind-the-scenes negotiators were hinting of a referendum for Cape Verdean independence by mid-to-late summer 1974.[22]

On 26 August 1974, events were whirling. Guinea-Bissau was admitted as the one hundred-thirty-eighth member of the United Nations and quickly recognized by almost a hundred other members. This group did not include the United States, which was secretly meeting with the Supreme Allied Command Atlantic (SACLANT) subdivision of NATO in Norfolk, Virginia, to discuss concerns about protecting valuable South Atlantic shipping lanes that carried oil and minerals.[23] U.S. Secretary of State Henry Kissinger was strongly opposed to a Cape Verdean union with Guinea-Bissau because he feared these countries might fall into Soviet hands.[24]

On 4 September, the first representatives of the CEL entered Bissau, and on 14 September, Portugal gave its de jure recognition to the new Republic of Guinea-Bissau, whose flag was raised for the first time at the United Nations on 18 September. The victorious Cape Verdeans Luís Cabral and Aristides Pereira officially entered Bissau on 19 October 1974. The war was over, Guinea-Bissau was liberated, and half of what they had fought for was now theirs.

Toward One Party, Two States, 1975 to 1980

In Cape Verde, the PAIGC had no military strength, only a clandestine political organization. Although Spínola was driven out of Guinea by the guns of the liberation fighters, he still hoped that Cape Verde's political future might be modeled after that of the Madeiras or the Azores. The PAIGC leaders were well aware of their weakness in the islands, but they also knew of the precarious state of the Portuguese during these critical months. This situation resulted in a power vacuum, which in turn created a classic revolutionary moment. The PAIGC rapidly developed a united front strategy for mass mobilization to take advantage of the deep political divisions within the MFA in Portugal and build upon the remarkable achievements of the PAIGC on the mainland.

The struggle intensified on 28 August when a PAIGC delegation arrived in São Vicente to establish a headquarters there. They were greeted by a crowd estimated at 20,000—in a town of about 35,000. The throng carried signs denouncing colonialism and neocolonialism and endorsing unity with Guinea-Bissau. Much alarmed by this, Spínola turned to the divide-and-rule strategy that had worked so well in the past. Fearing that a referendum in Cape Verde would only provide more legitimacy to the PAIGC, Spínola sent his overseas minister, Almeida Santos, to Praia to meet with representatives of the PAIGC, especially the opposition União Democrática de Cabo Verde (UDCV) and the União das Populações das Ilhas de Cabo Verde (UPICV). They hoped that a referendum in Cape Verde might split the rapidly expanding political base of the PAIGC. As the date set for Guinea-Bissau independence, 24 September 1974, drew closer, the pro-PAIGC rallies in Cape Verde became more frequent and intense.

In Lisbon, the situation degenerated to one of finger-pointing and deepening ideological struggle between those endorsing the neocolonialist position of Spínola and those taking the decolonization position of Gonçalves and the MFA majority. In August and early September, Portuguese attention was diverted to the troop withdrawal and the recognition of the independence of Guinea-Bissau. The ever-weakening Spínola then met at Sal, in the Cape Verde Islands, with Zaire's President Joseph D. Mobutu and with Angolans opposed to the MPLA to see if the same divisive policy might block Angolan independence. While at Sal, Spínola was confronted with a huge pro-PAIGC demonstration at the International Airport. He heard that Pedro Pires was trying to fly back to the islands from Bissau, so he denied landing rights to Pires's plane. In response, the PAIGC in Bissau told Spínola that he was not welcome there.

Political slogan in Bissau: "One People, One Country," 1975 (Photo by author)

This tug-of-war was to become even more serious. When a contingent of 150 bitter Portuguese marines being withdrawn from Guinea-Bissau arrived in São Vicente en route to Lisbon, they provoked ugly anti-PAIGC incidents there. To prevent more bloodshed, these troops were hurriedly recalled to Lisbon by Gonçalves. The way now appeared clear for Pires to return home to Cape Verde. An intransigent Spínola was still unwilling to discuss independence for Cape Verde, and he still thought he could salvage something from the situation. On 21 September, he gave orders to fire on the demonstrators in Mindelo. Meanwhile, two days later, Guinea-Bissau was completely free.

It was now too late to change the course of events. However, in searching Cape Verdean homes the following day, some of the remaining Portuguese troops injured many civilians and wrecked the homes. This repressive, even riotous violence continued for yet another day, when, during a search operation, the troops opened fire and provoked further confrontations with the PAIGC militants. This left more wounded, and at least two PAIGC militants were killed. A general strike was declared, and Aristides Pereira wired the United Nations to protest this violation of the spirit of the earlier Algiers Accords.

The Portuguese governor of Cape Verde, Silva Horta, tried to accommodate the demonstrators and refused to arrest the PAIGC leaders. Still clinging to some power in the army, Spínola responded by sacking Governor Horta; he was quickly

Portuguese troops in Praia, São Tiago, 1975 (Photo by author)

replaced by Serge Fonseca, an ardent colonialist who was told to arrest the leading PAIGC members and block the arrival of any others.

Applying still more pressure, the PAIGC backed an unprecedented wave of strikes by transit and construction workers led by the Democratic Workers Union. The workers won major wage increases: Construction workers, who had been paid only $1.66 per day, were able to negotiate for $2.90 per day.[25] Amid these struggles, the PAIGC called a general strike for 27 to 28 September in order to demonstrate their strength to the MFA. Spínola again called on loyal Portuguese troops in Cape Verde to open fire. But this crisis created serious tensions in Lisbon, and on 30 September, Spínola was pushed further out of MFA ruling circles by its leftist members.

Silvino da Luz, the hardened PAIGC military man who knew war firsthand in Guinea and as a Portuguese conscript in Angola, had already managed to return to Cape Verde. Fearing further Portuguese maneuvers and deceit, da Luz, a key PAIGC player at the moment, temporarily disappeared underground. His military instincts indicated that the situation was truly at the breaking point. Meanwhile, on 13 October, Pedro Pires personally arrived in Cape Verde to head the committee that would negotiate for Cape Verdean independence. In the Bissau he had just left, the very last of 30,000 Portuguese transitional troops had departed, to make way for the grand arrival on 19 October of the new president of Guinea-Bissau, Luís Cabral, and PAIGC Secretary-General Aristides Pereira.

With Spínola essentially out of the picture by October 1974, a new set of actors emerged. Since the colonial structure was now in tatters, the Cape Verdean lawyer Aguinaldo Veiga, who had served major judicial, corporate, and colonial enterprises in Luanda and Lisbon, began to call for an independent and democratic Cape Verde. He and his supporters were especially opposed to unity with Guinea-Bissau and were angered by the PAIGC leadership and their international socialist program. Veiga sent an open letter to the United Nations in which he protested the "foreign" activities of the PAIGC in the islands; he also presented his own development plan, which envisioned, among other things, a land where "Capeverdean young women ... will be dressed in 'elegant' and 'impeccable white uniforms' and will 'direct traffic with their sunny smiles and they will dispel agitators and lawbreakers with their black cudgels ... while robust men carry on their indispensable competitive work in industrial establishments.' "[26]

In the coming years, Aguinaldo Veiga, João Baptista Monteiro, António Cardoso, Harry Fernandes, Edmundo Ramos, Roy Teixeira and his son, and others in New England turned the "juridical congress" into a persistent opponent of the PAIGC. Another small group, the anti-Soviet UPICV, was strongly against unity with Guinea-Bissau. Both of these groups perceived the UDCV (later known as Unição Caboverdeano para a Independencia e Democrática [UCID]) and the UPICV as either divisive or bluntly opposed to decolonization. However, in these critical weeks, the battle-wise PAIGC and the left-leaning MFA were steadfast regarding decolonization under one-party rule.

From 22 to 23 February 1975 in faraway Boston, the Cape Verdean Juridical Congress (ancestor of the UCID) unilaterally declared the independence of the Republic of Cape Verde.[27] Fearing its own isolation, the Juridical Congress sought to block the PAIGC's assumption of power in the islands. According to the U.S.-based PAIGC support group Tchuba, this Boston declaration was a desperate fantasy. Inside the hotel where they met, the Cape Verdeans expressed a fear of losing their property to Africans and "Communist insurgents." PAIGC supporters, gathered outside, were forcefully excluded from the meeting hall, which was accessible by invitation only.[28] Once again, the deep connections between the islands and New England brought both regions into the struggle for independence.

In this continuing unstable situation, the long-moribund FLING movement, vying for a position in Guinea, was prompted to make another attempt at bringing down the PAIGC in a poorly planned coup d'état in Bissau on 21 March. Sensitive to the demands for broader participation and aware of the bids for power by FLING in Bissau and the Juridical Congress in Boston, the MFA and PAIGC delegations had agreed to hold an election of deputies for the Cape Verdean National Assembly; a declaration to this effect was published in Portugal on 15 April. Meanwhile, to put more pressure on Cape Verde, the new PAIGC state apparatus held its first national assembly from 28 April to 6 May in Bissau as an example of its parallel plan for Praia.

The stubborn Spínola, already sidelined in Portuguese politics, suddenly reappeared in Lisbon on 11 May 1975, where he staged an unsuccessful coup against the MFA. Now, the chaotic process of decolonization could be put into some order. On 20 to 26 June, the PAIGC delegation of Fidelis Cabral de Almeida (who would become the state commissioner for justice in Guinea-Bissau) and José Araujo (a long-standing and high-ranking party troubleshooter) went to Cascais, Portugal, to settle more details of the transition.

On 30 June 1975, the first Cape Verdean elections were held to choose representatives to the Peoples' National Assembly. This occurred under the supervision of a special United Nations mission headed by Syrian Ambassador Heisham Al-Kilani, who would later conclude that the PAIGC was "the only lawful representative" of the Cape Verdean people.[29] At polling stations, there was a serious but joyful atmosphere. In Mindelo, a place of supposed anti-PAIGC sentiment, there was no counterdemonstration, no public opposition, and no climate of intimidation, and the areas around the polling places were unguarded and relaxed. According to official results, 85 percent of the adult population participated, and 92 percent of the votes cast went to the PAIGC.

The efforts to block or dilute the PAIGC had failed. The PAIGC claimed that after more than a decade of armed struggle and a national referendum, there had been plenty of opportunity for other parties to express their interest in or opposition to independence for Cape Verde. The opposition by UCID, UPICV, and other later dissident formations such as the MpD has stressed that widespread exclusion took place because the process was completely dominated by the PAIGC. Others have opined that these groups or their policies essentially excluded themselves. Whatever the perspective, it is clear that this grievance was later to be well marketed by those opposed to PAIGC rule.

Since the PAIGC program called for unity between sister republics, there were already many agreements that united the two lands in commerce, transport, education, and communication. Most importantly, the PAIGC was the ruling party in both countries, although there were two separate national assemblies. As one African proverb states, "Even twins are not born at the same time."

As already shown in the war years, the Cape Verdean leadership of the PAIGC had a joint program for the joint liberation of two lands. Politically, the struggles were inseparable. Militarily, each region of the single party provided a depth of defense, with reserve troops to be called up if either part of the common nation was in jeopardy. Even though the lands were separated by water, their unity, especially from 1975 to 1980, was considered inviolable. Events in Bissau and Praia were inevitably linked.

Thus, in the early 1970s, although there *were* groups opposed to the PAIGC, their numbers and influence were marginal. The huge surge in support for the PAIGC was shown in the united front actions, the general strike, demonstrations, and the referendum. When, on 1 November, the MFA and PAIGC jointly de-

Voting poster, PAIGC referendum,
São Vicente, 1975: "To vote is a
form of participation in the
leadership of your country"
(Photo by author)

nounced Spínola and endorsed the PAIGC as the sole party of decolonization, this was a de facto elimination of any role for the UDCV and UPICV.

Because most of Africa had been led by nationalist, populist movements to one-party states, this was neither odd nor exceptional. So, at this point, the UPICV and UDCV were politically isolated not only by the MFA and PAIGC but also by a majority of the Cape Verdean people. The UDCV and UPICV offered too little, too late in their opposition to colonialism, and both remained opposed to the unity of Cape Verde and Guinea-Bissau.

The rapidly changing atmosphere led to a round of serious negotiations on 7 November between the PAIGC and the reconstituted leadership of the MFA. They agreed to grant independence in six months and hold a jointly supervised electoral referendum, from which the UDCV and UPICV would be excluded. In the interim, the PAIGC militants formed the Democratic Action Group of Cape Verde and Guinea (GADCVG), which organized a twenty-four-hour general strike in mid-November that shut down island services, and an estimated 90 percent of the Cape Verdeans in the Portuguese armed services left their barracks to express their support for decolonization, led by the PAIGC.[30] The rapid mobilization and general strikes were well orchestrated to coincide with the second return visit to Cape Verde by Pedro Pires on 23 November; he was there to hold the final discussions on self-determination.

The exclusion of the UDCV and UPICV was angrily broadcast by Radio Barlavento in São Vicente. This radio station had typically represented the pro-Portuguese views of the Gremio Club of Mindelo, a social and political meeting place for the local elite. Antagonized by these broadcasts, PAIGC militants organized by Silvino da Luz and Luís Fonseca occupied the radio station on 9 December—an impatient act of revolutionary justice, similar to the takeover of a São Tiago farm by its impoverished workers on 16 December.[31] Four days later, the six-member Executive Committee of the Transitional Government was able to reach a final agreement. This committee was composed of three MFA members, led by Almeida d'Eca, and three members of the PAIGC Cape Verdean National Committee. The accords promised elections on 30 June 1975, which would be "as representative as possible." Independence was promised for 5 July 1975, when the first elected and seated Cape Verdean National Assembly turned to its first act of business.[32] On that day, Assembly President Abílio Duarte announced the creation of the sovereign and independent Republic of Cape Verde, and a constitution was promised in ninety days. When Aristides Pereira arrived in Sal, some 7,000 people were on hand to meet him; this number surpassed the general population of the entire island. When he went to Mindelo, he found a crowd of 30,000.[33] Expressing his dream—and that of the Cape Verdean people—PAIGC Secretary-General Pereira said,

> Our state will be profoundly democratic and will guarantee the participation of all, without distinction of color, religion or sex in the conduct of the affairs of the state. In Cape Verde, with the Government of transition established, we have the inheritance of chronic abandonment of centuries and more than six years of drought, under the colonial and fascist government, that only worsened the situation instead of working for solutions. The country is in a disastrous situation that we do not however, consider desperate because we are sure that we are right and we firmly believe in the triumph of just causes that are never isolated.[34]

The people's joy was tempered by the ongoing drought, which was ultimately alleviated by $1.7 million in emergency relief from the UN Development Program. An additional $40 million was promised by the Portuguese government.[35] Sharing the birthday of this new nation, Vasco Gonçalves, the tough leader of the MFA, personally welcomed the dawn of the new era in an independent Cape Verde. The Republic of Cape Verde joined Guinea-Bissau as an OAU member on 18 July.

It is impossible to understand the events in Cape Verde from 1975 to the present without knowing more about at least four of its contemporary leaders. So much material is available on Amilcar Cabral that it seems unnecessary to repeat it here, beyond noting that he was born in Bafatá, not in Cape Verde, and tragically died before the liberation of the islands; thus, he was not actually a part of the events just described.

What follows are biographical sketches of those holding key positions in more recent years: Prime Minister Pedro Pires, President Aristides Pereira, President of the National Assembly Abílio Duarte, and Minister of Defense Silvino da Luz.

Pedro Verona Pires (1934–   ) was born in an isolated village on Fogo Island. After studying in Cape Verde, he went on to Lisbon to study engineering, but by 1959, he was already involved with the underground African liberation movement there. Threatened with conscription into the colonial army, he fled from Portugal to Ghana to meet Amilcar Cabral. After joining the PAIGC, he received additional military training in Algeria, and in 1966, he was sent to Cuba to prepare a thirty-man team to plan for a two-pronged invasion of the Cape Verde Islands. (This plan was never implemented.) During the armed struggle in Guinea-Bissau, he was the *responsável* (the person officially responsible for a specific aspect of administration) for health and education, and he rose to become the commander of the South Front.

In 1974, Pires led the PAIGC delegation in London and Algiers that helped bring about the independence of Guinea-Bissau. He was also the principal negotiator for the independence of Cape Verde. In one critical role, he convinced U.S. congressmen that Cape Verde would not be used as a Soviet base, thereby garnering crucial U.S. support—or at least, reduced opposition. Some people credit his efforts as pioneering achievements, but others now in the MpD have made his administration and important decisions he reached the focus of their criticisms. The first Cape Verdean Popular National Assembly elected him as the nation's first prime minister. Internationally, he advocated a foreign policy of nonalignment. Domestically, he developed programs of ecological conservation and fiscal accountability, both to donor nations and to his people.

In November 1980, Guinea-Bissau President Luís Cabral, half brother of Amilcar Cabral, was overthrown by his minister of defense, João "Nino" Vieira. Pires considered this a direct assault on the unity of Cape Verde and Guinea, and he subsequently became the architect of the transformation of the PAIGC to the PAICV.

The shock of this event in Bissau caused the PAICV leadership in Cape Verde to become more fearful of domestic opponents. Some opposed the PAICV's closeness to the Soviet Union, and others were antagonized by the extensive nationalization and land reform. In response, the PAICV took steps to isolate opponents within the party by expulsion and by arresting other opponents outside the party. Unfortunately, these measures may have actually created more opponents for Pires and the PAICV.

Aristides Maria Pereira (1924–   ) was one of the original founders of the PAIGC, born on Boa Vista Island. After attending the *liceu* ("secondary school") in Cape Verde, he received specialized training as a radio-telegraph technician. Pereira was one of the organizers of the Pijiguiti strike in 1959, and he worked in Bissau as the chief of telecommunications until 1960, when he left to join Amilcar

Cabral in Conakry as a member of the Political Bureau of the Party's Central Committee. In 1964, Pereira was the joint secretary-general of the PAIGC, and he was a member of the War Council after 1965. Following organizational restructuring in 1970, Pereira became a member of the Permanent Commission of the Executive Committee for the Struggle (CEL), along with Luís Cabral and Amilcar Cabral. In this position, his chief responsibilities were security, control, and foreign affairs. Before the death of Amilcar Cabral, Pereira was the deputy secretary-general of the party, but after Cabral's passing, he became the top political officer of the PAIGC. Then, with the independence of Cape Verde on 5 July 1975, Pereira became the first president of the Republic of Cape Verde. In this position, he maintained a policy of social democracy and nonalignment.

Abílio Augusto Monteiro Duarte (1931–   ) is also considered one of the PAIGC's "old guard," having played an early and critical organizational role. In 1958, he was the leading underground member of the PAIGC in the islands. The son of a Catholic priest, he studied at the *liceu* in Mindelo, while serving as a party organizer among the strategically important dockworkers. His recruits included Luis Fonseca, Silvino da Luz, Joaquim Pedro Da Silva, Ignacio Soares, and Manuel dos Santos. He fled from the islands to Paris in November 1960, narrowly avoiding arrest, and went on to Algeria for military training. He served the PAIGC in many ways, among them many vital foreign missions. He was also a key member of the Cape Verdean National Council. While serving as the president of the Assembleia Nacional Popular (ANP) (1975–1991), he was the individual who formally declared Cape Verde's independence on 5 July 1975. He was likewise the one who signed the important Agrarian Reform Law in April 1982.

Silvino da Luz (1939–   ) was a medical student in Coimbra, Portugal, when he was drafted as a lieutenant in the Portuguese army. Sent to Angola to help suppress the uprisings that began in 1961, he gained practical military experience, but he also witnessed the savagery of colonial "pacification," in which tens of thousands were killed. He deserted and escaped to Zaire and Nigeria, where he was almost captured. From there, he finally reached Conakry in 1963 to make contact with the PAIGC headquarters. He received additional military training in Algeria and was then sent to Dakar for more "medical studies," while actually spending most of his time working in the PAIGC underground. Later, he received military training in Cuba. He became a successful FARP commander during the armed struggle, he served as the Cape Verdean minister of defense and national security, and later, he was the minister of foreign affairs and a member of the Cape Verdean National Council. Depending upon one's point of view, da Luz is either credited with or blamed for organizing the takeover of Radio Barlavento, as well as implementing some of the measures that restricted the voices of the PAIGC opposition.

The first year of the PAIGC's governance of both lands was 1975. At this time, relations between Portugal and Guinea-Bissau were strained over the PAIGC's decision to nationalize the local branches of the Portuguese Overseas National Bank, and relations with Cape Verde's government-in-waiting were not much better. In Guinea, the peso was created to replace the Portuguese escudo, and in Cape Verde, the new escudo was introduced. Internal unity was solidified at the Second Session of the Guinean Peoples' National Assembly from 22 April to 3 May 1975; it was also aided by visits to Bissau from President Samora Machel of Mozambique and President Agostinho Neto of Angola. The Commission of Cape Verdean Trade Unionists was formed on 1 May 1976, and Guinean filmmaker Flora Gomes released his film *Le Retour de Cabral*. Taking firmer control of the economy on 1 July, the government of the Republic of Cape Verde nationalized banks, airports, airlines, shipping, harbors, and ports.

Somewhat ominously, the government also passed a law on 30 October 1975 that gave their internal security organ—the Direcção Nacional de Segurança (DiNaS)—the power to detain anyone in prison for ninety days without being charged. Later, opposition groups would point to this decision as the "thin entering wedge" that began (or perhaps continued) the erosion of the people's free expression. In December 1975, Cape Verde signed friendship accords with Angola and thereby gained an additional measure of security. Soon, Cape Verde and Guinea-Bissau jointly served as transit points for Cuban troops en route to aid the MPLA in Angola in its long and bloody civil war against its South African– and U.S.-backed rival, the União Nacional para Independência Total de Angola) (UNITA). Some 300 Cubans were stationed in Bissau, with roles in support, logistics, and police training, and Cuban doctors were also active in Cape Verde. Radical reforms in education in Guinea-Bissau and Cape Verde were designed to eliminate colonial influences and increase technical and practical skills, and another law was passed to allow the military to identify and try political criminals. It is clear that the PAIGC in Cape Verde was troubled by dissidents, and some PAIGC members felt the dissidents deserved these repressive measures. Aristides Pereira, secretary-general of the PAIGC of both lands, simultaneously served as the president of Cape Verde.

By 1977, President Luís Cabral in Guinea-Bissau was also facing economic and political problems. The problems were "resolved" with repression and the erosion of the relative democracy established under his brother, Amilcar Cabral. This only deepened the distrust the Cape Verdean leaders felt toward Bissau—a distrust that was nervously perceived in Praia.[36] Carlos Veiga, later the MpD prime minister of Cape Verde, was then a PAIGC member serving as the attorney general of the Republic of Cape Verde. Since the PAIGC was under criticism in its dual territories, it was reasonable for Veiga to begin thinking of an independent position.

From 15 to 20 November 1977, the PAIGC held its Third Party Congress. After some delays and almost a year of meticulous and widespread preparation, the central themes of this major event were unity between Guinea-Bissau and Cape Verde, economic development, and political consolidation. The former Permanent Secretariat, composed of 4 members, was enlarged to 8; the CSL was increased to 90 members; and the new CEL was expanded from 24 to 26 members. The newly elected members of the Permanent Secretariat were Pedro Pires, Umaro Djalo, Constantino Teixeira, and Abílio Duarte. Leaders hoped to reform the PAIGC as a vanguard political party that would organize, dynamize, and unify the peoples of both countries.

Armed with legal measures of repression in 1977 and 1978, the PAIGC arrested some opposition UCID members. UCID claimed that forty-four were arrested and a few were held for as long as one year. The PAIGC countered that it had broken up a plot to dynamite a power station and take over a radio station. Whatever the case, this conflict stimulated more anti-PAIGC opposition, now expressed mainly by the UCID and the UPICV. Both groups were still quite small; they had a long and ineffective presence in the islands and were largely based in exile groups.

As noted, the UCID opposed PAICV policies that they considered anti-American and pro-Soviet. The UCID was opposed to restrictions they believed were placed on the Catholic Church in Cape Verde. In a series of articles, written, in large part, by John C. Wahnon in the 1980s, they noted grievances concerning: political prisoners in Cape Verde, the PAICV's association with "international terrorism," the "illegitimacy" of the PAICV government, charges that the Cape Verde Islands were to be tranformed into a "Soviet submarine base," cultural and political ties with Libya and the Palestinians, and the expropriation of land. The PAICV intentions to introduce major agrarian reform were especially unpopular with UCID, for some of its members apparently were landowners of some note. This reform had become law in 1982 and was put into effect on 1 Jan 1983.

Whatever the merit of these grievances, it is clear that by the late 1970s, the PAIGC government in both Bissau and Praia rested upon an increasingly narrow base of popular support. In the small-scale, highly personal society of Cape Verde, many people who were not at all aligned with the policies of UCID found that the PAICV was excessive in its use of power.

In 1978, Prime Minister Pedro Pires was well aware of these opposition forces, but he was secure enough to set out on a long tour of the United States to visit Cape Verdean communities. His strength was also measured by his ability to send an honorary contingent of FARP soldiers to serve as personal bodyguards for the Angolan president. Some argued that this represented a reserve military force stored in Angola for PAICV security in Cape Verde. Meanwhile, within the PAIGC in both Bissau and Praia, anxieties were growing. Pires and Pereira understood the dangers of unaddressed internal dissidents—they had only to reflect on the dissident plot that resulted in the tragic death of Amilcar Cabral. Apart from the death of Cabral, all past measures taken for internal party discipline had succeeded, and there was no reason to suspect the current circumstances would be different. The PAIGC leadership believed that those who were complaining had not shared the risks of war in Guinea and were too young or too eager to find top places for themselves in the party.

Because these dissidents were of a younger generation in the party, they also were part of a reformist mode designed to secure some liberalization and more open access to party decisionmaking. Weighing all of these factors, the PAIGC determined that an internal shuffle was required to exclude some of these younger dissidents. By February 1979, such people as Manuel Faustino and José Veiga quit the PAIGC and the government due to criticism about the lack of internal democracy. From the vantage point of UCID or UPICV exiles, this was further proof of the validity of their earlier criticisms.

But this time, the internal dissent did not stop there. Therefore, in April 1979, the PAIGC continued with its internal "restructuring" and removed several more members charged with being "Trotskyists" after a meeting of the Cape Verdean National Council. Was this simply an intergenerational struggle for power? Or was this a more fundamental ideological struggle—or both? Additional PAIGC members who were young and independent, such as Eugénio Innocéncio, were aligned with the defectors. In a signal that something was now amiss, the joint military exercises for Guinea and Cape Verde planned for May did not take place. Another sign was the absence of the constitution that was promised to be delivered ninety days after the 1975 declaration of independence; it was now delayed for more than five years and would not be passed until 5 September 1980. Moreover, the united front that had originally brought liberation was no longer so united. In early 1980, this was not easy to see because so much successful work of the PAIGC was actively under way. With the party serving vital needs in education, health, and other practical areas, many observers missed this apparently small, internal "management problem."

One Party, One State, 1980 to 1990

Left untreated, these small lesions became an open wound in November 1980 when João "Nino" Vieira overthrew President Luís Cabral.[37] This coup was perceived by Pires as an act of moral, political, and personal treason.[38] In the Praia branch of the PAIGC, the coup was seen as grossly divisive and utterly opposed to one of the most precious policy goals of the PAIGC—unity. It was a treacherous violation of the sacred and noble struggle against colonialism.

But João Vieira in Bissau viewed this bold step as necessary for curbing the power wielded by a small group of Cape Verdeans who had "manipulated" the Guinean fighters in order to achieve their goal of independence for the islands. Put in the terminology of the seventeenth century, one might conclude that the *Crioulo lançados* had merely used the African *grumetes* and *tangomãos* to attack the Portuguese at their most vulnerable time. Whatever the perspective, there is no doubt that in the wake of the Vieira coup, the two republics became politically divorced. Suddenly, severe pressures were placed on the unity and solidarity manifest in (1) a shared party and overlapping political leadership; (2) a common armed struggle to free both lands; (3) the presence of Cape Verdeans in key posts in both nations; and (4) critical links in culture, economics, and military structure that had existed throughout the postindependence period.

For the PAIGC, this was another major turning point: The many years of effort to unify the two nations, peoples, and parties under a single flag had come to a sudden end. Even though the PAIGC still had thousands of other members in the islands, two prominent members were destined to leave—the bright, independent-minded Renato Cardoso and the former attorney general, Carlos Veiga. Both had determined that there was no longer a role for them within the PAIGC as it was then structured. And both were to be heard from again.

The erosion of the party's political self-confidence was also expressed by Prime Minister Pires, who noted on 31 December 1980 that the rupture in unity with Guinea-Bissau was a matter of internal security for the PAIGC in Cape Verde since reserve FARP troops from Guinea could no longer be counted on for support in the islands.

So deep was the personal hurt and the political cleavage that the leadership of the Cape Verdean branch of the PAIGC determined to sever its connection by discarding the name PAIGC and replacing it with a new name—African Party for the Independence of Cape Verde (PAICV). This party became the direct political successor, and it ruled in the Republic of Cape Verde until 1991. The PAICV was officially formed on 19 January 1981, with essentially the same structure and personnel as it had had before the Bissau coup. Other party organs were also renamed, such as the women's organization, which was changed from the Democratic Women's Union (UDEMU), found in both lands, to the Organization of Women of Cape Verde (OMCV), which was unique to the islands. Although there was hardly any significant change in the leading personnel, the Cape Verdean PAIGC was officially disbanded on 12 February 1981.

Anxieties caused by the Bissau coup were still running high at the end of the summer of 1981. In a particularly important case, the PAICV military and the Public Order Police (POP) raided and arrested UCID opponents in Santo Antão on the night of 31 August. This resulted in the detention (without charge), interrogation, and probably harsh treatment of roughly twenty people by the internal security officers at the Morro Branco military headquarters in São Vicente.

Within the small-scale Cape Verdean society, rumors traveled quickly and broadly. It was difficult for the new PAICV to regain public confidence, even though the UCID was not particularly well supported. By this time, there was fairly widespread apprehension and disgruntlement over PAICV methods. It must be said, however, that such instances of repression were comparatively rare. As if it had let the genie out of the bottle, the PAICV struggled to restore control of the restive spirit of opposition.

Some steps toward reconciliation were made by Bissau in January 1982 when President João Vieira released former President Luís Cabral from confinement to begin a life in exile. By June 1982, Cape Verde and Guinea-Bissau were at least able to restore the diplomatic relations that had been severed, but a coup attempt in Bissau in 1983 only raised suspicions once again. Those in the PAICV ruling circles attempted to conduct business as usual, and on 26 March, the Agrarian Reform Legislation was passed. Although the legislation was understandably justified by the backwardness and exploitive relations in land ownership and although it was well received by the poor, it was perceived by the opposition as another step toward socialism and state control, which they clearly did not want.

The 1980s also found new political winds blowing across continental Africa. The peaceful, multiparty election in adjacent Senegal brought Abdou Diouf to power as president, even with a few opposition members in his cabinet. Certainly, those in the large Cape Verdean community in Dakar and the mounting opposition in the islands took note of these events.

The hurricanes that hit the islands in the early fall of 1983 were especially severe in Fogo, São Tiago, Maio, and Brava, where hundreds were left homeless and crops were destroyed. This natural event paralleled the storm that battered the PAICV. Feeling politically isolated and economically vulnerable, the PAICV government signed a cultural accord with Libya, which the opposition marketed as "proof" that the PAICV was viewed as a pariah nation.

The situation appeared to be normalized in 1983 and 1984 when the PAICV began to rebuild its membership, recover from the destructive hurricane, and free the jailed opponents. On 20 January 1985, the twelfth anniversary of the death of Cabral, the Amilcar Cabral Institute and School was opened by Aristide Pereira, and on 28 October, Pereira inaugurated the new and impressive Peoples National Assembly building, which had been funded by the People's Republic of China.[39] But China's own poor record on democracy and human rights were used by the PAICV's opponents as more "evidence" of the government's bad company. For internationalist Cape Verdeans living in the diaspora, such alliances were discussed with lament, as was the granting of political asylum to Basque separatists (members of Euzkadi ta Azkatasuna [ETA]) from Spain in February and the Cape Verdean police unit sent to Cuba for training in June. The socialist world that had been so important during the war years was being transformed into a political liability. It was even alleged that the PAICV in Cape Verde supported an abortive military coup led by Paulo Correia in Bissau in order to recover their weakened ties to Africa. President Vieira sentenced Correia and others to death in 1986.[40]

To its credit, the PAICV was still making advances: constructing infrastructure and monumental works, increasing party membership, developing the new German-PAICV airport construction project in Brava, and establishing the Transportes Aéreos de Cabo Verde (TACV) direct flights to Boston. However, deep inside the Cape Verdean *saudade,* corrosive grudges, frustrated personal ambitions, and ideological differences festered.

Only coincidental with this loss in spirit was the tragic and premature death of Carlos "Chachass" Martins, the "King of *Funana,"* in a car crash on 29 March 1988. He had come to symbolize the liberated and authentic spirit of the *Crioulos* of Cape Verde. The rapidly expanding younger generation of Cape Verde who loved the *funana* of "Chachass" felt marginalized, while the heroic but old guard remained in power.

When the Third Congress of the PAICV was held from 25 to 30 November 1988, further achievements were cited in an accounting of the projects under way, the land reclaimed, the children educated, the health conditions improved, and the trees planted. Yet amid these advances, the people were still missing their fuller empowerment. Even for this rather well-served population, with a notably honest government, there was still a demand for free and diverse political expression, which the people saw expanding in the West African movement for political pluralism.

The confusion of those times is captured in the mystery of the so-called Cardoso affair. The bright Renato de Silos Cardoso (1951–1989) had been a PAIGC member until 1980, when the party was facing the various dilemmas just examined. Cardoso was dismissed from the party for "Trotskyism," but this may have only demonstrated that his liberalism was just ahead of the party leadership. Cardoso went to Brazil for practical training, and upon his return to Cape Verde in 1985, he was readmitted to the party and appointed as a special adviser to Prime Minister Pires; later, he was a secretary in the Ministry of Labor and Public Affairs. But on 29 September 1989, Cardoso was found mortally wounded at a Praia beach. Although an arrest took place, the lack of solid evidence resulted in an unsuccessful prosecution. Cardoso's closeness to influential circles of the PAICV caused his mysterious demise to become a much-manipulated political issue that was often cited in the 1991 Cape Verdean elections.

Two Parties, One State, 1990–

Probably the first public reference to the Movimento para a Democracia (MpD) was in the public declaration of March 1990 by Carlos Veiga, which called for greater democracy within the PAICV. Veiga's leadership of the MpD was tolerated by the National Assembly because of a rising apprehension among many delegates about efforts within the PAICV to centralize further powers. By April, the PAICV, still the only party in the land, accepted the suggestion to call assembly elections in order to resolve disputes within that body. In the Fourth PAICV Congress on 25 July 1990, there was no special indication to outside observers that the political structure of Cape Verde was about to experience a major shift. By August, rumors were circulating that the PAICV, completely confident of victory, would allow the elections to proceed in order to isolate its opposition.

On 2 September, the party, operating from this perceived position of strength, officially adopted the policy of transition to pluralism. This shift was possible only with a revision of the constitution that would require a two-thirds majority vote to permit an official change from a one-party state to a multiparty state. The PAICV was convinced that the opposition could not muster anything close to this level of support and that it would be politically humiliated in the effort. Even Veiga and his supporters thought their defeat likely, but they also believed that the PAICV needed to be formally notified of opposing views. Both the PAICV and MpD underestimated the sentiment of the voters at the time.

Seeing this electoral opening, other PAICV dissidents and defectors aligned themselves with the embryonic MpD, mainly to restrain the PAICV's appetite for greater powers. However, the possibility of challenging and rejecting the PAICV leadership exploded in unanticipated popularity, and the MpD won the two-thirds majority necessary for a constitutional reform allowing plural democracy. By November, the MpD published its first political program in an attempt to capture these repressed sentiments.

These changes were not made in a political vacuum. In the same year, Mozambique and the Ivory Coast had legalized political opposition, and the former anticolonial ally, São Tomé and Príncipe, had also passed a referendum for a multiparty constitution. Buoyed by these parallel events and by their own new liberties, the MpD campaigned intensely throughout November and December to criticize the PAICV on the issues on which they were most vulnerable: party democracy, human rights, relations to the church, abortion, and the innuendo about Cardoso. It is alleged that the MpD also received campaign advice and assistance from groups that would benefit from privatization and economic and religious liberalization. In two words, the MpD marketed *change* and *youth*. It was just what the young Cape Verdean people wanted after sixteen years of the PAICV.

Since the 1975 referendum for independence under one party, the PAIGC, there had never been plural elections in Cape Verde. As a result of the weakened position of the PAICV and the emergence of the dissident MpD, all this would now change. The other Cape Verdean political groups—the UCID and the UPICV—were not participants in the 1990 elections.

The UCID had failed to file on time with the Electoral Commission, and, indeed, it has never been tested in the ballot box. The exclusion of the UCID from political life in Cape Verde dates back to 1974. As a party of exiles, the UCID has representatives in Portugal, Germany, Holland, and southern New England. In the United States, the then first secretary of UCID, John C. Wahnon, is a longtime opponent of the policies and practices of the PAICV. There is a reasonable expectation that the UCID will continue to seek a political presence in the islands, and their party congress in August 1993 helped them formulate an electoral strategy to run candidates in the expected elections of 1995–1996. The UCID might win some seats in the National Assembly, especially for the Barlavento Islands. When UCID President Lido Silva failed to compete in the 1991 elections, he did not swing his support to any of the other candidates. He was replaced as UCID president by Antero Barros, who was then removed from UCID leadership in August 1993. Another rising star is identified as Caldeira Marques, the regional UCID president in Iberia, and only months after Barros stepped down, Celso Celestino became the UCID presidential candidate. As this account implies, internal rivalries for UCID leadership must be resolved if this group is to have an effective electoral role.

It is noteworthy that the UCID stands by the former National/PAIGC flag and opposes the changes in the national colors brought about by the MpD. Likewise, UCID is a supporter of newly elected independent President Monteiro, but it is opposed to MpD Prime Minister Carlos Veiga. A small splinter group of UCID, led by João Alem in the early 1990s, created the Partido Social Democrática (PSD). But the PSP has not competed in elections, nor demonstrated any degree of support.

The União Popular das Ilhas de Cabo Verde (UPICV) had its roots in 1959 as a Cold War rival to the PAIGC. The UPICV aligned itself more closely with the People's Republic of China, while the PAIGC tended to seek its significant support from the Soviet Union and Eastern Europe. The date 12 November 1977 is significant to UPICV supporters, for it marks the day they met in Holland and Belgium to draft their eight-point program. This included provisions for: the political and judicial structure, the armed forces and finance, human rights, private property, freedom of religion and conscience, freedom to learn and teach, and freedom in work, health, and emigration, as well as a design for a three-color flag with ten stars representing the islands of the archipelago. Portuguese was to be the official language, but with provisions to advance the development of *Crioulo* culture and language. The most persistent leaders in the UPICV are José Leitão da Graça and his wife, Maria Querido, who held discussions and concluded formal agreements with the PAICV in 1990 as the UPICV (Reconstructed), which may also become a participant in future elections.

The moment of truth for the PAICV and the MpD arrived on 13 January 1991 in the National Assembly elections, held under close scrutiny and codes of electoral ethics. Of the 79 elected seats, 56 went to the MpD, and only 23 went to the PAICV in 515 electoral precincts. For reasons that are still unclear, about 20 percent of 159,988 registered voters abstained. The fairness of the elections is proven by the fact that the ruling PAICV was voted out of power and the *partido unico* ("single party") of sixteen years became the minority party. The election results by island are provided in Table 4.1.

With the assembly reconstituted by the January elections, the people could then turn to the elections for a new prime minister and president in February. Onofre

TABLE 4.1 Results of 1991 Elections

	Electoral Seats (by parish)	PAICV	MPD
Boa Vista	S. João Baptista/Santa Isabel	2	0
Brava	S. João Baptista/N.S. Do Monte	1	1
Fogo	N.S. Ajuda	2	0
	N.S. Conceicao/Santa Catarinha	2	1
	S. Lorenco	1	1
Maio	N.S. Da Luz	1	1
Sal	N.S. Das Dores	1	1
São Tiago	Praia Urbano	4	8
	Praia Rural I	0	2
	Praia Rural II	1	1
	S. Catarina	1	5
	S. Salvador do Mundo	0	2
	S. Lorenco dos Orgaos/Santiago Maior	1	4
	S. Amaro Abade/S. Miguel	1	4
Santo Antão	N.S. do Livramento/N.S. Do Rosario	0	2
	S. Crucifixo/S. Pedro Apostolo	0	2
	S. Antonio Das Pombas	0	2
	S. Andre	0	2
	S. Joao Baptista	0	2
S. Nicolau	N.S. Do Rosario	1	2
	N.S. Da Lapa	0	2
S. Vicente	N.S. Da Luz	2	10
Diaspora:	Africa	1	0
	America	1	0
	Europe	0	1
Totals		23	56

NOTES: The Comissão Eleitoral Nacional reported 15–20 percent abstentions among the 159,988 registered voters in the islands; 6,830 emigrants voted in the elections. The MpD won 69 percent of the votes for 56 assembly seats; the PAICV had 22 percent of the vote for 23 seats. Three seats in the National Assembly of 79 are reserved for emigrants, i.e., two for the PAICV from Africa and the United States and one for the MpD from Europe. S. stands for "Saint" in Portuguese; the N.S. stand for "Our Lady."
SOURCE: Comissão Eleitoral Nacional.

Lima, the head of the Electoral Commission, announced that in the contest for president, 72.2 percent had voted for António Mascarenhas Monteiro, and only 26.2 percent voted for Aristides Pereira. In absolute numbers, among the 159,667 registered voters, Monteiro received 70,582 votes, and Pereira got 25,722; there were also 372 blank votes (0.28 percent) and 1,363 nullified votes (1.39 percent).

The elections had proceeded in a calm and tranquil fashion, although hardly a wall was left unpainted with rival political slogans. In the urban area of Praia, the vote was 70 percent for Monteiro, and in Santa Catarina, it reached an amazing 89 percent. There was also strong support for Monteiro in São Vicente and Santo Antão. After the MpD electoral victories, a new government was formed.

Prime Minister Carlos Wahnon de Carvalho Veiga (21 October 1949–) was born and attended school in Mindelo, São Vicente, and went to Classical University in Lisbon in 1971 to obtain a law degree. He then went to work in Bie, Angola, as a registrar in the colonial Civil Registry until 1974. After the independence of Guinea-Bissau, he returned to Cape Verde to work in Praia as the director general of internal administration until 1978. Then, the PAIGC government asked him to become attorney general for the nation.

Since Veiga could not agree with certain PAICV practices, he opposed its strong state control and sought more liberal democracy in the party, as well as a greater role for private investment. Veiga left government service to form his own law firm in 1980. In his successful private practice, he gained valuable legal experience as the counsel for a variety of private and public enterprises. He also served as deputy and vice president of the National Assembly Special Constitutional Commission and on the Praia Municipal Council.

As prime minister, he has taken steps to expand the free-market political economy and end the fifteen years of a socialist-statist economy system. He seeks a mixed economy guided by private initiative and an irreversible multiparty democracy guaranteeing human rights. As the prime minister of Cape Verde, he has also attended meetings of the UN General Assembly and its Security Council, where Cape Verde served as a rotating member nation.

President António Mascarenhas Gomes Monteiro (1943–) studied law at the Universities of Lisbon and Coimbra. He joined the PAIGC in 1969 but left in 1971 over policy disagreements. He then continued his study of law at the Catholic University of Louvain in Belgium and became a researcher at the International Center for Public Law there. He returned to Cape Verde after independence to be appointed by the Popular National Assembly as a judge in the Cape Verde Supreme Court in July 1977, where he served until his election to the presidency of Cape Verde in 1991.[41]

The electoral defeat of former Prime Minister Pedro Pires led to his resignation on 14 January 1991. Although initially shocked by the result, he philosophized by noting that his historic role in freeing Cape Verde from colonialism had ultimately made democracy possible. Pires has now become a member of the "loyal opposition," and his party leadership has been criticized. The position of PAICV secretary-general has already been turned over to Aristides Lima, to make the PAICV more competitive in the 1995 elections. Pires is not expected to be the PAICV candidate for Prime Minister. In July 1992, Pires attended the Democratic National Convention in the United States.[42] Since the elections, former President Aristides

Jorge Barbosa Preparatory School, São Vicente Island, 1992 (Photo by author)

Pereira has often been a mediator and senior statesman among the Third World nations, and he has distanced himself from some previous PAIGC policies.[43] Former Minister of Defense Silvino da Luz now works for a commercial firm in Mindelo, São Vicente.

In Cape Verde, the new actors on the political scene have raised fresh issues. Some complain that the MpD has taken too much license with its electoral victory, which was perhaps as much an indictment of the ruling PAICV as it was a victory for the MpD. Some members of the National Assembly felt neglected or isolated after the MpD gained power and no longer needed their support. There were also some allegations of scandal over the sale of military planes by Brazil. However, whatever its detractors might say, the MpD was democratically elected, and its promise for change and a new constitution with provisions for multiparty participation was promptly realized. All sides praise the move to plural democracy, and widespread congratulations were given to the MpD.[44]

Elsewhere in Lusophone Africa, the Cape Verdean model of political pluralism has been studied with interest. In May 1994 in Bissau, the constitutional provision holding that the party was "the leading political force in the state and society" was abolished, as it had been earlier in Cape Verde. This move paved the way for pluralistic elections. In Bissau, elections were held on 3 July 1994; it took two electoral rounds before João Vieira won a majority and was democratically elected as the PAIGC candidate for president. Vieira finally defeated the young and surprisingly popular Koumba Yala of the Partido da Renovação Social (PRS). The elections in Angola also took place and brought the MPLA to democratic power over UNITA, which soon reverted to civil war to protest the election results. Cape Verde was an OAU-appointed overseer of the Angolan elections and is expected to be an observer in proposed elections in Mozambique. The opposition also won elections in São Tomé and Príncipe. Elsewhere in Africa, the movement for democratization is still advancing—in Mali, Togo, Ivory Coast, Zambia, the Gambia, Ghana, Benin, and Cameroon.

On 15 December 1991, there was another test of electoral strength in Cape Verde. Still nursing its political wounds, the PAICV backed Nuno Duarte against the MpD candidate, Jacinto Santos, for mayor of Praia in the Municipal Council elections. On 17 December, the election results showed that the MpD won ten of fourteen contested councils. But Praia—the nation's capital and thus politically important to the MpD government housed there—was another story. It seems that the PAICV campaign workers had gone all out to make this local election into a better version of the national election they had lost.

During the official polling period, Duarte of the PAICV had pulled ahead of Santos of the MpD. When the MpD learned about this, they reacted with alarm and extended the voting beyond the proscribed polling period to get friendly voters to the polls. There was no allegation of fraudulent balloting, but there *was* a procedural irregularity in which Duarte was finally, though narrowly, defeated. In

São Vicente, an independent candidate, Onésimo Silveira, who was opposed to the PAICV and backed by the Catholic Church, won the municipal election for Mindelo.[45]

In 1992, the second year of the MpD government, Cape Verde assumed international prominence by taking a nonpermanent seat on the UN Security Council. On 3 January 1992, the United States, Great Britain, and France, the permanent and powerful members of the council, sought support to: (1) extradite Libyans accused of the Lockerbie, Scotland, aircraft bombing, and (2) further investigate the UTA plane that blew up over Chad. Formerly, Cape Verde had a policy of non-alignment and a cultural exchange treaty with Libya, which made them reluctant to fall into line behind the superpowers. Previously unsupportive Cuba and Yemen were sitting at the Security Council, and it was hoped that the new Cape Verdean delegate would now be more supportive of the Western positions. On 22 January, the Security Council unanimously called on Libya to hand over the suspects and cooperate in the inquiry on Chad. Finally, Cape Verde's prime minister, Carlos Veiga, personally appeared at the Security Council to advocate support for such UN actions.

On 25 June 1992, the MpD also took steps to liberalize and extend electoral suffrage and expand the right of Cape Verdean immigrants to vote in future presidential elections and participate more fully in the National Assembly. However, during the Assembly sessions in the summer of 1992, the discussions over the flag and constitutional revisions grew so heated that on 20 July, the PAICV minority delegation withdrew from this special session. The PAICV opposition complained that the MpD had limited the PAICV's access to the press, television, and radio and had generally exceeded its electoral mandate. The MpD responded by reminding the PAICV of the recent electoral results. The following day, the assembly turned to the significant matter of privatization and denationalization, which was backed by the U.S. government.

In September 1992, as Prime Minister Veiga set off for a visit to the United States, the privatization process was beginning to be concretized. Plans included outright sale, mixed ownership, continued national ownership, and, in the case of the state trading company—EMPA—some basic commodities and foodstuffs remaining under state control, while others were to be privatized. Some inefficient enterprises, such as the fishing fleet, may be closed. Some public sector companies in tourism and hotels, perhaps even the national airline and communication systems, may be sold, in part, to private investors. One fear is that the enterprises that would not be sold would be those public enterprises which are not profitable, thereby leaving the state burdened with them. The MpD government even requested reimbursement for PAICV facilities originally built with state funds.

A Cape Verdean epoch is over. To summarize and understand why this happened requires a deeper reflection about the context and history. Certainly, the end of the Cold War and the remarkable collapse of the former Soviet Union and

Eastern European socialist regimes added to the force and direction of this change. These allies had been strong and long supporters of Cape Verde. Likewise in Africa, many one-party and military regimes have been followed by multiparty democratic governments. Cape Verde is part of an African trend. The MpD perceives that the election of 1991 represented a revolution of equal proportion. The PAICV understands its failures but believes that the new government, drawn from PAICV dissidents, will soon face the same challenges that they knew earlier. Moreover, the issues of inflation, drought, scarce water supplies, underemployment, and privatization are a potentially explosive mixture that needs careful handling by the MpD.

Given these differing perceptions, one may understand the depth and intensity of feeling about the new national flag that was adopted in July 1992. The former flag was modeled after many other West African flags, and the cultural identity of the African roots of Cape Verde was featured. The new flag, however, has similarities with the flag of the European Economic Community. Clearly, the issue of Cape Verdean cultural identity is central. Did the former flag symbolize only the PAIGC party that liberated the islands? Or was it truly a Cape Verdean national flag? Was this a flag symbolizing the unity of Cape Verde with Guinea-Bissau? The debate continues.

Anticipating that the 1992 session of the National Assembly would result in a new flag, the PAICV called a rally on independence day to express support for the former flag. Although this rally was not very large, the topic was revisited in demonstrations in September that were more heated. Some opposition polls in the summer of 1992 claimed that 46 percent of the population was opposed to the change in the flag. However, on 24 July, the new flag was officially adopted and the Second Republic of Cape Verde proudly proclaimed. The MpD government will be in office at least until the next democratic elections, scheduled for the end of 1995.

As one young worker from Sal explained the situation, "The PAIGC has lost its raison d'être now the country is sovereign. It is the party of the past. Most Cape Verdeans are young, and they are looking for something to develop the islands."[46] Thus, there is a race in the Cape Verdean political arena between the aspirations of the young and the new political leadership of the MpD. Will development come fast enough? Or will the problems of the past result in instability and emigration? What new parties will appear on the scene as suddenly and forcefully as the MpD?

The new prime minister, Carlos Veiga, has said, "We think that winning creates an obligation to work hard and do better than before. Some results can be obtained rapidly. It isn't easy and we have told the people that there will be problems and that they have to understand them. There are some problems we will not be able to solve over the next five years, but we are going to do what we can to improve the various situations here in Cape Verde as much as we can."[47]

5

PEASANTS, SOCIALISTS, AND CAPITALISTS: ECONOMICS IN CAPE VERDE

Parallel to the struggle against colonialism, political oppression, and the harsh environment, there has been a movement to strengthen the integrity and autonomy of the Cape Verdean economy. The economic structure can be divided into three spheres. First, is the domestic subsistence economy of foodstuffs, including fruits such as bananas, papayas, mangos, and coconuts. Vegetables such as tomatoes, potatoes, squashes, and melons are also important, and the principle starches have long included rice and, after the New World discoveries, corn. To this grassroots economy can be added livestock production for consumption, with chickens, turkeys, and especially pigs, goats, cattle, and horses being of special importance.[1] Finally, there is a maritime aspect of local production, which includes a variety of fish but especially cod and tuna, as well as crustaceans, conches, cephalopods, and sea turtles. The vast majority of these foods are consumed within the islands—if, indeed, a given year has produced sufficient food. In the past, the only minor exception to this were the foods from this list that could be sold to passing ships seeking provisions for long voyages. Vegetables could be stored, and poultry, swine, and turtles were kept on deck until slaughter. Dried and salted fish were sometimes added to this menu of victualing goods. There was also an intra- and interisland trade in slaves, hides, and *panos*.

From Subsistence to Consumption

In the 1980s, domestic consumption patterns rather consistently required that 47 to 52 percent of the family income be spent on food. During the same period, housing costs ranged from 12 to 14 percent of family income, and bottled drinks and tobacco followed, absorbing 10.6 to 12.9 percent of family income. The remaining income was typically spent on clothes, shoes, and transportation.[2] The amount of domestic income available for health care was virtually negligible.

As a result of heavy expenditures devoted to household survival and basic subsistence, there were usually few funds available for investment or savings. Housing expenditures proved the exception to this rule. The most recent available data shows that construction was regularly the largest sector of investment, accounting for 56.4 to 68.5 percent of all investments. Normally, the biggest proportion of construction expenditures were devoted to either housing or public works. These two areas were important in meeting the needs of the increasing population and in making up for deficiencies from the colonial inheritance. Capital equipment expenditures ranged from 21.7 to 31.9 percent during this period, as the Cape Verdean economy was directed toward creating a basic infrastructure that had not been adequately provided by Portuguese colonialists.[3]

The second sphere of economic activity incorporates the cash crops primarily used for export. An absolutely firm line cannot be drawn here because some part of local production was exported and some percentage of cash crops were consumed locally. The earliest crop produced especially for export markets and sold to monopolies was sugarcane. Freshly cut cane was processed in the local presses, then exported as molasses, sugar, or grog (rum); it also was used to make some syrupy wine from the vineyards of Fogo. Grog, horses, salt, and *panos* could also be exported to the coast for use in the slave trade.[4] In fact, these commodities are still traded.

Cape Verdean exports also include mountain-grown coffee, bananas, citrus fruits, castor beans, physic nuts, animal hides, salt and salted fish and meat, and, in certain periods in the past, the plant dyes like urzella and indigo. These were usually exported in bulk and unprocessed or used in dyeing the cotton *panos* that were (and are) always woven with white and dark indigo fibers. The mineral puzzolane, used as a cement or plaster additive, has sometimes been produced in commercial and exportable quantities (6,455 tons, or 6,558 metric tons, in 1981), especially from the mines in Santo Antão.

Table 5.1 summarizes the main Cape Verdean exports in the 1980s. Manufactured items and primary goods produced in Cape Verde are few, and in this postindependence period, their modest role has rather steadily deteriorated. Overwhelmingly, the Cape Verdean export economy is built upon services. Important among these are transport and related export services, which have been part of the Cape Verdean economy for centuries. In the future, development plan-

TABLE 5.1   Cape Verdean Exports of Goods and Services

	1980	1982	1984	1986	1988
Export of goods	19.9	10.1	8.3	13.0	7.5
Export of services	71.8	80.6	83.6	77.0	81.4
Ship repair	0.3	0.1	2.5	5.0	5.2
Transport	30.9	37.0	52.0	50.2	57.5
Communication	1.5	1.1	1.4	3.0	5.8
Insurance	3.4	1.2	1.4	0.8	1.5
Re-exports	35.8	41.1	26.5	18.0	11.4
Exports to absentee Cape Verdeans	8.4	9.3	8.1	10.0	11.0

NOTE: These statistics represent the percentage of total exports for these selected years.
SOURCE: Ministério das Finanças e do Plano, Direcção-Geral de Estatística, *Boletim de Contas Nacionais*, 1991, p. 38.

ners may take further advantage of this service economy by seeking improvements in storage, container shipping, and regional break-of-bulk strategies whereby large-scale, bulk shippers break down loads into small units for more economical, small-scale routes and markets.

The third and last sphere of the Cape Verdean economy is that of imports and re-exports. Items in this category have included wild animal skins, spices, food grains, gold, ornamental bird feathers, beeswax, honey, plant and bark dyes, woods, goat and cattle hides, cacão, and ivory. With little question, this third sphere has been the most lucrative for those involved in it. In Cape Verdean commerce to and from the coast, slaves clearly were the most valuable imports. Since the coast and islands were jointly administered, one may consider the coastal exports to the archipelago as an internal exchange. In the islands, slaves had either labor value or re-export value when they were sent to the New World plantations.

When the PAIGC came into power in Cape Verde beginning in 1975, their leaders' principal economic experience was limited to models of state-run enterprises, such as those operating in the socialist nations that had provided important support to the local government. The PAIGC also had practical economic experience in running the *Armazens do Povos* in the liberated areas during the war. These Peoples' Stores met local needs for basic supplies such as knives, textiles, tools, blankets, salt, sugar, pots, pans, thread, sandals, and paper. They also received local produce—animal hides, rice, peanuts, palm nuts, honey, seeds and nuts, ivory, wax, kola, and corn—in exchange for the manufactured items. Another objective of the Peoples' Stores was to undermine the Portuguese trading monopolies, such as the Companhia União Fabril (CUF), by taking business from them and thereby increasing the cost of colonialism. However, this formative economic experience of the PAIGC in Guinea-Bissau had little application in Cape Verde.

Table 5.2 illustrates the Cape Verdean predicament as a heavy importer of goods, especially of consumer items (which are relatively expensive). Although this places a major burden on the Cape Verdean economy, data on the domestic

TABLE 5.2   Cape Verdean Imports of Goods and Services

	1980	1982	1984	1986	1988
Import of goods	88.3	79.5	82.1	79.3	74.0
Consumer goods	40.0	29.7	30.2	32.4	26.0
Intermediate goods	19.7	21.6	22.0	22.1	23.2
Capital goods	19.7	18.3	19.7	16.1	19.7
Combustibles	9.0	10.0	10.1	8.7	5.1
Import of services	9.5	18.9	16.0	18.7	23.7
Imports from absentee Cape Verdeans	2.2	1.6	1.9	1.9	2.3

NOTE: These statistics represent the percentage of total imports for these selected years.
SOURCE: Ministério das Finanças e do Plano, Direcção-Geral de Estatística, *Boletim de Contas Nacionais*, 1991, p. 44.

economy show that the bulk of these items are foods and primary subsistence goods, which are absolute necessities. Thus, the poor export record, coupled with a notable need for imported goods, perpetuates the deficit economy of the islands. In 1986, Cape Verdean exports totaled US$4.5 million, and imports stood at US$108 million. Data for 1991 show that Cape Verdean exports had risen to US$8.9 million, and imports had reached US$124 million.[5] Approximately half of the GNP is spent on payments for imports.

In short, the traditional economic inheritance had changed little, except that slavery was replaced by free labor export before the PAIGC arrived. The PAIGC's own economic experience was limited. Thus, the PAIGC had to make basic choices about which portion of the Cape Verdean economy they would emphasize: local subsistence, supply, and exchange; Cape Verdean cash exports; or imports and re-exports. Such fundamental decisions shaped the postcolonial era from 1975 to 1990.

The PAIGC's primary goals were: (1) to liberate the economy from colonialism; (2) to increase self-reliance and reduce imports; and (3) to gain hard currency from export sales and services. A retrospective view of the postcolonial period quickly shows that although progress has been made, the colonial economic inheritance, the lack of capital and experience, and the poor resources of the islands have weighed very heavily against the achievement of these goals.

The Economics of Island Ecology

The ecological struggle was one of the first economic battlegrounds. The majority of the rural population was tied to an agricultural economy that was perilous and not even self-sufficient. For centuries, the soil had been degraded and eroded, and trees either died or were cut for fuel. Indeed, Cape Verde was about to join its related ecosystem, the Sahara Desert: To define the situation as desperate may be inadequate. The ecological struggle also forced many Cape Verdeans to abandon the islands and thus not apply their labor, skills, and knowledge to the economic development of their homeland. Despite these discouraging circumstances, the PAIGC leaders were morally committed to confronting the problems because of their own sacrifices in the armed struggle and their deeply felt attitude of "serve the people."

Consequently, in a Herculean effort, the PAIGC started to plant some 3 million drought-resistant trees and build more than 600 miles (960 km) of erosion control dykes, plus water tanks and extensive catchment basins. A poster campaign for water conservation was launched, and desalinization programs were expanded so that the water resources would be better managed and conserved. In terms of the reforestation effort, it should be noted that at independence, there were only 7,304 acres (2,957 ha) of forest, but from 1976 to 1980, another 16,477 acres (6,671 ha) were added; from 1981 to 1988, this was followed by an additional 86,954 acres (35,204 ha), bringing the present total to well over 111,150 acres (45,000 ha).

These efforts, often coordinated by the Cape Verdean Center for Agrarian Studies, have produced numerous positive results in ecological stabilization, drought relief, natural and human resource development, and improved potential for agriculture and animal resources. Of the extremely limited water supply, it is estimated that 89 percent is consumed for agricultural uses, 2 percent for industry, and 9 percent for domestic purposes.[6]

The Macroeconomic Structure

To see the larger picture, these three spheres—domestic economy, cash crops, and imports and exports—must be integrated at the macroeconomic level. In the structure of imports and exports, Table 5.3 illustrates the notable skew in the Cape Verdean economy toward the tertiary service sector. The economy is presently dominated by services—but this is a long-standing pattern that can be expected to show little change in the future. Little change is likely in primary production in Cape Verde, given the paucity of minerals and the limited agriculture. But unless manufactured items can play a larger role in the future, services and remittances will keep the economy afloat.

To explore this dynamic more fully, Table 5.4 presents a survey of the 10 largest contributors to the Cape Verdean gross national product. Commerce and construction have been continuously dominant in the postindependence period. It is still too early to see the effects of the MpD economic policy of increased privatization; however, it is likely that commerce and construction will continue making a dominant contribution to the Cape Verdean economy.

Overall, the islands' economy is growing in absolute and relative terms. Statistics from the Ministry of Planning and Development show the GNP (in millions

TABLE 5.3   Gross Production by Economic Sector

	1980	1982	1984	1986	1988
Primary sector	16.2	11.5	12.0	13.5	15.5
Secondary sector	24.6	27.8	25.6	27.3	24.8
Tertiary sector	54.4	56.6	58.0	54.7	55.8

NOTE: These statistics represent the percentage of gross value to the economy in current prices.
SOURCE: Ministério das Finanças e do Plano, Direcção-Geral de Estatística, *Boletim de Contas Nacionais,* 1991, p. 14.

of Cape Verdean escudos growing from 11,214.1 in 1984 to 20,634.5 in 1988 (1 escudo = 100 centavos; 72 escudos = 1 U.S. dollar, as of 1991). This impressive gain far exceeds the rate of increase for the population, yet it fell short of targeted development goals. Statistics provided by the World Bank for 1992 reveal that the standard of living in Cape Verde is one of the highest in the West African region. The per capita GNP for Guinea-Bissau is only US$180; for São Tomé and Príncipe, it is US$400, and at its lowest in Mozambique, it is a mere US$80. On one hand, according to the World Bank, Cape Verde has shown a steady rise from US$329 GNP per capita in 1982 to US$402 in 1984 to US$798 in 1988 and a regional high of US$890 in 1990.[7] On the other hand, some of this gain has been lost to inflation. With 1983 as a base year set at 100, the overall consumer price index by 1991 had already risen to 170, thereby reducing a substantial measure of the gain in GNP.[8] Setting the food price index at 100 for 1983, it had already reached 152 by 1989. For the prices of shoes and clothing, the index had reached 201.3, and housing costs had gone up to 129. In 1989, the annual rate of inflation was put at 7.7 percent, and by 1993, it reached about 9.5 percent.

There is some optimism about the Cape Verdean economy, but there are also very real concerns. For the poorer economic strata in Cape Verde who may not have had commensurate increases in wages and compensation relative to inflation, these rapidly increasing costs are alarming. For years, unemployment has been a serious domestic problem, and the European and U.S. recessions have slowed remittances and foreign aid and offered fewer overseas possibilities for Cape Verdean job-seekers. If unemployment is not ameliorated, the economic situation may well intrude into the political sphere, which now stresses privatization and a reduction in state-backed services.

The composition of the economy reveals its inherent weaknesses. The primary sector of agriculture, fishing, and extractives—in which the majority of the population struggles for a living—generated only 19 percent of the gross national product in 1980 and 20 percent in 1988. The secondary sector —skilled, manufacturing, and small-scale industrial or state workers (a smaller group in terms of the overall population)—earned about 16 percent of the GNP in 1980 and 17 percent in 1988. This sector is primarily based in fish processing, textile and shoe production, rum distilling, a small bottling industry, and ship repair. The tertiary sector

TABLE 5.4   Ten Main Contributors to the Cape Verdean GNP

| | *Percentage by Selected Years* | | | | |
	1980	*1982*	*1984*	*1986*	*1988*
Commerce	25.2	24.3	21.3	20.1	19.2
Construction	16.3	20.2	16.6	16.6	14.8
Government services	9.9	11.8	13.5	10.7	12.8
Agriculture	7.1	3.5	3.9	4.8	7.8
Duties and taxes	4.9	4.1	4.3	4.5	3.9
Local housing	4.8	4.6	4.9	5.0	5.0
Shipping	2.8	1.8	2.7	2.3	2.8
Road transport	2.7	2.3	2.1	2.6	2.5
Artisanal fishing	2.7	2.5	2.3	2.2	2.1
Cattle	2.5	2.1	2.3	2.7	2.5

NOTE: These figures are calculated from current annual prices. No column adds to 100 percent, for other smaller categories are excluded.
SOURCE: Ministério das Finanças e do Plano, Direccção Geral Estatística, *Boletim de Contas Nacionais,* 1991, p. 8.

of the economy, including the commercial and service industries, was responsible for 59 percent of the GNP in 1980 and 58 percent in 1988; within this sector, the communication and maritime transport industries usually showed a profit, but the national airline (TACV) often lost money.

Not only is the island economy heavily tilted toward imported goods and exported services, it is also further skewed by the very unequal exposure to foreign and domestic commerce. Only one main city in each half of the archipelago has the port infrastructure needed to handle any substantial degree of commerce. Consequently, the principal trade takes place in Praia and in Mindelo, as shown in Table 5.5.

Bilateral foreign aid to Cape Verde is considerable, reaching US$87 million in 1987 and US$84 million in 1990; this amounts to about US$256 per capita.[9] From 1985 to 1990, bilateral foreign aid represented about 60 to 70 percent of foreign assistance, with the rest derived from multilateral agencies such as the World Food Program, the European Community, the UN Development Program, and the African Development Fund. Generally, the main donor nations are among Cape Verde's main trading partners, but they also include Sweden, France, and Germany, which all give financial support for special projects in such areas as health, infrastructure, and food. Because it has a relatively favorable GNP compared to neighboring nations and because it has a rather small population, the major development funds of the World Bank, the International Development Agency (IDA), and the International Bank for Reconstruction and Development (IBRD) offered grants and credits to Cape Verde of only US$20 million in 1991. However, since Cape Verde is a small nation with a rather honest government, donor nations have often seen a conspicuous and tangible effect from their aid. An example

TABLE 5.5   Cape Verde Island Commerce in 1988

	Percent of Merchandise Exchanged	
At Ports of:	*Foreign*	*Domestic*
São Tiago	42.0	35.7
São Nicolau	0.5	3.4
Fogo	3.9	2.5
Brava	0.1	0.6
São Vicente	52.1	46.6
Maio	0.1	1.2
Sal	0.9	0.2
Boa Vista	0.0	0.0

SOURCE: These percentages are calculated from Ministério do Plano e da Cooperação, Direccção Geral de Estatística, *Cabo Verde em Números*, Novembro 1990, pp. 14–15.

is the increased energy output for expanded power grids coming from electricty generation plants that were largely financed through foreign aid. For the small distances in Cape Verde, urban and rural electrification projects can be installed relatively quickly.

U.S. aid to Cape Verde had totaled US$6 million in 1990 but will likely be cut to about US$4.6 million by 1994.[10] The main objectives for the USAID program are to supply foodstuffs such as American corn, improve the Cape Verdean watershed, encourage private investment, improve food crop research, support human resource training programs, encourage democratization, and support family planning and AIDS awareness programs. The USAID office for Cape Verde was almost closed, but it will remain open until 1996, when it will likely be moved to the Dakar regional office.

Since 1977, Cape Verde has been a member of the Economic Community of West African States (ECOWAS), which enables it to trade freely within the sixteen cooperating nations of West Africa. Similarly, the island republic has been a signatory to the Lomé Accords I–IV since 1977. These accords between the European Community (EC) and most African, Caribbean, and Pacific (ACP) nations allow the ACP countries to trade with Europe without duties on specified commodities. This has resulted in funding for projects ranging from urban sanitation to water and power supply. Cape Verde also has had fruitful cooperation with the EC, which has resulted in funding for reforestation and water conservation. Italy has assisted in improvements in roads and airports, and other contributing nations have provided emergency food aid for famine relief and in times of natural disasters, such as floods and locust control.[11]

Throughout the 1980s, trade with Africa accounted for only 3 to 11 percent of Cape Verde's imports, while that with the Americas ranged between 9 and 18 percent. Trade with Europe at this time accounted for 71 to 81 percent of Cape Verde's imports, and in the data for 1989, the vast bulk of European imports were from member nations of the European Economic Community.[12] More than one-third of Cape Verde's exports are sent to Algeria, which receives mostly fish. And despite the end of colonialism, Portugal still accounts for about one-third of all imports and exports. The Netherlands accounts for about 1 percent of Cape Verde's exports and 9 to 12 percent of its imports. Other lesser trade partners are France, Spain, Belgium, Germany, Brazil, Argentina, Italy, Great Britain, Angola, and the United States.

Significant imports include petroleum and petroleum products, foodstuffs, beverages, manufactured items, textiles, and cement and other construction materials. Portugal is the primary supplier of Cape Verde: In 1981, for example, 39.9 percent of all imports to Cape Verde were from Portugal, as were 62.5 percent of all exports. If Portugal's former colonies are included, then 75 percent of Cape Verdean imports are from this group of Lusophone nations.

The major recipients of Cape Verdean exports were Portugal and the former Portuguese African colonies, which received about two-thirds of the meager volume of total exports—chiefly fish, lobster, salt (sometimes accounting for 10 to 15 percent of exports), and bananas. The other major recipient of Cape Verdean exports is the United States, which purchases 15 to 25 percent of the total exports, especially fish products. Exports of goods and services increased substantially between 1979 and 1983, rising from 30 percent of the GDP to 44 percent. This expansion was largely a consequence of increased aviation services through the still underutilized international airport at Sal and improvement in services at the port of Mindelo.

The 1981 deficit was US$103 million; in 1983, it dropped to US$90 million. Data from 1991 show that this deficit between imports and exports has only widened; the trade deficit has grown steadily from a negative US$81.9 million in 1986 to a negative US$117.2 million in 1991.[13] A contributing reason for this fundamental economic imbalance has been the prolonged need for major food imports (about two-thirds of the total import value). Paralleling this deficiency is the steady rise of Cape Verdean external debt, from US$99.6 million in 1985 to US$152.0 million in 1990, according to the World Bank.

By value, exports in recent years have covered only 5 to 6 percent of all imports; thus, heavy government subsidies, emigration, burdensome poverty, and remittances are needed to absorb the deficit. Economic development plans include improved port and aviation infrastructure, shipping and fishing fleets, a small textile industry, a fish-processing factory, tourism, and commercial production of salt and puzzolane. Therefore, the forseeable future shows more of the same economic picture, and it will only worsen with drought, high transport and energy costs, and inflation. It will improve, however, with the development of the domestic market, expansion of the manufacturing sector, better management, and efficiency in the ground transport and maritime services.

The Microeconomic Structure

Agriculture

Many types of West African and New World cultigens are found in Cape Verde. From West Africa, Cape Verde has received grains including fonio, sorghum or millet, some Guinea yam, and okra. Calabash gourds and watermelons are important. Sudanic or Sahelian crops with commercial usages also include cotton, oil palm, and sesame, with special mention due to the kola nuts that have been important on the coast as a trade item and in social relations as a condiment.

In Cape Verde, valuable and scarce arable land was used to raise cash crops at a time when the production of basic subsistence crops was declining. The significant cash crop exports have been sugarcane and bananas, but other cash crops have included coffee, citrus fruits, and castor beans. For example, in recent years, the production of maize as a basic staple equaled only 4 percent of the total demand; the balance has long been imported at great cost in hard currency reserves or in terms of political dependency upon donor nations.

The plant dyes—urzella, orchil, and indigo—have often been exported from Cape Verde, although they originated from the Rio Nuno area on the Guinea coast. Indigo is a leguminous plant, and urzella is a lichen collected in the mountains of Cape Verde. Both produce a blue dye. Indigo and urzella were used to dye Cape Verdean textiles, especially the economically and socially important *panos*. Orchil is a red plant dye. Today, the importance of these dyes has been dwarfed by other cash crops, and synthetic dyes have often replaced the natural ones.

Table 5.6 presents data on the main crops of Cape Verde in terms of overall volume. Banana cultivation has fluctuated quite markedly in recent years, but overall production has remained very high relative to other crops. For example, bananas were produced at 1.58 tons per acre (3.92 tons per ha), and the next highest productivity was recorded for peanuts, at 0.29 tons per acre (0.76 tons per ha). Moreover, some of the land used for bananas is among the best-watered land in the archipelago, including rather large, privately owned plantations. The 74.1-acre (30-ha) banana plantation of Fazenda Santa Cruz on São Tiago, which once employed 1,000 workers, was taken over by its workers after April 1974. Perhaps it will be slated for denationalization and a return to private ownership in the 1990s.

Many of the important West African and Cape Verdean crops today are, in fact, native to the Americas and were only introduced to the region in the sixteenth century. Chief among these is maize or American corn (*Zea mays*), which is well suited to rain-fed areas or to places cultivated by irrigation. Lima and haricot beans are common American legumes now used in numerous Cape Verdean dishes. The island diet also includes such American crops as pineapples, pumpkins, squash, tomatoes, and papaya. The Cape Verdean state-run supply enterprise, EMPA, is the major importer of corn and typically imports 10,000 to 15,000

TABLE 5.6   Agricultural Production (in metric tons)

Crop	1971	1975	1983	1985	1988	1989	1992
Sugarcane	9,070	10,000	9,000	13,200	15,000	18,150	18,000
Bananas	5,400	3,000	3,000	5,000	6,400	5,400	6,000
Cassava	1,660	2,500	950	2,100	5,700	3,000	2,000
Sweet potatoes	1,450	1,200	1,600	2,600	12,000	1,600	3,000
Maize (corn)	910	1,500	2,700	1,300	16,500	7,300	6,000
Potatoes	—	1,200	800	3,300	3,400	1,920	3,000
Beans	270	3,000	2,200	2,100	14,200	8,900	4,000
Coffee	185	103	—	40	50	—	—

SOURCES: Data from 1971 to 1988 are from the Ministério do Desenvolvimento Rural e Pescas, Gabinete de Estudos e Planeamento, *Estatísticas Agricolas*, Dezembro 1989, Quadro 7.1; data for 1989 are from the same ministério, but the publication is: *Cabo Verde em Números*, Novembro 1990, p. 4; data for 1992 are from *Europa World Year Book, 1994*, vol. 1, pt. 2 (London: Europa World Publications), p. 720.

tons each year. Unfortunately, even though Cape Verde produces about 15,000 tons of sugarcane yearly, it must still import 8,000 to 13,000 tons of refined sugar to meet domestic demand, especially for beverage production.

Peanuts or groundnuts (*Arachis hypogaea*), or *mancarra* in Portuguese, are grown in Cape Verde, especially on Fogo, but this crop has far less significance in the islands as compared to the neighboring mainland. Production fluctuates very widely according to rainfall. Even the high figure for 1964 was a small 164 tons; the production of peanuts in 1970, a year of major drought, was just 14 tons.

About 80 percent of the Cape Verdean working population (some 172,000 workers) live by agricultural production (mostly subsistence farming). This figure can vary from over 90 percent in the larger and more populated islands of Fogo, São Tiago, and Santo Antão to less than 25 percent in São Nicolau and Sal. Thus, when subsistence production falls drastically during a drought, there is a devastating and extensive impact.

Statistics for the early 1960s showed that only 130,090 acres (52,688 ha) of the total land area of Cape Verde was being cultivated; in 1981, this number had fallen to 90,856 acres (36,784 h), and in 1987, there were only 86,109 acres (34,862 ha) under cultivation. The limitations on agriculture are even more obvious when one considers that about 30 percent of the farmland in Cape Verde is being fallowed, and only 50 percent is used for permanent, regular cultivation. Although agriculture accounts for the greatest portion of all water consumption and although almost all urban residents have access to safe water, less than half of the rural residents have a convenient water supply.

Since Cape Verde is such a young nation, its inherited systems of colonial land tenure still have a notable effect. Even at independence, 69.4 percent of the 36,309 farms were operated by sharecroppers or tenant farmers. For those minority farmers who owned their own land, the holdings were usually small. Today, major owners of Cape Verdean land include private capitalists and the Catholic Church.

The best land on some islands is along coastal strips that receive rain runoff and in the high, moisture-bearing altitudes on Fogo (which are particularly good for peanut and coffee cultivation). However, the largest amount of agriculture is concentrated on São Tiago, Santo Antão, and São Nicolau, all of which have more regular sources of water.

Aside from food and cash crops, Cape Verdean agriculture is also concerned with animal wealth as a source of meat and hides and for some export. Although drought and famine have devastated livestock herds at times, the relatively stable animal production offers distinct benefits: food security, wealth accumulation, and import substitution. Table 5.7 shows recent levels of Cape Verdean animal wealth.

Banking, Commerce, and Supply

A main feature of the economic burden in colonial times was represented by the Companhia União Fabril (CUF)—one of the largest Portuguese conglomerates, holding perhaps 10 percent of all Portuguese corporate capital. CUF also had important financial links to other major commercial and banking enterprises, especially in France and the United States. Not only did CUF have huge investments in Portuguese Africa and elsewhere, it also was dominant by virtue of the diversity of its goods. Textiles, petroleum products, chemicals, steel, and shipbuilding supplies were carried by its critical transport services, which included its own fleet of merchant ships and tens of thousands of employees. In form, function, and relative scale, CUF in Cape Verde in the twentieth century was the equivalent of the mid-eighteenth-century Companhia do Grão Pará e Maranhão. The general structure of the political economy in both periods and the companies' relations to Portugal's capital and its ruling classes were remarkably similar.

In a serious effort to break these exploitive and monopolistic ties, the PAIGC government set up its own banking and supply establishments. In 1976, the PAIGC established the Bank of Cape Verde (BCV) from a merger of the local branches of the Overseas National Bank (BNU) and the Banco de Fomento. The BNU was a major Portuguese banking organization, first established in Cape Verde in 1868. The BNU board of directors was intimately connected—personally, politically, and economically—with the colonial administration; two former colonial secretaries as well as major shareholders were associated with CUF and its overseas linkages. Net profit to the BNU in the years just before independence was some US$3 million, with dividends commonly yielding a generous 9 percent profit. With extensive political connections, the BNU bankers exerted a critical influence in financing and shaping the development (or lack of development) in many aspects of the Cape Verdean economy and society—insurance, agriculture, transport, and petrochemicals, among others. Following independence, the BNU was renamed the Bank of Cape Verde (BCV), which now functions as the central bank issuing currency and as the government's banker. Since the BCV was estab-

TABLE 5.7   Number of Head of Major Livestock

	1970	1975	1980	1985	1986	1988	1992
Cattle	25,000	15,000	11,000	10,000	11,500	17,996	19,000
Goats	60,000	50,000	66,000	75,000	78,000	95,338	110,000
Sheep	1,800	1,600	1,600	1,700	2,300	4,193	6,000
Pigs	30,000	24,000	35,000	58,000	67,000	57,977	86,000

SOURCE: *Europa World Year Book, 1994*, vol. 1, pt. 2 (London: Europa World Publications), p. 720.

lished, its monetary policy has stressed maintaining a strong foreign reserve position. The BCV has its central office in Praia, with branches on the other islands.

To reinforce the financial structure of the young economy, the PAIGC also established the Empresa Public de Abastecimento (EMPA), which was legally created in July 1975. To a great degree, it was modeled after and inspired by the People's Stores that had evolved in the years of military struggle on the mainland. Its formal functions involve meeting the social, economic, and political needs of Cape Verde by supplying foodstuffs and diverse building materials. Its basic objective is to help the nation achieve economic independence. In short, EMPA became the state-operated public monopoly of basic supplies. In practice, it functioned as the national importer, distributor, and seller of those goods deemed essential for national reconstruction and development. It also regularized commerce and established a standard price structure. Typical imports of EMPA included corn, rice, beans, sugar, milk, coffee, olive and vegetable oils, lard, margarine, potatoes, onions, butter, cement, pipes and tubing, diverse construction materials, and sanitary ware. Exports from Cape Verde through EMPA have included dyes, varnishes, solvents, puzzolane, salt, potatoes, onions, vegetables, corn meal, eggs, cigarettes, and chickens. EMPA is represented on each island, and in the late 1980s, it had a total staff of 1,013 employees. For a small nation, this is a very large and complex operation, involved trucking, office staff, warehouses, port facilities, and communications. Like most centrally planned state enterprises in the socialist world, it must be credited with providing basic supplies at low prices. But due to the lack of competition and the scale of the operation, there was little incentive for economy in staffing, which often had redundant employees. In the wake of the MpD victory, EMPA has been subject to close scrutiny, and it will probably be targeted for privatization in full, in part, or through long-term leases. In keeping with these new policies, Cape Verde held its first international trade fair in July 1993; various firms (mostly Portuguese) were invited to explore investments in Cape Verdean tourism, industry, construction, and trade. Notably, the current management of EMPA is associated with the MpD government.

Maritime Trades: Fishing, Bunkering, and Repairs

Fishing is a mainstay of the Cape Verdean economy, and it can help reduce agriculture's vulnerability to recurrent drought. Without the easily accessible fishing

TABLE 5.8   Recent Values of Fish Catches (in millions of Cape Verdean escudos)

	Type of fishing activity	
	Artisanal	*Industrial*
1986	556.0	79.6
1987	645.7	131.9
1988	713.5	32.9

NOTE: In 1985, one U.S. dollar equaled 90 Cape Verdean escudos.
SOURCE: Ministério do Plano e da Cooperação, Direcção Geral de Estatística, *Cabo Verde em Números,* Novembro 1990, p. 16.

resources, it is certain that famines would have resulted in increased mortality rates. Fishing can be divided into two sectors: the small-scale artisanal fishing for local sale and consumption and the small, state-supported industrial fishing, geared to tuna and lobster exportation. Fishing can be an important part of the economy; in the past, it represented from 28 percent to 36 percent of all export earnings.[14] Before independence, annual fish catches were commonly 5,500 tons (5,000 metric tons). By 1980 this had risen to 9,680 tons (8,800 metric tons), and in 1982, it grew still further to 11,440 tons (10,400 metric tons) per year. Since then, the catch has either fluctuated or declined, although the potential catch in offshore waters could be 44,000 tons (40,000 metric tons) annually. In addition, fish-processing could produce 5,500 tons (5,000 metric tons) each year if efficiently managed. Under proper management and with appropriate technology, the Cape Verdean fishing industry has a great untapped potential in the islands' underfished offshore waters. (See Tables 5.8 and 5.9.)

The volcanic origins of the islands produced a very narrow coastal shelf, which provides for limited trawling for some species of commercial fish. The fishing industry has significant potential for expansion, but it has been limited by lack of investment capital, inadequate port facilities and fishing technology, and small-scale seafood-processing facilities. There is a substantial potential for the development of light industry related to the canning and freezing of fish products. In recent years, the state-run fishing enterprise has been criticized for its ineffective operation, and in the current move toward privatization, it may be scrapped and fishing rights may be sold to those who have appropriate technology to fish in Cape Verdean waters, perhaps with some conditions of joint ownership or use of Cape Verdean port facilities.[15] Despite the important maritime traditions of Cape Verde in the small-scale cargo packet trade, artisanal fishing, and the oceanic location, its fishing fleet has not been productive or effective because of: the limited amount of capital available for the purchase of large-scale, factory-type fishing ships and large-scale canning facilities for export; low wages; high risk; and foreign competition.

Closely related to fishing are the facilities for ship fuel bunkering, supply, and repair, services that are provided in the smaller ports in the archipelago and are available on a large scale at the port of Mindelo. Even though a great deal of ship

TABLE 5.9   Fish Exports, 1982 to 1988 (in thousands of Cape Verdean esducos)

	1982	1983	1984	1985	1986	1987	1988
Fresh fish	148,279	105,339	0	66,628	0	773	2,183
Frozen fish	0	0	0	71,668	126,461	270,988	77,819
Live lobsters	15,494	11,769	12,785	30,954	29,882	31,335	22,194
Preserved fish	11,796	46,893	46,812	70,493	42,883	18,112	12,942

NOTE: One U.S. dollars equals about 90 Cape Verdean escudos.
SOURCES: Ministério do Desenvolvimento Rural e Pescas, Gabinete de Estudos e Planeamento, *Estatísticas Agricolas,* Dezembro 1989, Quadro 10.5; Ministério do Plano e da Cooperação, Direcção Geral de Estatísticas, *Cabo Verde em Números,* Novembro 1990, p. 7.

traffic passes through the Suez Canal rather than down the Atlantic coast of West Africa, there is still an ongoing maritime role for Cape Verde due to its strategic position in the sea lanes to South America and Africa. This potential has been recognized for five centuries, as has the skill and low cost of Cape Verdean merchant mariners. Future development plans may build on this long-standing link to the sea. For example, there are discussions among Brazilian merchants and shippers about using the vacant lands in Cape Verde for warehousing goods to be sold in Africa: Bulk items would be sent directly from Brazil to Mindelo, and then, in smaller ships with smaller cargos and a faster turnaround, these goods could be sold more economically in the numerous West African port towns.[16] Certainly, these links are maintained by remittances and *mantanas* ("sustaining messages") from the widely scattered maritime communities of Cape Verdeans in Rotterdam, New Bedford (Massachusetts), Lisbon, and many other places.

Tourism

Tourism has often been discussed as a primary resource for Cape Verde, given the almost yearround sun and warm temperatures in the islands. The potential for tourist development is also enhanced by dramatic scenery; points of archaeological, ecological, geological, and historical interest; and especially by the fine beaches and the potential for sports fishing and scuba diving. Yet tourism only accounted for about 2 percent of the 1986 GDP. The main difficulties to be faced involve the limited or high cost infrastructure—including expensive water, electricity, fuel supply, and inadequate roads. Some of the political objections to tourism as a corrupting influence were bypassed with the electoral defeat of the PAICV. However, important issues of ownership or leasing of land for foreign tourist development are still very sensitive.

To date, the overwhelming number of tourists are Cape Verdeans in the diaspora who return home to see family and friends. The role of the emigrants in the Cape Verdean economy is extremely important, not only as returning "tourists" but also in the remittances sent back to the islands. Recent statistics on tourism clearly show a modest but steady increase in tourist traffic—and, of course, in the hard currency that tourists bring. (See Table 5.10.)

Town and harbor at Mindelo, São Vicente Island (Photo by author)

It is clear that tourism has consistently grown in importance in terms of construction, hotel jobs and related services, and taxes. Aside from the substantial costs involved in the required infrastructure, tourism is relatively "clean" development, for it has little associated industrial or chemical pollution. According to the Ministry of Planning and Development, the number of hotel employees in Cape Verde rose from 577 to 705 between 1986 and 1990, and in the period between 1986 to 1989, the number of "hotel-nights" likewise increased, from 129,437 to 194,315.

Sal Island had the greatest number of hotel-nights in 1989 (99,660) and it has the vast majority of direct international air connections to Europe, North America, and Africa; magnificent, extensive beaches; and high-standard hotels. For many who come to Sal, that is the beginning and end of their Cape Verdean experience. Next on the list is São Tiago, with a total of 57,880 hotel-nights in 1989. As the oldest settled island, São Tiago has the impressive ruins of Ribeira Grande and numerous other sites of historical or scenic interest. But at points *between* the main towns, there is still little reason for the average tourist to stop, and the small scale of industry at present provides little incentive for investment.

Sal is not the only island with tourist potential. The development of Boa Vista may also be considered, for it is relatively flat and low (maximum altitude, 1,280 feet [389 m]) and sandy. Recently, a fast trimaran has been introduced that can sail from Sal to Boa Vista in about one hour.[17] During the last years of Portuguese

TABLE 5.10   Origin of Tourists to Cape Verde, 1986 to 1988

	1986	1987	1988
Nonresident Cape Verdeans	14,232	17,068	18,273
Portugal	4,346	4,483	5,319
France	1,661	1,286	1,542
Germany	408	538	1,046
Holland	1,033	1,113	1,069
United States	632	956	1,156
Italy	515	493	711
South Africa	528	394	515
Senegal	389	396	379
Miscellaneous	4,114	4,134	4,593
Total	27,858	30,861	34,603
Percent Change		+10.4%	+12.4%

SOURCE: Ministério do Plano e da Cooperação, Direcção Geral de Estatística, *Cabo Verde em Números*, Novembro 1990, p. 10.

colonialism, a West German company, AIP, had planned to develop three hotels in Boa Vista with a 6,000-bed capacity for tourists, but this plan was never realized. Another firm called TURMAIO had a similar plan for Maio Island, but it, too, had little result. With improved interisland air transport facilities and aircraft, as well as improved accommodations, tourism in Cape Verde does offer some promise for economic development.

São Vicente's pleasant capital has tourist potential and is highly regarded for both the carnival at Bai do Gatos and for the excellent wind-surfing conditions, which can produce world-speed records. Finally, the security issues that trouble tourism in some nations are virtually no problem at all in Cape Verde.

Other Contributors to the Economy

A variety of small contributors to the Cape Verdean economy deserve mention. The salt extraction industry, especially in Sal at Pedro Lune, suffered in recent years and is now closed, in spite of the rather steady role that salt played in the economic history of Cape Verde. Production of puzzolane, the cement additive produced in Santo Antão, also is in decline, but presumably, it could be revived with some potential benefit. Poultry, egg, milk, agricultural, and livestock producers, as shown in Tables 5.6 and 5.7, are faring relatively well by meeting an increasing demand in local consumption and in the export of animal hides. Until recently, these enterprises had been under state control; they may be highly tempting for Cape Verdean entrepreneurs or their backers, for they can be very lucrative businesses.

Construction and transportation services in Cape Verde contribute little to export directly, but they can play a role in import substitution. Manufacturing and

Salt works, Sal Island, 1992 (Photo by author)

small-scale assembly has not been well developed but a certain potential exists in this area if utility costs can be managed and if foreign investors can be assured that their capital is secure and that they can obtain a reasonable level of profits. Likewise, trained professionals in health and education contribute to national development by curbing the reliance on outside consultants, who are paid and accommodated at much greater cost.

Finally, the role of remittances is extremely important to the Cape Verdean economy. The greatest number of Cape Verdean emigrants in the 1980s left for the United States, Portugal, and Angola, to mention only a few of the nations to which they have moved. It is estimated that well over US$1 million in U.S. social security benefits reach Cape Verde annually, and the amount from other European nations must be even greater. The amount that is sent regularly or carried back during holidays and visits is not known precisely, but this certainly represents an extremely important source of foreign currency. One report indicates that remittances reached US$29 million in 1986 and rose to US$35 million by 1988.[18] Meanwhile, the MpD government has been very active in trying to increase the flow of remittances and investments by diaspora Cape Verdeans, who are encouraged to invest in the islands with tax benefits and other enticements in the area of fishing and light industry; however, there is inadequate evidence of the effectiveness of this policy.[19]

The MpD Strategies for Economic Development, 1991–

It is very clear that the MpD intends to forge an economic revolution in Cape Verde. A wide-ranging, free market economy is planned, and there will be a major push toward private investment and sales of state-run and state-owned enterprises. In addition, operations that are not deemed economically viable will be closed. The fundamental shifts proposed may attract foreign capital for investment if terms for the repatriation of profits are favorable or competitive. New services and infrastructure are projected, as well, but by 1994, none had yet made a notable appearance.

Parallel to the transition from a state-run to a private economy in Eastern Europe, Cape Verde is experiencing some rising social and political tensions, increased unemployment, and active class formation. Although few precise political polls have been conducted, it is widely believed that the huge popularity enjoyed by the MpD in the election has been reduced substantially, for the party's economic program is perceived in some circles to have benefited only a small group. A major cabinet reshuffling in March 1993, unsubstantiated rumors of a coup in August, the emergence of a faction within the MpD, and the intervention of the neutral president in the National Assembly all suggest a degree of dissatisfaction both inside the MpD and "on the street."

Few data related to the drive toward privatization inaugurated in late 1992 are available as yet. The falling yields of the state-run fishing industry hint that the entire industry may be completely dissolved, then privatized or subcontracted. The national airline has a strong potential for profit if it is run as a national but privately owned monopoly; the same is true for the national shipping industry. Tourism and associated services such as skin-diving, travel agencies, car rentals, hotels, and entertainment are usually considered quite unpredictable but potentially lucrative. If EMPA is broken down, its monopoly in supplying basic foodstuffs, fuels, and construction materials is almost guaranteed to attract private investors. Whether parts of EMPA will remain under state control to ensure food supply, or whether parts will fall under mixed ownership remains to be seen.

The MpD is ready to privatize wherever it can and to eliminate nonproductive enterprises wherever it must. For the sake of economic efficiency, these steps are to be applauded; for the sake of national economic sovereignty, they must be scrutinized. This present free market and relatively open-door economy of Cape Verde is a bold experiment that has been tried before, but in the past, its limited successes have been more the exception than the rule. One recalls the brief period when early settlers were allowed to trade freely on the coast, when the *lançados* were engaged in smuggling, or when the PAIGC/PAICV grabbed the economic controls from 1975 to 1990. Such efforts to achieve economic autonomy were generally short-lived or of limited success. Far more often, the Cape Verdean economy has fallen under foreign economic influences, and this appears to be the case under the MpD administration. Most Cape Verdeans have benefited little, some have suffered greatly, and a few have made their fortunes.

The great promise of Cape Verdean unity with Guinea-Bissau died with the 1980 coup in Bissau. But even under the PAIGC/PAICV leadership, this dream was driven by nationalist and liberation ideology because the total trade with Africa was very small—a fraction of the trade with Europe. The slight trade with African nations that are members of CEDEAO (West African Economic Community) has increased recently, although overall trade with Africa is usually less than that with the Americas so many thousands of miles away. Whatever the coming years bring for Cape Verde, it is certain that the lessons and models from the past will direct and illuminate its future.

6

CONCLUSION: CAPE VERDE AT THE END OF THE TWENTIETH CENTURY

Dᴜʀɪɴɢ ᴛʜᴇ ᴡᴀʀ ʏᴇᴀʀs, the PAIGC moved cautiously and confronted its political and military enemies when it had the strength to defeat, resist, or absorb them—whether these enemies were internal dissidents, colonialists presenting ideological challenges, military rivals on the battlefield, or assassins. The PAIGC was also able to isolate competitive movements such as FLING, UCID, and the UPICV. It was also extremely effective in conducting international and diplomatic affairs and in building united fronts at critical moments. As a result of its organizational strength, it was even able to overcome the significant loss of Amilcar Cabral. On Guinean battlefields, the military wing of the PAIGC defeated the well-armed Portuguese, and it was able to turn this victory into decisive negotiations with the MFA for the independence of Cape Verde. The PAIGC sought to combine a revolution against colonialism with a social revolution liberating the urban poor, the rural peasants, women, and others who were victimized and stranded by colonial policies.

After 1975, the Cape Verde branch of the PAIGC recruited masses of Cape Verdean members, but those in the old guard, battle-hardened and tempered in the Cold War, were not about to loosen their grip on the state they had given so much to create. These veteran leaders of the PAIGC were committed to the collective liberation of the two lands, although the newly recruited members could not appreciate this objective as fully. In those days, Carlos Veiga and António

Monteiro were at the margins of the PAIGC. They had not experienced the daily risks of the armed struggle. They were younger and more inclined toward political and economic liberalism rather than the socialist ideals of the preceding generation. The liberation of and unity with Guinea was probably not so significant for those who had not been galvanized by the struggles there. Another difference was that Cape Verdeans dominated the top leadership positions of the PAIGC in Guinea. The vast majority of the combatants were Guineans, and this made the old guard sensitive or vulnerable in their position vis-à-vis the African majority. In Cape Verde, both leaders and followers were Cape Verdean, but though the party was projected as two branches of the same organization, its composition was notably different from that in the mainland. Thus, such distinctions laid the foundation for a dissident generation within the PAIGC/PAICV that, almost overnight, formed the MpD in 1991.

Cultural Identity as "Currency"

In this study, Cape Verdean cultural identity is shown to have been transformed into a source of political power. "Cape Verdeanity" was counterposed to Portuguese culture as a means of asserting self-determination and achieving national liberation. For some, a derivative of this same spirit of Cape Verdean nationalism led to a separation of the ties to Africa, in addition to those with Portugal. The MpD, seeking its own political identity, had to reject the strengths of the PAIGC, which lay with its highly developed association with Africa. From the view of the PAIGC, Cape Verde was intimately linked to and built from their African power base. This linkage was seriously damaged by the 1980 coup d'état against the key PAIGC official, President Luís Cabral, in Bissau. The resultant break was symbolized by the ruling party in Cape Verde in the change in nomenclature from PAIGC to PAICV. Perhaps some bitter Cape Verdean leaders may have projected themselves as the unfortunate victims of Africans who were "not sufficiently grateful" for their liberation, and Guineans naturally perceived such attitudes as patronizing. Since the political and military strength of the PAIGC was based in Africa, the opposition MpD turned to Euro-American economic ties and cultural models for its strength.

Without stretching the model too far, the historical battles between Crown and *capitãos,* on one hand, and the *lançados* and *grumetes,* on the other, can illuminate some of the dimensions of the modern PAICV and MpD rivalries. The power of the *capitãos* rested in Lisbon; the power of the *lançados* was based on their economic and military ties to Africa. The *lançados* and the PAIGC/PAICV Cape Verdean leadership both held power because they were at a key economic, military, and political intersection. Both relied on a military force made up of African irregular soldiers. Both carried the *Crioulo* language and culture deeper into Africa, and both pushed an African identity deeper into the Atlantic. Both were simultaneously central and yet strangely peripheral to the political processes in Africa. Both were expelled from Africa and experienced strategic retreat to the Cape Verde Islands. And both commanded the flow of wealth from primary production, imports, and exports—with all their critical links to the peoples of Africa.

In the archipelago, the *badiu* population of runaway slaves might also be added to this list of marginally empowered people. Their flight and resistance gave them a measure of autonomy and respect: At least they were empowered to the extent that their freedom of movement on isolated mountain hillsides—and even the Africanity of their identity—posed a threat to the monopoly of colonial, religious, and cultural forces. The combination of colonial Portugal's vulnerability and the united front of these traditionally unempowered people brought the reins of the state into the hands of the PAIGC.

Only on rare instances was the bipolar model of "colonized and colonizer" in Cape Verdean society, culture, and history challenged. Only when the external Lisbon power base was shaken at home did the colonial rulers become vulnerable in their far-flung colonial empire. It was even less common for the complex divisions of the colonized people in the islands to be transcended. Only in the liberation war were the islanders sufficiently articulated with the mainland to acquire enough strength to achieve full independence. In terms of regional political history, the victory of the PAIGC was clearly quite exceptional.

In Cape Verde, with its small internal power base, culture has become "currency" that can be "spent" in the African or Western marketplaces of power. Inevitably, all of the various contemporary rulers of impoverished Cape Verde have sought to trade in this currency. The PAIGC and PAICV used the Africanity of their currency to acquire the human, military, and cultural wealth of Africa, and the MpD has attempted to trade its "Europeanness" to attract Western capital and alliances to achieve economic and political stability.

The dilemma of defining the Cape Verdean self-image and empowering its people exists within this framework of acquiring external power bases. Which cultural currency will be spent to purchase this power? Are Cape Verdeans southern Europeans, westernmost Africans, or easternmost West Indians? And who are *Crioulos* anyway? Spiritually and culturally, just where is the Cape Verdean *saudade*? These questions cannot be answered decisively because the answers depend upon who is asked, when he or she is asked, who is asking, and what the motivation is for asking the question in the first place.

In 1991, the struggle for the icons of Cape Verdean identity was at least partially centered on the issue of a new flag. The former PAIGC/PAICV flag was defended as an African flag, bearing the color of the blood shed by Cape Verdeans and Guineans. Since that party symbolized the nation, it was considered by some the only proper emblem for African self-pride.

The MpD sought—and continues to seek—scarce political and economic capital in a manner similar to that of the *capitãos*. The MpD is very open to foreign investment, and it encourages privatization. The MpD's leaders seem to be serious activists in the democracy movement sweeping Africa, and they have been active in courting the West, now without its long-standing socialist opponents.[1]

MpD leaders have pointedly attacked the former flag for being only a partisan banner. Indeed, they saw it as the emblem of the party that had excluded a generation of Cape Verdeans from leadership and had isolated the islands in an outmoded statist and socialist economy, leading the nation to ruin. A break with the past was necessary if there was to be hope for the future. Consequently, a flag with a star for each island and an archipelago free of symbolic ties to an impoverished and undemocratic Africa was deemed appropriate by the new leaders.

There was no problem with a European icon; after all, Europe is multiracial, and Portuguese passports had been valid for half a millennium. But the issue of Cape Verdean symbols in the flag and national hymn is likely to persist. To conclude, contemporary Cape Verdean politics can be compared to the contrasting models and historical reality of the *capitãos* and the *lançados*. The search for Cape Verdean cultural identity may be seen as a struggle between competitive African and Euro-American powers. The unique flexibility of "Cape Verdeanity" makes this cultural currency valid tender in both markets.

Cape Verdean Politics: From Populism to Pluralism

To address the issue of Cape Verde's political future, three models of political democracy are offered:[2] populism, plural democracy, and Madisonian federalism.

Under populist models, the people as a whole seek to govern themselves, but this requires popular mobilization and participation. Collective and egalitarian relations are advocated, involving popular organizations and groups that had been neglected by former regimes. Efforts are made to have direct popular control. In populist models, problems typically arise due to inadequate representation of socioeconomic, cultural, or gender divisions. In the past, such problems were often addressed by muffling the claims of competitive groups, which resulted in a tendency toward authoritarianism and against liberal democratic expression. This model has been very common in societies with weak class formation—including immediate postcolonial Africa. As class formation emerges, populist models are stressed. It is not hard to see that this was the experience of the PAIGC/PAICV when it was attaining power from 1975 to 1980 and trying to consolidate it from 1980 to 1991.

The second model—plural democracy or multiparty representation—is designed to protect or develop meaningful economic or ideological choices in complex societies. With competitive parties, there is a structural recognition of the different interests in the various social strata. Political institutions and party leaders become more important than the daily expression of citizens' concerns, and each party exists on the basis of the issues it represents and the interest groups it serves.

Typically, no party really reflects all views of the citizenry. To win elections, each party must represent a plurality of views, which are strategically reduced to the singularity of one party. Party candidates are essentially political entrepreneurs competing in the electoral marketplace. So it was in the 1991 elections, which led to the MpD victory. These are the new rules in the Cape Verdean multiparty, electoral democracy.

A third model, that of Madisonian democracy, is intended to preserve individual freedoms with institutional or governmental guarantees to limit the power of the elected leaders in multiparty representative democracy. Such federalism is supposed to protect the minority against a majority that might not be so democratic in practice. Madisonian models are common in internally diversified states in which minorities (whether defined by class, ethnicity, or gender) need safeguards against democratically elected authoritarians. This provides a system of checks and balances against tyranny by counterbalancing executive, judicial, and legislative branches of government. Discussions with the leadership of UCID indicate that, if they compete in the 1995 elections, they will advocate such a model. Heavily influenced by the U.S. Constitution, this party, largely composed of emigrants, intends to promote a federal system for Cape Verde in which a governor on each island will have considerable self-rule. The intent is for this form of government to balance Praia's drive for centralization and bureaucratization. This model may provide an alternative to the first two, but this would require a second round of constitutional revisions.

For Cape Verde, one may have pessimism about the drought and lack of natural resources, but the small-scale society and highly interconnected personal relations do keep the islands working as a totality. The loss of the united front approach of the PAIGC/PAICV does risk divisive class formation and rising youth unemployment. However, as long as plural democracy remains, these tendencies will also have their counterbalances. The geography of the archipelago has an inherent federalism with its insularity and self-reliance, which is reminiscent of the anthropological model of "ordered anarchy" usually known in stateless societies.

The decades ahead will reveal whether this will be part of the new world order—or disorder. Certainly, there is a new context without the Cold War and with Europe's civil wars and revived racism, a populous Third World, plural democracy, ecology and energy crises, AIDS, rising global poverty, massive urbanization, and new patterns of class formation apparently under way.

Realistic Social and Economic Development

After probing the questions regarding the sources and models of power in Cape Verde and the search for a national and cultural identity, practical concerns must be addressed if realistic plans are to be made for social and economic development. Since the majority of the Cape Verdean population is female, it seems that the issues around gender and the status of Cape Verdean women will need to become more central in order to tap the fullest potential of this human resource. Sexism is a universal social pathology, and it is no different in Cape Verde than anywhere else. However, the plan for social development should consider formal women's organizations as more than auxiliaries of political parties. Likewise, it is better to deliver domestic water by pipes and pumps than to have it carried on the heads of girls or women.

Labor-intensive road brigades may be replaced with appropriate heavy machinery as women expand their presence in the National Assembly, in factories, in commerce, in education, and in the social services. When physical abuse of Cape Verdean women is tolerated at home and a father can neglect his parental responsibility, the overall development of Cape Verdean society is lessened. In turn, scarce financial and institutional resources are consumed to attend to the issues in courts, hospitals, and schools, rather than in more constructive ways.

Some of the most pressing concerns regard the amelioration of poor health conditions. Great credit must be given for the huge strides made in a very short period; life expectancy has risen, and death rates have dropped. Still, there is room for improvement in maternal prenatal and postnatal care, and infant mortality rates could be reduced if infant nutrition, oral rehydration, and diarrhea control are improved. With anticipated declines in the infant death rate, family planning information and strategies must be physically and socially accessible, or population pressures will severely tax the small-scale infrastructure. Data on AIDS in Cape Verde are precious few, but we know that it is present; much more will have to be done to block or retard its spread there and in all nations that continue to lack any effective approach beyond education and behavioral modification. Diseases such as malaria and cholera, though not major, also need to be monitored more closely in the health programs of Cape Verde.

The levels of illiteracy continue to fall in the islands, and most development budgets have been rather generous in their funding of education. Cape Verdeans have long treasured education—for its intrinsic value and for the social and geographic mobility it encourages. Cape Verde's finest leaders have had homegrown educations, through the *liceu*-level at least. Educators will likely revisit the issue of Crioulo as the national language when and if the standardization of its grammar and spelling are achieved.

Between 1975 and 1995, advances in soil and water conservation have shown how much can be done in a short time and how tragic the neglect during Portuguese colonialism actually was. Water conservation will remain a critical limiting factor and a major cost in Cape Verdean development unless innovations in desalinization technology make this resource more manageable. Solar and wind power are making some inroads, but further development and expansion seems appropriate. Even though there have been droughts since independence, the present

Faces of the future, São Tiago (Photo by author)

food reserves have prevented the outrageous famines and mortality known commonly in the recent past.

The natural resources of Cape Verde have never been great, and they have often been underutilized. First on this list are the fishing resources, which, if managed effectively, could have a tremendous spin-off in processing and attracting hard currency from foreign markets. Maritime services in ship repair, bunkering, and construction need to be regularized and expanded to make full use of the well-honed seafaring skills of Cape Verdeans. The natural resources of endless warm sun and lovely long beaches have been marketed more effectively, and tourism promises to be an area of continued development; the primary dangers here involve the degree of foreign control and the inherent vagaries of tourist trade and service sector employment.

The people of Cape Verde have always been its best renewable resource. Forever recovering from hardship, sending remittances back home, creating a dynamic music and literature, and spreading the Cape Verdean diaspora to Africa and to Europe, the *povo Crioulo* will find a way. Faith in their creative energies is the note on which this book ends—and the development of the Cape Verdean future begins.

Acronyms

ACP	African, Caribbean, and Pacific (countries)
AID	Agency for International Development
ANP	Assembléia Nacional Popular
	Popular National Assembly
BCV	Bank of Cape Verde
BNU	Banco Nacional Ultramarino
CDR	Crude death rate
CEDEAO	West African Economic Community
CEI	Casa dos Estudantes do Império
	House of Students from the Empire
CEL	Comité Executivo da Luta
	Executive Committee of the Struggle
CONCP	Conferência das Organisações Nacionalistas das Colónias Portuguesas
	Conference of Nationalist Organizations of the Portuguese Colonies
CSL	Conselho Superior da Luta
	High Council of the Struggle
CUF	Companhia União Fabril
	Industrial Union Company
DGS	Direcção Geral de Segurança
	General Directory of Security
DiNaS	Direcção Nacional de Segurança
	National Directorate of Security
EC	European Community
ECOMAG	Economic Community Military Assistance Group (of ECOWAS)
ECOWAS	Economic Community of West African States
EMPA	Empresa Pública de Abastecimento
	Public Supply Enterprise
ETA	Euzkadi ta Azkatasuna
	(Basque) Nation and Liberty (Party)
FAL	local militia forces of the PAIGC
FARP	Forças Armadas Revolucionárias do Povo
	People's Revolutionary Armed Forces
FLGC	Frente de Libertação da Guiné Portuguesa e Cabo Verde
	Liberation Front of Portuguese Guinea and Cape Verde
FLING	Frente de Luta Pela Independência Nacional da Guiné-Bissau
	Front of the Struggle for National Independence of Guinea-Bissau
FRAIN	Frente Revolucionária Africana para a Independência Nacional das Colónias Portuguesas

	African Revolutionary Front for the National Independence of the Portuguese Colonies
FRELIMO	Frente de Libertação de Moçambique Liberation Front for Mozambique
FULGPICV	United Front for the Liberation of Portuguese Guinea and the Cape Verde Islands
GADCVG	Grupo de Acção Democrática de Cabo Verde e Guiné Democratic Action Group of Cape Verde and Guinea
GDP	gross domestic product
GNP	gross national product
IBRD	International Bank for Reconstruction and Development
ICS	Instituto Caboverdeano de Solidaridade Cape Verde Solidarity Institute
IDA	International Development Agency
IDR	infant death rate
INIA	National Institute for Agricultural Research
ITCZ	Inter-Tropical Convergence Zone
JAAC	Juventude Africana Amilcar Cabral Amilcar Cabral African Youth
MAC	Movimento Anti-Colonialista Anti-Colonial Movement
MFA	Armed Forces Movement
MFDC	Mouvement des Forces Democrátique de la Casamance Movement of Democratic Forces of the Casamance
MLGCV	Mouvement de Libération de la Guiné "Portugaise" et les Iles du Cap Vert Liberation Movement of "Portuguese" Guinea and the Cape Verde Islands
MLICV	Mouvement de Libération des Iles du Cap Vert Liberation Movement of the Cape Verde Islands
MpD	Movimento para Democracia Movement for Democracy
MPLA	Movimento Popular de Libertação de Angola Popular Movement for the Liberation of Angola
NATO	North Atlantic Treaty Organization
OAU	Organization of African Unity
OMCV	Organização das Mulheres do Cabo Verde Organization of Women of Cape Verde
PAICV	Partido Africano da Independência de Cabo Verde African Party of Independence of Cape Verde
PAIGC	Partido Africano da Independência da Guiné e Cabo Verde African Party of Independence of Guinea and Cape Verde
PIDE	Polícia Internacional e de Defesa do Estado International and State Defense Police
POP	Public Order Police
PSP	Partido Social Democrática Social Democratic Party

TACV	Transportes Aéreos de Cabo Verde
	Cape Verde Air Transport
UCID	União Caboverdeana para A Independente e Democrátia
	Cape Verdean Union for Independence and Democracy
UDCV	União Democrática de Cabo Verde
	Cape Verde Democratic Union
UDEMU	União Democrática das Mulheres
	Democratic Union of Women
UN	United Nations
UNITA	União Nacional para Independência Total de Angola
	National Union for the Total Independence of Angola
UNTG	National Union of Guinean Workers
UPICV	União das Populações das Ilhas de Cabo Verde
	Union of the Peoples of the Cape Verde Islands
USAID	United States Agency for International Development
UTA	Union des Transportes Ariennes

Notes

Chapter 1

1. The foremost references to Cape Verde include António Carreira's studies, such as *Cabo Verde: Classes Sociais, Estrutura Familiar, Migrações* (Lisbon: Biblioteca Ulmeiro, 1977); *O Crioulo de Cabo Verde, Surto e Expansão* (Lisbon: Fundação Gulbenkian, 1982); *The People of the Cape Verde Islands* (London: Hurst, 1982); *Panaria Cabo-Verdeano-Guineense* (Praia, Cape Verde: Instituto Caboverdeano do Livro, 1983); and especially his masterful work *Cabo Verde: Formação e Extinção de uma Sociedade Escravocrata (1460–1878)* (Praia, Cape Verde: Instituto Caboverdeano do Livro, 1983) and his *Cabo Verde: Aspectos Sociais, Secas e Fomes do Seculo XX* (Lisbon: Biblioteca Ulmeiro, 1984).

Also consult Cristiano José de Senna Barcellos, *Subsídios para História de Cabo Verde e Guiné*, 7 vols., (Lisbon: Tipografia da Academia Real das Ciências, 1899–1913). For information about Cape Verdean linkages to the coast, see Avelino Teixeira Da Mota, *As Viagens do Bispo D. Frei Vitoriano Portuense a Guine e a Cristianização dos Reis de Bissau* (Lisbon: Centro de Estudos de Cartografia Antiga, 1974), and Andre Donelha, *Descrição da Serra Leoa e dos Rios de Guine do Cabo Verde* (1625; reprint, Lisbon: Centro de Estudos de Cartografia Antiga, 1977); Fausto Castilho Duarte, *Os Caboverdeanos no Colonização da Guine, Boletim de Propaganda e Informação*, nos. 1, 2, and 13, 1949–1950. An excellent source on seventeenth-century Cape Verdean history is T. Bentley Duncan, *Atlantic Islands* (Chicago: University of Chicago Press, 1972). For studies of recent politics, consult: Basil Davidson, *The Fortunate Isles: A Study in African Transformation* (Trenton, N.J.: Africa World Press, 1989), and Colm Foy, *Cape Verde: Politics, Economics and Society* (London: Pinter Publishers, 1988). Other important Cape Verdean issues are discussed in the following: Baltazar Lopes da Silva, *O Dialecto Crioulo de Cabo Verde* (Lisbon: Agencia Geral do Ultramar, 1957); Baltazar Lopes da Silva, *Antologia da Ficção Cabo-Verdiana Contemporânea* (Praia, Cape Verde: Imprensa Nacional, 1960); Robert Harrison, "Famine and Poverty: The Cape Verde Islands," *Africa Today*, 10 (March 1963): 8–9; Richard Lobban, "Cape Verde Islands: Portugal's Atlantic Colony," *Africa* 21 (May 1973): 36–39; Emílio Moran, "The Evolution of Cape Verde's Agriculture," *African Economic History* 2 (1982): 63–86; Dierdre Meintel, *Race, Culture, and Portuguese Colonialism in Cabo Verde* (Syracuse, N.Y.: Syracuse University Press, 1984); Daniel A. Pereira, *Estudões da Historia de Cabo Verde* (Praia, Cape Verde: Instituto Caboverdiano do Livro, 1986); Michel Renaudeau, *Cape Verde Islands* (Boulogne, France: Delroisse, 1985). Readers will also find a comprehensive research bibliography in Richard Lobban and Marilyn Halter, *Historical Dictionary of the Republic of Cape Verde* (Metuchen, N.J.: Scarecrow Press, 1988).

2. For more specific reference to Portugal along the Guinea coast, see João Barreto, *Historia da Guineé* (Lisbon: Edição do Autor, 1938); Jean Boulegue, *Les Luso-Africains de Senegambie* (Lisbon: Ministerio da Educação, 1989), John Vogt, *Portuguese Rule on the Gold*

Coast, 1569–1682 (Athens: University of Georgia Press, 1979); and Gomes Eanes Zurara, *The Chronicle of the Discovery and Conquest of Guinea,* 2 vols. (1452; reprint, London: Hakluyt Society, 1896–1899). A research bibliography for Guinea-Bissau appears in Richard Lobban and Joshua Forrest, *Historical Dictionary of Guinea-Bissau* (Metuchen, N.J.: Scarecrow Press, 1988).

Also important are the many relevant works of George E. Brooks, such as *Yankee Traders, Old Coasters and African Middlemen* (Boston: Boston University Press, 1970); *Luso-African Commerce and Settlement in the Gambia and Guinea-Bissau Region,* Working Paper No. 24, (Boston: Boston University African Studies Center, 1980); *The Kola Trade and State-Building: Upper Guinea Coast and Senegambia, 15th–17th Centuries,* Working Paper No. 38 (Boston: Boston University African Studies Center, 1980); *Landlords and Strangers: Ecology, Society, and Trade in Western Africa, 1000–1630* (Boulder: Westview Press, 1993).

For general reference to Portugal's history in Africa, readers can consult David M. Abshire and Michael A. Samuels, eds., *Portuguese Africa: A Handbook* (New York: Praeger, 1969); Eric Axelson, *Congo to Cape: Early Portuguese Explorers* (New York: Harper and Row, 1973); C. R. Boxer, *Race Relations in the Portuguese Colonial Empire, 1415–1825* (Oxford: Oxford University Press, 1963); and C. R. Boxer, *Four Centuries of Portuguese Colonial Expansion, 1415–1825* (Berkeley: University of California Press, 1972); Ronald H. Chilcote, *Portuguese Africa* (Englewood Cliffs, N.J.: Prentice-Hall, 1967); James Duffy, *Portugal in Africa* (Cambridge, Mass.: Harvard University Press, 1962); Felipe Fernandez-Armesto, *Before Columbus: Exploration and Colonisation from the Mediterranean to the Atlantic, 1229–1492* (London: Macmillan Education, 1987); Richard Hakluyt, *Voyages and Discoveries* (1589; reprint, Baltimore: Penguin Books, 1972); Richard J. Hammond, *Portugal and Africa, 1815–1910* (Stanford: Stanford University Press, 1966); A. W. Lawrence, *Trade Castles and Forts of West Africa* (Stanford: Stanford University Press, 1963); A. H. De Oliveira Marques, *History of Portugal,* 2 vols., 2d ed. (New York: Columbia University Press, 1976); William Minter, *Portuguese Africa and the West* (Baltimore: Penguin Books, 1972); and Duarte Pacheco Pereira, *Esmeraldo de Situ Orbis,* Memoria No. 19. (1508; reprint, Bissau: Centro de Estudos da Guine Portuguesa, 1956).

3. Those seeking additional sources and bibliography on general African history are referred to the *Cambridge History of Africa* (Cambridge: Cambridge University Press, 1977), especially vols. 3, 4, and 5; *General History Of Africa* (Paris: UNESCO, 1972), especially vols. 4 and 5; J.F.A. Ajayi and Michael Crowder, eds., *History of West Africa,* 2 vols. (New York: Columbia University Press, 1972); Philip D. Curtin, *The Atlantic Slave Trade: A Census* (Madison: University of Wisconsin Press, 1969); Philip D. Curtin, *Economic Change in Precolonial Africa* (Madison: University of Wisconsin Press, 1975); Robert W. July, *A History of the African People,* 3d ed. (New York: Scribner's, 1980); and Walter Rodney, *A History of the Upper Guinea Coast, 1545–1800* (New York: Oxford University Press, 1970). A source for Brazilian references to West Africa is Gilberto Freyre, *The Masters and the Slaves: A Study in the Development of Brazilian Civilization* (Berkeley: University of California Press, 1986).

4. One of the most comprehensive and detailed studies of Cape Verdean climatology and hydrology is that of Ilidio do Amaral, *Santiago de Cabo Verde: A Terra e os Homens,* Memoria no. 48 (Lisbon: Junta de Investigações do Ultramar, 1964).

5. For readers interested in the struggle for the liberation of Cape Verde and Guinea-Bissau, there is a large recent literature, including: Gerard Chaliand, "The PAIGC Without

Cabral: An Assessment," *Ufahamu*, 3, no. 3 (December 1973): 87–95, and Patrick Chabal, *Amilcar Cabral: Revolutionary Leadership and People's War* (New York: Cambridge University Press, 1983). There are many writings by Cabral himself, such as his *Revolution in Guinea* (New York: Monthly Review Press, 1970); *Return to the Source* (New York: Africa Information Service, 1973); and *Unity and Struggle: Speeches and Writings of Amilcar Cabral* (New York: Monthly Review Press, 1980). Ronald Chilcote has also written extensively on Cabral; for example, see his "The Political Thought of Amilcar Cabral," *Journal of Modern African Studies,* 6, no. 3 (October 1968): 378–388; "Amilcar Cabral: A Bio-Bibliography of His Life and Thought, 1925–1973," *Africana Journal* 4 (1974): 289–307; and *Amilcar Cabral's Revolutionary Theory and Practice: A Critical Guide* (Boulder: Lynne Rienner, 1991). Also see Basil Davidson, *The Liberation of Guinea: Aspects of an African Revolution* (Harmondsworth, England: Penguin, 1969); Lars Rudebeck, *Guinea-Bissau: A Study in Political Mobilization* (Uppsala, Sweden: Scandinavian Institute of African Studies, 1974); Eduardo da Sousa Ferreira, *Portuguese Colonialism in Africa: The End of an Era* (Paris: UNESCO, 1972); Ruth First, *Portugal's Wars in Africa* (London: Christian Action Publications, 1972); Richard Gibson, *African Liberation Movements: Contemporary Struggles Against White Minority Rule* (London: Oxford University Press, 1972); Arslan Humbaraci and Nicole Muchnik, *Portugal's African Wars* (New York: Third World Press, 1973); Carlos Lopes, *Guinea-Bissau: From Liberation Struggle to Independent Statehood* (Boulder: Westview Press, 1987); Richard Lobban, "Guinea-Bissau: 24 September and Beyond," *Africa Today,* 21, no. 1 (1974): 15–24; Bernard Magubane, "Amilcar Cabral: Evolution of Revolutionary Thought," *Ufahamu* 2, no. 2 (September 1971): 71–87. The most recent analyses include Joshua Forrest, *Guinea-Bissau* (Boulder: Westview Press, 1992), and Mustafah Dhada, *Warriors at Work: How Guinea Was Really Set Free* (Niwot: University Press of Colorado, 1993).

6. The U.S. connection to Cape Verde is very deep, and readers will benefit from: Raymond A. Almeida and Patricia Nyhan, *Cape Verde and Its People: A Short History* (Boston: American Committee for Cape Verde, 1976); Ron Barboza, "Cape Verde: Portrait of an Archipelago," *Spinner* 2 (1981): 27–31; Sam Beck, *Manny Almeida's Ringside Lounge: The Cape Verdean's Struggle for Their Neighborhood* (Providence, R.I.: Gavea-Brown, 1992); Norman R. Bennett and George E. Brooks, *New England Merchants in Africa: A History Through Documents* (Boston: Boston University Press, 1965); Briton Cooper Busch, "Cape Verdeans in the American Whaling and Sealing Industry, 1850–1900," *The American Neptune* 45, no. 2 (March 1985): 104–116; Sidney M. Greenfield, "In Search of Social Identity: Strategies of Ethnic Identity Management Amongst Capeverdeans in Southeastern Massachusetts," *Luso-Brazilian Review* 13, no. 1 (June 1976): 3–17; Robert C. Hayden, *African-Americans and Cape Verdean-Americans in New Bedford: A History of Community and Achievement* (Boston: Select Publications, 1993); Waltraud Coli and Richard Lobban, *The Cape Verdeans in Rhode Island* (Providence: Rhode Island Publication Society, 1990); Richard Lobban, Waltraud Coli, and Robert Tidwell, "Patterns of Cape Verdean Migration and Social Association," *New England Journal of Black Studies* 5 (1985): 31–45; Meintel, *Race, Culture, and Portuguese Colonialism; Elsie Clews Parsons, Folklore from the Cape Verde Islands* (Cambridge, Mass.: American Folklore Society, 1923); and Michael Platzer and Michael Cohn, *Black Men of the Sea* (New York: Dodd, Mead, 1978). Special research collections having material on Cape Verde can be found at: the New Bedford Whaling Museum

(New Bedford, Mass.); the Kendall Whaling Museum (Sharon, Mass.); Mystic Seaport (Mystic, Conn.); and Rhode Island College (Providence, R.I.).

Chapter 2

1. This thinking about African ethnogenesis follows the approach in J. H. Greenberg, *Studies in African Linguistic Classification* (New Haven: Compass, 1955); Malcolm Guthrie, "Bantu Origins," *Journal of African Languages* 1 (1962): 9–21; and George Peter Murdock, *Africa, Its People and Their Culture History* (New York: McGraw-Hill, 1959). A summary of some of the issues raised on African cultural origins appears in Richard Lobban, "Ethnogenesis in Africa: Some Models of Unity and Diversity," *Reviews in Anthropology* 16 (1991): 245–255.

2. The claim is widely made; see especially Lionel Casson, *The Ancient Mariners* (Princeton: Princeton University Press, 1991), p. 116.

3. Reference to the smoking volcano, which one may interpret as being Fogo Island, is made by Herodotus in Manuel Komroff, ed., *The History of Herodotus,* bk. 4 (New York: Tudor Publishing, 1956). See also Casson, *The Ancient Mariners,* p. 122.

4. The Phoenician navigation and trade on the Atlantic coast is known through archaeological evidence at Mogador, and there is reference to it in Komroff, ed., *The History of Herodotus,* p. 263. Other details on the Phoenician relations with Africa are found in G. Mokhtar, *General History of Africa,* vol. 2, *Ancient Civilizations of Africa* (Paris: UNESCO, 1990), especially in chap. 18.

5. Casson, *The Ancient Mariners,* pps. 168–169.

6. Roman relations with Africa are reviewed in Mokhtar, *General History of Africa,* chap. 19.

7. The history of the savanna kingdoms at this period is very well summarized by I. Hrbek, *General History of Africa,* vol. 3, *Africa from the Seventh to the Eleventh Century* (Paris: UNESCO, 1992), especially chaps. 2–6, 16, and 18. The presence of Jews in Iberia at this time is noted in Gilberto Freyre, *The Masters and the Slaves: A Study in the Development of Brazilian Civilization* (Berkeley: University of California Press, 1986), p. 9.

8. The connections between the regions north and south of the Sahara are reviewed in Hrbek, *General History of Africa,* chap. 11.

9. An excellent source on Islam in Africa in this period is R. Oliver, ed., *The Cambridge History of Africa,* vol. 3, *From c. 1050 to c. 1600* (New York: Cambridge University Press, 1977).

10. A. H. De Oliveira Marques, *History of Portugal,* 2 vols., 2d ed. (New York: Columbia University Press, 1976), p. 136, suggests that Muslims may have reached Sal Island and the Canaries before the Portuguese. See also Ivan Van Sertima, *They Came Before Columbus: The African Presence in Ancient America* (New York: Random House, 1976), p. 234.

11. Van Sertima, *They Came Before Columbus,* pps. 232 and 237.

12. A very comprehensive survey of this history is found in Marques, *History of Portugal,* vol. 1, chap. 1.

13. Kenneth Nebenzahl, *Atlas of Columbus and the Great Discoveries* (New York: Rand McNally, 1990), pps. 6–7.

14. J. Devisse and S. Labib, "Africa in Inter-Continental Relations," in D. T. Niane, ed., *General History of Africa,* vol. 4 (Berkeley: University of California Press/UNESCO, 1984), pps. 664–666.

15. One of the best recent studies of early Iberian maritime innovation is Felipe Fernandez-Armesto, *Before Columbus: Exploration and Colonisation from the Mediterranean to the Atlantic, 1229–1492* (London: Macmillan Education, 1987).

16. The story of early Portuguese navigation is well known through the chronicles kept by the pilots and the records of the Portuguese Crown, such as Gomes Eanes Zurara, *The Chronicle of the Discovery and Conquest of Guinea*, 2 vols. (1452; reprint, London: Hakluyt Society, 1896 and 1899), or, much later, Andre Donelha, *Descrição da Serra Leoa e dos Rios de Guiné do Cabo Verde* (1625; reprint, Lisbon: Centro de Estudos de Cartografia Antiga, 1977). A concise, popular account is Eric Alexson, *Congo to Cape: Early Portuguese Explorers* (New York: Barnes and Noble, 1973).

17. Fernandez-Armesto, *Before Columbus*, p. 190.

18. Ibid., p. 193; and George E. Brooks, *Landlords and Strangers: Ecology, Society, and Trade in Western Africa, 1000–1630* (Boulder: Westview Press, 1993), p. 128.

19. Marques, *History of Portugal*, p. 270.

20. Orchil is a violet-colored lichen (*Rocella sp.*) used in dyes. Orchil, indigo, and urzella have long been exported from Cape Verde; see Fernandez-Armesto, *Before Columbus*, p. 202.

21. Fernandez-Armesto, *Before Columbus*, pps. 227–228, and Jean Boulegue, *Les Luso-Africains de Senegambie* (Lisbon: Ministério da Educação, 1989), pps. 18, 22, have stated that some Wolof notables fled to São Tiago in 1489 following a rebellion against their own authority. Clearly, they felt more secure with their *lançado* allies in the Cape Verde Islands.

22. Brooks, *Landlords and Strangers*, p. 133.

23. António Carreira, *The People of the Cape Verde Islands* (London: Hurst, 1982), pps. 22–25; António Carreira, *Cabo Verde: Formação e Extinção de uma Sociedade Escravocrata (1460–1878)* (Praia, Cape Verde: Instituto Cabo-Verdeano do Livro, 1983), p. 479.

24. Philip D. Curtin, *The Atlantic Slave Trade: A Census* (Madison: University of Wisconsin Press, 1969), p. 211.

25. Luís de Albuquerque and Santos and Maria Emília Madeira (coordinations), *Historia Geral de Cabo Verde* (Lisbon: Centro de Estudos de História e Cartografia Antiga, Instituto de Investigação Científica Tropica, 1991), p. 271.

26. Curtin, *The Atlantic Slave Trade*, pps. 112 and 189.

27. A. G. Hopkins, *An Economic History of West Africa* (New York: Columbia University Press, 1973), p. 91.

28. Carreira, *Cabo Verde: Formação*, p. 89.

29. The role of criminals and prostitutes in Brazil is discussed in Freyre, *The Masters and the Slaves*, p. 220; their role in Cape Verde is described in Brooks, *Landlords and Strangers*, p. 186.

30. Further detail about the formation of the *Crioulo* population between the islands and the coast in this period is provided in Boulegue, *Les Luso-Africains de Senegambie*, and in the short essay by António Carreira, *O Crioulo de Cabo Verde, Surto e Expansão* (Lisbon: Fundação Gulbenkian, 1982).

31. T. Bentley Duncan, *Atlantic Islands* (Chicago: University of Chicago Press, 1972), chap. 9.

32. Jay Coughtry, *The Notorious Triangle: Rhode Island and the African Slave Trade, 1700–1807* (Philadelphia: Temple University Press, 1981), pps. 5–6; R. J. Cottrol, *The Afro-*

Yankees: Providence's Black Community in the Antebellum Era (Westport, Conn.: Green-wood Press, 1982), p. 14.

33. Coughtry, *The Notorious Triangle*, pps. 27–28.

34. Ibid., pps. 45 and 254.

35. Ibid., pps. 97 and 100.

36. Cottrol, *The Afro-Yankees*, p. 15.

37. Ibid., p. 16.

38. Coughtry, *The Notorious Triangle*, pps. 81 and 83.

39. Marques, *History of Portugal*, pps. 465–467; Duncan, *Atlantic Islands*, pps. 227–228.

40. Marques, *History of Portugal*, pps. 436–441.

41. Ibid., pps. 407, 413, 466, and 471.

42. Duncan, *Atlantic Islands*, pps. 221–222.

43. George E. Brooks, *Yankee Traders, Old Coasters and African Middlemen* (Boston: Boston University Press, 1970), p. 30.

44. Ibid., p. 29.

45. N. R. Bennett and George Brooks, *New England Merchants in Africa* (Boston: Boston University Press, 1965), especially chaps. 2, 3, and 4, give rich primary data on the nature of New England trade with West Africa in the nineteenth century.

46. Captain T. Conneau, *A Slaver's Logbook* (Englewood Cliffs, N.J.: Prentice-Hall, 1976), pps. 74–77; 214–215, 246.

47. Marques, *History of Portugal*, p. 87.

48. Brooks, *Yankee Traders*, p. 124.

49. Ibid., pps. 311–312.

50. Ibid., pps. 117–118.

51. Ibid., pps. 194–196.

52. I am grateful for Francis T. McNamara's work on this subject, which was brought to my attention while he served as the U.S. ambassador to Cape Verde from 1990 to 1993; see McNamara, *France in Black Africa* (Washington, D.C.: National Defense University Press, 1989).

53. The history of São Vicente is covered in great detail in D. J. Gaitlin, *A Socio-Economic History of São Vicente de Cabo Verde, 1830–1970* (Los Angeles: History Department, University of California, 1990).

54. Ibid., p. 88; Duncan, *Atlantic Islands*, p. 163.

55. Gatlin, *History of São Vicente*, pps. 179–181.

56. Marques, *History of Portugal*, vol. 2, pps. 177–224.

57. Richard Lobban and Joshua Forrest, *Historical Dictionary of Guinea-Bissau* (Metuchen, N.J.: Scarecrow Press, 1988), pps. 108–109, 125–126. These "special facilities" were designed for beatings, electric shocks, psychological torture, and solitary confinement in the dark. They are now abandoned but serve as a monument to those terrible years.

58. Basil Davidson, *The Liberation of Guinea: Aspects of an African Revolution* (Harmondsworth, England: Penguin, 1969), pps. 142–160; W. A. Nielsen, *African Battleline*, (New York: Harper & Row, 1965), pps. 1–13.

59. H. Galvão, *Santa Maria: My Crusade for Portugal* (Cleveland, Ohio: World Press, 1961).

60. Some of the works documenting NATO ties to Portugal include James Duffy, "Portugal's Colonies in Africa," *Foreign Policy Bulletin*, 40 (March 1961); James Duffy, *Portugal in*

Africa (Cambridge, Mass.: Harvard University Press, 1962); and William Minter, *Portuguese Africa and the West* (Baltimore: Penguin Books, 1972).

Chapter 3

1. Many have worked on the topic of Lusotropical multiracialism; relevant are the works of Gilberto Freyre, *The Masters and the Slaves: A Study in the Development of Brazilian Civilization* (Berkeley: University of California Press, 1986); Marvin Harris, *Portugal's African "Wards"* (New York: American Committee on Africa, 1958); Marvin Harris, *Patterns of Race in the Americas* (New York: Walker, 1964); Marvin Harris, "Referential Ambiguity in the Calculus of Brazilian Racial Identity," *Southwestern Journal of Anthropology* 26, no. 1 (1970): 1–14; Charles Wagley, ed., *Race and Class in Rural Brazil* (New York: Columbia University Press, 1952); G. T. Bender, *Angola Under the Portuguese: The Myth and the Reality* (Berkeley: University of California Press, 1978); and Deirdre Meintel, *Race, Culture, and Portuguese Colonialism in Cabo Verde* (Syracuse, N.Y.: Syracuse University Press, 1984).

2. The fundamental distinctions between race, language, and culture, long recognized by the discipline of anthropology, have seemed to require endless reexamination since the time of the classic work on this topic by Franz Boas, *Race, Language And Culture* (New York: Macmillan, 1948).

3. These Portuguese racial terms are all drawn from my survey of the 1856 Registry of Slaves, Cape Verde National Historical Archives, Praia.

4. Additional perspectives on the specifics of twentieth-century racial classification for Cape Verde can be found in Meintel, *Race, Culture, and Portuguese Colonialism,* pps. 98–105.

5. Wagley, ed., *Race and Class,* pps. 29 and 94.

6. The overall sparred length of the *Ernestina* is 152 feet (46.2 m); the hull length is 112 feet (34.0 m). Its maximum breadth is 24 feet and 5 inches (7.4 m), and it draws 13 feet (3.9 m). The sail area is 7,937 square feet (317.5 m^3), and it weighs 98 gross tons (99.6 metric tons). These data are supplied by the Schooner Ernestina/Morrissey Historical Association, New Bedford, Mass.

7. Harris, *Portugal's African "Wards,"* p. 7.

8. James Duffy, "Portugal's Colonies in Africa," *Foreign Policy Bulletin* 40 (1961): 90.

9. This famous talk by Amilcar Cabral, given in honor of Eduardo Mondlane at Syracuse University in February 1970, has been reprinted in many places but is easily accessible in Amilcar Cabral, *Unity and Struggle: Speeches and Writing of Amilcar Cabral* (New York: Monthly Review Press, 1980), pps. 138–154. The important work by Ronald Chilcote, *Amilcar Cabral's Revolutionary Theory and Practice: A Critical Guide* (Boulder: Lynne Rienner, 1991), pps. 47–64, explores Cabral's revolutionary concepts in a stimulating chapter on his sophisticated understanding of the theory of class and class struggle.

10. The *badius* are discussed in the ethnomusicological entries by Peter Manuel in Richard Lobban and Marilyn Halter, *Historical Dictionary of the Republic of Cape Verde* (Metuchen, N.J.: Scarecrow Press, 1988), as well as in ongoing ethnomusicological research by Susan Hurley-Glowa at Brown University.

11. Calculated from the 1990 census of Cape Verde; see Direcção-Geral de Estatística, Divisão de Censas e Inquéritas, *2{d} Recenseamento da População e Habitação, 16–30 Junho 1990* (Praia: Republic of Cape Verde, 1990), p. 50, table 13.

12. Meintel, *Race, Culture, and Portuguese Colonialism,* pps. 55–72; K. David Patterson, "Epidemics, Famines, and Population in the Cape Verde Islands, 1580–1900," *The International Journal of African Historical Studies* 21, no. 2 (1988): 303–309.

13. William A. Cadbury, *Labour in Portuguese West Africa* (London: George Routledge Publisher, 1910); António Carreira, *Cabo Verde: Classes Socais, Estrutura Familiar, Migraóalcões,* No. 9 (Lisbon: Biblioteca Ulmeiro, 1977) pps. 33–53; Antonio Carreira, *Cabo Verde: Aspectos Sociais. Secas E Fomes Do Seculo XX* (Lisbon: Biblioteca Ulmeiro, 1984); Meintel, *Race, Culture, and Portuguese Colonialism,* pps. 64–67.

14. Marilyn Halter, "Cape Verdean–American Immigration and Patterns of Settlement, 1860–1940," Ph.D. diss., Boston University, 1986.

15. Marilyn Halter, "Working the Cranberry Bogs: Cape Verdeans in Southeastern Massachusetts," in D. Huse, ed., *Spinner* (New Bedford, Mass.: Spinner Publications, 1984), pps. 70–83.

16. Halter, *Cape Verdean–American Immigration.*

17. Michael Platzer and Michael Cohn, *Black Men of the Sea* (New York: Dodd, Mead, 1978).

18. Sam Beck, "Longshoremen's Union, Local 1329," in Paul Buhle, Scott Molloy, and Gail Sansbury, eds., *A History of Rhode Island Working People* (Providence, R.I.: Regine Printing, 1983) pps. 76–77; Waltraud Coli and Richard Lobban, *The Cape Verdeans in Rhode Island* (Providence: Rhode Island Publication Society, 1990), pps. 24–25.

19. Lobban and Halter, *Historical Dictionary,* pps. 94–95.

20. Timothy J. Finan and Helen K. Henderson, "The Logic of Cape Verdean Female-Headed Households: Social Response to Economic Scarcity," *Urban Anthropology* 17, no. 1 (March 1988): 87–103, have noted a high correlation between matrifocal households and subsistence agriculture in the context of widespread poverty and male migration, particularly in the island of São Tiago.

21. The 1856 Registry of Slaves, now housed in the Cape Verde National Historical Archives in Praia, are considered the only surviving record of this kind in Cape Verde. Other slave registries are believed to exist in Portugal, but they were not consulted for this study.

22. António Carreira, *Cabo Verde: Formação e Extinção de uma Sociedade Escravocrata (1460–1878)* (Praia, Cape Verde: Instituto Cabo-Verdeano do Livro, 1983), p. 506.

23. Finan and Henderson, "The Logic of Cape Verdean Female-Headed Households," p. 94.

24. Cabral, *Unity and Struggle,* pps. 144–145.

25. Lobban and Halter, *Historical Dictionary,* p. 57.

26. Ibid., p. 51.

27. Ibid., p. 37.

28. Ibid., p. 108.

29. Ibid., p. 75; Luís Romano, *Cabo Verde—Renascenço de uma Civilazação no Atlântico Medédio* (Lisbon: Edição da Revista "Ocidente," 1970), pps. 126–132.

30. Lobban and Halter, *Historical Dictionary,* pps. 67–68.

31. A great deal has been written about Cape Verdean literature and the *Claridade* movement. Early and well-informed contributions are found in Donald Burness, ed., *Fire: Six Writers from Angola, Mozambique and Cape Verde* (Washington, D.C.: Three Continents Press, 1977); in O. R. Dathorne, *The Black Mind: A History of African Literature* (Minneapolis: University of Minnesota Press, 1974), pps. 339–355; in the rich folkloric collection by

Romano, *Cabo Verde—Renascenço*, and especially in Russell Hamilton, *Voices from an Empire: A History of Afro-Portuguese Literature* (Minneapolis: University of Minnesota Press, 1975), pps. 237–357, who devotes four chapters to the study of Cape Verdean literature in this seminal work. Also see Hamilton's short but provocative article about politics and poetry in Cape Verde, "Cape Verdean Poetry and the PAIGC," in Richard K. Priebe and Thomas A. Hale, eds., *Artist and Audience: African Literature as a Shared Experience* (Washington, D.C.: Three Continents Press, 1979), pps. 103–125. Several more recent works show the established maturity of Cape Verdean literary traditions and of those who have made critical surveys of it: Donald Burness, ed., *Critical Perspectives on Luso-Phone Literature from Africa* (Washington, D.C.: Three Continents Press, 1981); Donald Burness, ed., *Wanasema: Conversation with African Writers* (Athens: Ohio University African Series, 1985); and the long introduction and very comprehensive literary anthology by Maria M. Ellen, ed., *Across the Atlantic: An Anthology of Cape Verdean Literature* (North Dartmouth: Center for the Portuguese-Speaking World, University of Massachusetts, 1988).

32. A rich exploration of the connection between Cape Verdean poetry and the armed political struggle led by the PAIGC is found in Hamilton, "Cape Verdean Poetry and the PAIGC."

33. Lobban and Halter, *Historical Dictionary,* pps. 68–69; Ellen, *Across the Atlantic,* pps. 82–83.

34. Lobban and Halter, *Historical Dictionary,* p. 20; Ellen, *Across the Atlantic,* p. 71.

35. Lobban and Halter, *Historical Dictionary,* p. 69.

36. Ibid., p. 69; Ellen, *Across the Atlantic,* pps. 93–106.

37. Lobban and Halter, *Historical Dictionary,* p. 109.

38. Ellen, *Across the Atlantic,* pps. 22, 38–39, 74–75.

39. Romano, *Cabo Verde—Renascenço,* pps. 109–125; Elsie Clews Parsons, *Folklore from the Cape Verde Islands* (Cambridge, Mass.: The American Folklore Society, 1923).

40. Lobban and Halter, *Historical Dictionary,* p. 73.

41. Cape Verdean foods and recipes are featured in newspapers and in some *Crioulo* cookbooks. Identification of specific Cape Verdean foods and cooking instruments is provided by Romano, *Cabo Verde—Renascenço,* pps. 146–155.

42. These musical instruments are reported in ibid., pps. 80–81. In earlier sections of this chapter, I have recorded the musical and dance forms that have links to the African coast.

43. These children's games were listed in the Crioulo glossary in ibid., pps. 162–205.

44. The unequaled reference on Cape Verdean *panos* is António Carreira, *Panaria Cabo-Verdeano-Guineense* (Praia, Cape Verde: Instituto Cabo-Verdeano do Livro, 1983). In this focused work, Carreira has compiled, analyzed, and richly illustrated the social, economic, and aesthetic history of these textiles in Cape Verde.

45. Stephanie Urdang, *Fighting Two Colonialisms: Women in Guinea-Bissau* (New York: Monthly Review Press, 1979).

46. Specific works and short biographies of these women writers are provided by Ellen, *Across the Atlantic.*

47. Urdang, *Fighting Two Colonialisms,* p. 267.

48. Ibid., p. 270.

49. Richard Lobban and Joshua Forrest, *Historical Dictionary of the Republic of Guinea-Bissau* (Metuchen, N.J.: Scarecrow Press, 1988), pps. 134–135.

50. Ibid., p. 106.

51. Basil Davidson, *The Fortunate Isles: A Study in African Transformation* (Trenton, N.J.: Africa World Press, 1989), p. 72.

52. Dulce Almada Duarte, "The Cultural Dimension in the Strategy for National Liberation: The Cultural Bases of the Unification Between Cape Verde and Guinea-Bissau," *Latin American Perspectives* 11, no. 2 (1984): 55–56.

Chapter 4

1. Cabral is one of the most popular West African revolutionary thinkers, about whom a great deal has been written. A scholarly biography and comprehensive analysis of Cabral is found in Patrick Chabal, *Amilcar Cabral: Revolutionary Leadership and People's War* (New York: Cambridge University Press, 1983). Gerard Chaliand, *Armed Struggle in Africa* (New York: Monthly Review Press, 1969), and Basil Davidson, *The Liberation of Guinea: Aspects of an African Revolution* (Harmondsworth, England: Penguin, 1969), which give firsthand accounts of the liberation war. The work by Carlos Lopes, *Guinea-Bissau: From Liberation Struggle to Independent Statehood* (Boulder: Westview Press, 1987), provides a detailed socioeconomic and historical survey of the context of the liberation struggle. Lars Rudebeck, *Guinea-Bissau: A Study in Political Mobilization* (Uppsala, Sweden: Scandinavian Institute of African Studies, 1974), gives a detailed account of the political strategies of mass mobilization. Analysis of the role of women in the struggle in Guinea is found in Stephanie Urdang, *Fighting Two Colonialisms: Women in Guinea-Bissau* (New York: Monthly Review Press, 1979). As a basic reference and for a bibliography on Guinea-Bissau, see Richard Lobban and Joshua Forrest, *Historical Dictionary of Guinea-Bissau* (Metuchen, N.J.: Scarecrow Press, 1988). A penetrating scholarly account of the war in Guinea-Bissau recently appeared in Mustafah Dhada, *Warriors at Work: How Guinea Was Really Set Free* (Niwot: University Press of Colorado, 1993).

2. Some writers add the name of Rafael Barbosa to this list, but he became persona non grata in the course of the struggle and is usually excluded. Because so much has been written on the specific history of the PAIGC, I have focused on the ways in which the struggle in Guinea-Bissau relates to parallel or subsequent events in Cape Verde.

3. Dr. Eduardo Mondlane, founder of FRELIMO, described this movement in *The Struggle for Mozambique* (Baltimore: Penguin Books, 1969); it was published the year he was assassinated by the Portuguese. Researchers are referred to Ronald Chilcote, *Emerging Nationalism in Portuguese Africa* (Stanford: Hoover Institution, Stanford University, 1972), and Richard Gibson, *African Liberation Movements: Contemporary Struggles Against White Minority Rule* (London: Oxford University Press, 1972), for the evolution and terminology of these other groups.

4. Richard Lobban and Marilyn Halter, *Historical Dictionary of the Republic of Cape Verde* (Metuchen, N.J.: Scarecrow Press, 1988).

5. Journalists visiting PAIGC offices in Conakry were sometimes told that they were welcome to criticize the PAIGC, then asked to refrain from making any negative reports about Guinea-Conakry.

6. Mondlane, *The Struggle for Mozambique*.

7. Rudebeck, *Guinea-Bissau*, gives an excellent account of the grassroots political organization constructed by the PAIGC in the liberated zones.

8. Basil Davidson, *The Fortunate Isles: A Study in African Transformation* (Trenton, N.J. Africa World Press, 1989), p. 83.

9. This is typical of the simple and direct expressions of Cabral. Full citations to his published works are best found in Chilcote, *Amilcar Cabral's Revolutionary Theory,* pps. 180–231.

10. The criticism by opponents of the PAIGC was that it was dominated by Cape Verdeans. The effort to divide Cape Verdeans from Guineans was also an element in the plot to assassinate Amilcar Cabral in 1973 and in the coup d'état against Luís Cabral in 1980.

11. The vast network of "people's stores" in the liberated areas supported three goals: (1) providing basic subsistence items and food to the people living in these areas who supported the PAIGC; (2) purchasing local agricultural produce for sale and barter and for small-scale export; and (3) undermining the Portuguese colonial economy.

12. At secret meetings in New York City, New Bedford, Massachusetts, and Providence, Rhode Island, in 1972 and 1973, PAIGC officials were engaged in building their political support and conducting informational programs. The Cape Verdean diaspora community and individual families were deeply divided at this time over the issue of Cape Verdean identity and support for or opposition to the PAIGC.

13. In the United States, there were numerous African liberation support groups, such as the African Information Service, Africa Research Group, Southern Africa Committee, American Committee on Africa, Liberation Support Movement, and other liberal and radical groups.

14. Dulce Almada Duarte, "The Cultural Dimension in the Strategy for National Liberation: The Cultural Bases of the Unification Between Cape Verde and Guinea-Bissau," *Latin American Perspectives* 11, no. 2 (1984): 61.

15. From about 1972 to 1974, there was a substantial increase in the number of Portuguese aircraft lost, including spotter planes, helicopters, and fighter-bombers, because the PAIGC was using Soviet bloc Estrella SAM missiles. This improvement in military technology decisively strengthened the PAIGC political presence at this point.

16. Further details are provided in Richard Lobban, "The Fall of Guiledge," *Africa,* no. 21 (May 1973): 36–37.

17. "PAIGC Official Addresses UN Colonialism Committee," *Southern Africa* 7, no. 6 (June 1974): 24.

18. Spinola saw service with Nazi forces as an observer on the Russian front and also fought with the Fascists in Spain. While serving for four years in Portuguese Guinea, he was linked to the invasion of Guinea-Conakry and to the assassination of Amilcar Cabral. Spinola was also a top-ranking colonial military officer, who served in Angola. As the war in Guinea-Bissau advanced, he was recalled to Lisbon in August 1973 and appointed in January 1974 as the deputy chief of staff of the Portuguese armed forces. In the context of colonial fascism, he was considered liberal. His liberal attitude was most clearly expressed in his book *Portugal e o Futura* (Lisbon: Arcadia, 1974), which recognized the failures of the military and advocated a political solution to the wars; this, he believed, could result in a neo-colonial Lusitanian federation. By 14 March 1974, the tumult in the Portuguese military caused Spinola's ouster, but on 25 April, he personally presided over Caetano's surrender of power.

19. The speech by the figurehead president Spinola was broadcast on 29 July 1974 on Radio Portugal; the text can be found in *Africa News* for that date.

20. *Washington Post,* 22 May 1974; *O Seculo,* 21 May 1974.

21. "Portugal: The Road Ahead," *Southern Africa* 8, no. 9 (October 1974): 21–22.

22. This was rumored in accounts in the *New York Times,* 5 and 11 August 1974, and *Le Monde,* 10 July 1974.

23. *Guardian,* London, 16 May 1974.

24. *Le Canard Enchaine,* Paris, mid-October 1974.

25. "On the Cape Verde Islands," *Southern Africa* 8, no. 9 (October 1974): 23.

26. Veiga is quoted in "Reactionary Cape Verdeans Plan Action in US," *Southern Africa* 8, no. 3 (March 1975): 25.

27. The information on UCID is compiled here for the first time. It is derived from undated ephemera, field observations, and informal interviews.

28. These are my personal and direct observations; I was both inside and outside the hotel on this occasion.

29. *United Nations Delegates World Bulletin,* 21, April 1975.

30. *Sunday Nation,* Dar es Salaam, 17 November 1974.

31. *O Seculo,* Lisbon, 8 January 1975.

32. *Le Monde,* Paris, 27 December 1974.

33. *Zambia Daily Mail,* Lusaka, 24 February 1975.

34. This is taken from Pereira's New Year's Day address of 1975 and appears in "The Struggle Continues: The Cape Verde Islands," *Southern Africa* 8, no. 7 (July-August 1975): 30–31.

35. *International Herald Tribune,* Paris, 20 February 1975.

36. Basil Davidson, "Practice and Theory: Guinea-Bissau and Cape Verde," in Barry Munslow, ed., *Africa: Problems in the Transition to Socialism* (London: Zed Books, 1986), pps. 102–104.

37. The topic of the Vieira coup in Bissau against Luís Cabral is noted in Lobban and Forrest, *Historical Dictionary,* pps. 35, 133–134. Numerous explanations are offered; they commonly include: (1) tensions between the African population and the *Crioulo* leadership of the PAIGC, (2) repressive measures taken by Cabral against dissident units in the military, and (3) factors involved in a personal power struggle against supposed or potential rivals.

38. I met with Luis Cabral in Dakar and in Ziguinchor on several occasions in 1973. After independence was granted, I privately interviewed him in the Bissau statehouse in 1975. This interview was published in Richard Lobban, *Third World Coalition Newsletter No. 3* (Binghamton, N.Y.: Department of Sociology, SUNY, 1975), pps. 9, 13, 14. I have met Cabral once since then, in Paris. I also spent about a week with "Nino" Vieira at his military camp in the South Front in June 1973.

39. These dates and events were noted from memorial markers placed at the two sites.

40. A brief interview and biography of Correia is given in Ronald Chilcote, *Amilcar Cabral's Revolutionary Theory,* pps. 117–119. Some have judged that his effort to topple Vieira was motivated by a desire to restore the political links between Guinea and Cape Verde.

41. President Monteiro did not visit the United States with Prime Minister Veiga.

42. I first met Pires in the forests of the South Front in Guinea-Bissau in 1973. Subsequently, we met in the Providence, Rhode Island, city hall, and I conducted an in-depth interview with him in August 1992 in Praia.

43. I first met Pereira at the Conakry office of the PAIGC just a few months after the assassination of Amilcar Cabral. I recall that he was still nursing his injured wrists after being roughly bound during the attempted overthrow of the PAIGC. In a controversial interview in the Portuguese paper *Expresso,* in November 1993, Pereira suggested that Cape Verdeans may have been better served by political autonomy from Portugal rather than full independence.

44. See my two-part editorial published in *The Providence Rhode Island Journal,* 1 and 2 October 1992, released during Prime Minister Veiga's visit to New England.

45. This information is derived from the official results of the Electoral Commission; from the local press, especially *Voz di Povo* of the period; and from personal interviews with representatives of the PAICV and MpD, who have requested confidentiality.

46. Quoted from Amadou Traore's interview with José Chantre Oliviera, in "Cape Verde Country Report," *The Courier,* no. 127 (May-June 1991): 10.

47. Quoted from A. Traore's interview with Prime Minister Carlos Veiga, in ibid., p. 14.

Chapter 5

1. Republico de Cabo Verde, Ministério de Desenvolvimento Rural e Pescas, Gabinete de Estudos e Planeamento, *Estatísticas Agricolas,* December 1989; Richard Lobban and Marilyn Halter, *Historical Dictionary of the Republic of Cape Verde* (Metuchen, N.J.: Scarecrow Press, 1988), pps. 13–16.

2. Ministério des Finanças e do Plano, Direcção-Geral de Estatística, *Boletim de Contas Nacionais,* 1991, p. 52.

3. Ibid., p. 58.

4. Lobban and Halter, *Historical Dictionary,* pps. 45–46; Amadou Traore, "Cape Verde: A Mundança—Change," *The Courier,* no. 127 (May-June 1991): p. 19.

5. The 1986 data are from *The World Almanac and Body of Facts* (New York: Pharos Books, 1992), p. 746; the 1991 data are found in Jeffress Ramsey, ed., *Global Studies, Africa* (Guildford, Conn.: Annual Editions, 1991), p. 24.

6. *Environmental Almanac* (Boston: Houghton Mifflin, 1992), pps. 318–319.

7. World Development Report 1992, Development and the Environment, *World Development Indicators* (Washington, D.C.: Oxford University Press, 1992).

8. Republica de Cabo Verde, Ministério de Plano e da Cooperação, Direcção Geral de Estatística, *Boletim Anual de Estatística* 1989, pps. 157–162. *Global Studies, Africa,* puts Cape Verdean inflation at 12 percent for 1991.

9. Amadou Traore, *A Mundança—Change, The Courier,* no. 127 (May-June 1991): 10–19; "Country Profile for Cape Verde," *The Economist Intelligence Unit, 1992–93,* p. 65.

10. *The World Almanac and Body of Facts* (New York: Pharos Books, 1992), p. 831.

11. J. M. Sampaio, *Cape Verde,* pps. 23–24.

12. Republica de Cabo Verde, *Boletim Anual de Estatística,* p. 84

13. *Boletim Trimestral do Comércio Externo* (Praia, Cape Verde: Direcção-Geral de Estatistica, 1990), p. 1; "Country Profile for Cape Verde," p. 65.

14. Lobban and Halter, *Historical Dictionary,* pps. 51–52; Sampaio, *Cape Verde,* p. 26.

15. Traore, *A Mundança,* p. 18.

16. This suggestion was raised by Gustavo Araujo, minister of industry, trade, and tourism in 1991.

17. Traore, *A Mundança,* p. 17.

18. *The Courier,* no. 127 (May-June 1991): p. 19.

19. K. A. Hamilton, *Lusophone Africa, Portugal and the United States* (Boulder: Westview Press, 1992), p. 40.

Chapter 6

1. As this book enters its final draft, there are some reports of growing internal opposition to the Veiga government. Apparently, the frustration is based on the slow pace of promised changes; the movement toward privatization has also led to a degree of abuse. But both opposition parties, the PAICV and UCID, experienced internal shuffles as their focus turned toward future elections. It also appears that other new partners are emerging, such as Eurico Monteiro of the Partido da Convergência Democrática and Onésimo Silveira's Espaço Democrático.

According to the *Marktest* polls in the spring of 1994, the minority PAICV appears to be making some progress toward political recovery, but UCID still has a distance to travel before seriously competing for electoral seats in the future.

2. I am pleased to credit Nels Kasfir for his assistance on these models, derived from his unpublished papers, conversations spanning decades, common research on parallel issues in the Sudan, and shared summer retreats in New Hampshire.

Selected Bibliography

Abshire, David M., and Michael A. Samuels, eds. *Portuguese Africa: A Handbook* (New York: Praeger, 1969).

Ajayi, J.F.A., and Michael Crowder, eds. *History of West Africa*, 2 vols. (New York: Columbia University Press, 1972).

Albuquerque, Luís de, and Maria Emília Madeira Santos, coordinators. *Historia Geral de Cabo Verde*, vol.1 (Lisbon: Centro de Estudos de História e Cartografia Antiga, Instituto de Investigação Cientifica Tropica, 1991).

Almeida, Raymond A., and Patricia Nyhan. *Cape Verde and Its People: A Short History* (Boston: American Committee for Cape Verde, 1976).

Alves, Miguel. "The Cape Verdeans and America." *The Courier*, no. 127 (May-June 1991): 22.

Amaral, Ilidio do. *Santiago de Cabo Verde: A Terra e os Homens*, Memoria no. 48. (Lisbon: Junta de Investigaçãos do Ultramar, 1964).

Araujo, Norman. "A Study of Cape Verdean Literature." Master's thesis, Boston College, 1966.

Axelson, Eric. *Congo to Cape, Early Portuguese Explorers* (New York: Harper and Row, 1973).

Barboza, Ron. "Cape Verde: Portrait of an Archipelago." *Spinner* 2 (1981): 27–31.

Barcellos, Cristiano Josá de Senna. *Subsídios para História de Cabo Verde e Guiné*, 7 vols. (Lisbon: Tipografia da Academia Real das Ciências, 1899–1913).

Barreto, João. *História da Guiná* (Lisbon: Edição do Autor, 1938).

Beck, Sam. "Longshoremen's Union, Local 1329," in Paul Buhle, Scott Molloy, and Gail Sansbury, eds. *A History of Rhode Island Working People* (Providence, R.I.: Regine Printing Company, 1983).

_____. *Manny Almeida's Ringside Lounge: The Cape Verdeans' Struggle for Their Neighborhood* (Providence, R.I.: Gavea-Brown, 1992).

Bender, Gerald T. *Angola Under the Portuguese: The Myth and the Reality* (Berkeley: University of California Press, 1978).

Bennett, Norman R., and George E. Brooks. *New England Merchants in Africa: A History Through Documents, 1802–1865* (Boston: Boston University Press, 1965).

Boas, Franz. *Race, Language and Culture* (New York: Macmillan, 1948).

Boulegue, Jean. *Les Luso-Africains de Senegambie* (Lisbon: Ministério da Educação, 1989).

Boxer, C. R. *Race Relations in the Portuguese Colonial Empire, 1415–1825* (Oxford: Oxford University Press, 1963).

_____. *Four Centuries of Portuguese Expansion, 1415–1825* (Berkeley: University of California Press, 1972).

Brooks, George E. *Yankee Traders, Old Coasters and African Middlemen* (Boston: Boston University Press, 1972).

_____. *Luso-African Commerce and Settlement in the Gambia and Guinea-Bissau Region,* Working Papers no. 24 (Boston: African Studies Center, Boston University, 1980).

_____. *Kola Trade and State-Building: Upper Guinea Coast and Senegambia, 15th–17th Centuries,* Working Papers no. 38 (Boston: African Studies Center, Boston University, 1980).

_____. *Landlords and Strangers: Ecology, Society, and Trade in Western Africa, 1000–1630* (Boulder: Westview Press, 1993).

Burness, Donald, ed. *Fire: Six Writers from Angola, Mozambique and Cape Verde* (Washington, D.C.: Three Continents Press, 1977).

_____. *Critical Perspectives on Luso-Phone Literature from Africa* (Washington, D.C.: Three Continents Press, 1981).

_____. *Wanasema: Conversations with African Writers* (Athens: Ohio University African Series, 1985).

Busch, Briton Cooper. "Cape Verdeans in the American Whaling and Sealing Industry, 1850–1900." *The American Neptune* 45, no. 2 (March 1985): 104–116.

Cabral, Amilcar. *Revolution in Guinea* (New York: Monthly Review Press, 1972).

_____. *Return to the Source* (New York: Africa Information Service, 1973).

_____. *Unity and Struggle: Speeches and Writings of Amilcar Cabral.* (New York: Monthly Review Press, 1990).

Cadbury, William A. *Labour in Portuguese West Africa* (London: George Routledge Publisher, 1910). Reprinted by Negro Universities Press, 1969.

Carreira, António. *Cabo Verde: Classes Sociais, Estrutura Familiar, Migrações,* no. 9 (Lisbon: Biblioteca Ulmeiro, 1977).

_____. *O Crioulo de Cabo Verde, Surto e Expansão* (Lisbon: Fundação Gulbenkian, 1982).

_____. *The People of the Cape Verde Islands: Exploitation And Emigration* (London: C. Hurst, 1982). Translation by C. Fyfe of the 1977 Portuguese edition.

_____. *Panaria Cabo-Verdeano-Guineense* (Praia, Cape Verde: Instituto Caboverdeano do Livro, 1983).

_____. *Cabo Verde: Formação e Extinção de uma Sociedade Escravocrata, 1460–1878* (Praia, Cape Verde: Instituto Caboverdeano de Livro, 1983).

_____. *Cabo Verde: Aspectos Socias, Secas e Fomes do Seculo XX* (Lisbon: Biblioteca Ulmeiro, 1984).

Casson, Lionel. *The Ancient Mariners: Seafarers and Sea Fighters of the Mediterranean in Ancient Times* (Princeton: Princeton University Press, 1991). 2d ed.

Chabal, Patrick. *Amilcar Cabral: Revolutionary Leadership and People's War* (Cambridge: Cambridge University Press, 1983).

Chaliand, Gerard. *Armed Struggle in Africa* (New York: Monthly Review Press, 1969).

_____. "The PAIGC without Cabral: An Assessment," *Ufahamu* 3, no. 3 (December 1973): 87–95.

Chilcote, Ronald H. *Portuguese Africa* (Englewood Cliffs, N.J.: Prentice-Hall, 1967).

_____. "The Political Thought of Amilcar Cabral," *Journal of Modern African Studies* 6, no. 3 (October 1968): 378–388.

_____. *Emerging Nationalism in Portuguese Africa* (Stanford: Hoover Institution, Stanford University, 1972).

_____. "Amilcar Cabral: A Bio-Bibliography of His Life and Thought, 1925–1973," *Africana Journal* 4 (1974): 289–307.

_____. *Amilcar Cabral's Revolutionary Theory and Practice: A Critical Guide* (Boulder: Lynne Rienner, 1991).

Coli, Waltraud Berger. "Cape Verdean Ethnicity." Unpublished Master's thesis, Program of African and Afro-American Studies, Rhode Island College, 1987.

Coli, Waltraud Berger, and Richard A. Lobban. *The Cape Verdeans in Rhode Island* (Providence: Rhode Island Heritage Commission and Rhode Island Publication Society, 1990).

Conneau, Captain Theophilus. *A Slaver's Log Book, or 20 Year's Residence in Africa* (Englewood Cliffs, N.J.: Prentice-Hall, 1976). First published in 1853.

Cottrol, Robert J. *The Afro-Yankees: Providence's Black Community in the Antebellum Era* (Westport, Conn.: Greenwood Press, 1982).

Coughtry, Jay. *The Notorious Triangle: Rhode Island and the African Slave Trade, 1700–1807* (Philadelphia: Temple University Press, 1981).

Curtin, Philip D. *The Atlantic Slave Trade: A Census* (Madison: University of Wisconsin Press, 1969).

_____. *Economic Change in Precolonial Africa* (Madison: University of Wisconsin Press, 1975).

da Mota, Avelino Teixeira. *As Viagens do Bispo D. Frei Vitoriano Portuense a Guiná e a Cristianização dos Reis de Bissau* (Lisbon: Centro de Estudos de Cartografia Antiga, 1974).

Dathorne, O. R. *The Black Mind: A History of African Literature* (Minneapolis: University of Minnesota Press, 1974).

Davidson, Basil. *The Liberation of Guinea: Aspects of an African Revolution* (Hardmondsworth, England: Penguin, 1969).

_____. "Practice and Theory: Guinea-Bissau and Cape Verde." In Barry Munslow, ed., *Africa: Problems in the Transition to Socialism* (London: Zed Books, 1986).

_____. *The Fortunate Isles: A Study in African Transformation* (Trenton, N.J.: Africa World Press, 1989).

Dhada, Mustafah. *Warriors at Work: How Guinea Was Really Set Free* (Niwot: University Press of Colorado, 1993).

Dickinson, Margaret. *When Bullets Begin to Flower: Poems of Resistance from Angola, Mozambique and Guinea* (Nairobi: East Africa Publishing House, 1973).

Donelha, Andre. *Descrição da Serra Leoa e dos Rios de Guiná do Cabo Verde* (Lisbon: Centro de Estudos de Cartografia Antiga, 1977). First published in 1625.

Duarte, Dulce Almada. "The Cultural Dimension in the Strategy for National Liberation: The Cultural Bases of the Unification Between Cape Verde and Guinea-Bissau." *Latin American Perspectives* 11, no. 2 (1984): 55–66.

Duarte, Fausto Castilho. *Os Caboverdeanos no Colonização da Guiná. (Boletim de Propaganda e Informação,* nos. 1, 2, and 13, 1949–1950).

Duffy, James. "Portugal's Colonies in Africa." *Foreign Policy Bulletin* 40 (March 1961): 89–96.

_____. *Portugal in Africa* (Cambridge, Mass.: Harvard University Press, 1962).

Duncan, T. Bentley. *Atlantic Islands* (Chicago: University of Chicago Press, 1972).

Ellen, Maria M., ed. *Across the Atlantic: An Anthology of Cape Verdean Literature* (North Dartmouth: Center for the Portuguese Speaking World, University of Massachusetts, 1988).

Fernandez-Armesto, Felipe. *Before Columbus: Exploration and Colonisation from the Mediterranean to the Atlantic, 1229–1492* (London: Macmillan Education, 1987).

Ferreira, Eduardo da Sousa. *Portuguese Colonialism in Africa: The End of an Era* (Paris: UNESCO, 1972).

Ferreira, Manuel. *Introdução a Ficção Cabo-Verdiana Contemporanea* (Cabo-Verde: Boletim de Propaganda e Informação, 11, 129, 1959–1960).

Figueiredo, Jaime de. *Modernos Poetas Caboverdianos: Antologia* (Praia, Cape Verde: Edições Henriques, 1961).

Finan, Timothy J., and John Belknap. *The Characteristics of Santiago Agriculture* (Praia, Cape Verde: Instituto Nacional de Investigação Agraria, 1984).

Finan, Timothy J., and Helen K. Henderson. "The Logic of Cape Verdean Female-Headed Households: Social Response to Economic Scarcity." *Urban Anthropology* 17, no. 1 (March 1988): 87–103.

First, Ruth. *Portugal's Wars in Africa* (London: Christian Action Publications, 1972).

Flint, John, ed. *The Cambridge History of Africa, ca. 1790 to ca. 1870*, vol. 5 (New York: Cambridge University Press, 1977).

Forrest, Joshua. *Guinea-Bissau: Power, Conflict, and Renewal* (Boulder: Westview Press, 1992).

Foy, Colm. *Cape Verde: Politics, Economics and Society* (London: Pinter Publishers, 1988).

Freyre, Gilberto. *The Masters and the Slaves: A Study in the Development of Brazilian Civilization* (Berkeley: University of California Press, 1986). 2d English ed., rev.

Galvão, Henrique. *Santa Maria: My Crusade for Portugal* (Cleveland: World Press, 1961).

Gatlin, Darryle John. "A Socio-Economic History of São Vicente de Cabo Verde, 1830–1970." Ph.D. diss., Department of History, University of California, 1990.

Gibson, Richard. *African Liberation Movements: Contemporary Struggles Against White Minority Rule* (London: Oxford University Press, 1972).

Gray, Richard, ed. *The Cambridge History of Africa, ca. 1600 to ca. 1790*, vol. 4 (New York: Cambridge University Press, 1977).

Greenberg, J. H. *Studies in African Linguistic Classification* (New Haven: Compass, 1955).

Greenfield, Sidney M. "In Search of Social Identity, Strategies of Ethnic Identity Management Amongst Capeverdeans in Southeastern Massachusetts," *Luso-Brazilian Review* 13, no. 1 (June 1976): 3–17.

Guthrie, Malcolm. "Bantu Origins," *Journal of African Languages* 1 (1962): 9–21.

Hakluyt, Richard. *Voyages and Discoveries* (Baltimore: Penguin Books, 1972). First published in 1589.

Haladay, Joan, and N'Koumba Karamoko. *Cape Verde: A Case Study in African Migration* (New York: Afro-Portuguese Research Center, ca. 1979).

Halter, Marilyn. "Working the Cranberry Bogs: Cape Verdeans in Southeastern Massachusetts." In D. Huse, ed., *Spinner*, vol. 3 (New Bedford, Mass.: Spinner Publications, 1984).

———. "Cape Verdean-American Immigration and Patterns of Settlement, 1860–1940." Ph.D. diss., Boston University, 1986.

———. *Between Race and Ethnicity: Cape Verdean American Immigrants, 1860–1965* (Chicago: University of Illinois Press, 1993).

Hamilton, Russell G. *Voices from an Empire: A History of Afro-Portuguese Literature* (Minneapolis: University of Minnesota Press, 1975).

_____. "Cape Verdean Poetry and the PAIGC." In R. K. Priebe and T. A. Hale, eds. *Artist and Audience: African Literature as a Shared Experience* (Washington, D.C.: Three Continents Press, 1979).

Hammond, Richard J. *Portugal and Africa, 1815–1910: A Study in Uneconomic Imperialism* (Stanford: Stanford University Press, 1966).

Harris, Marvin. *Portugal's African "Wards"* (New York: American Committee on Africa, 1958).

_____. *Patterns of Race in the Americas* (New York: Walker, 1964).

_____. "Referential Ambiguity in the Calculus of Brazilian Racial Identity," *Southwestern Journal of Anthropology* 26, no. 1 (1970): 1–14.

Harrison, Robert. "Famine and Poverty: The Cape Verde Islands," *Africa Today* 10 (March 1963): 8–9.

Hayden, Robert C. *African-Americans and Cape Verdean-Americans in New Bedford: A History of Community and Achievement* (Boston: Select Publications, 1993).

Herodotus. (Manuel Kormrof, ed.) *The History of Herodotus* (New York: Tudor Publications, 1956).

Humbaraci, Arslan, and Nicole Muchnik. *Portugal's African Wars* (New York: Third World Press, 1973).

July, Robert W. *A History of the African People* (New York: Scribner's, 1980). 3d ed.

Lawrence, A. W. *Trade Castles and Forts of West Africa* (Stanford: Stanford University Press, 1963).

Lobban, Richard. "Cape Verde Islands: Portugal's Atlantic Colony," *Africa* 21 (May 1973): 36–39.

_____. "The Fall of Guiledge," *Africa* 24 (August 1973): 36–37.

_____. "Guinea-Bissau: 24 September and Beyond," *Africa Today* 21, no. 1 (1974): 15–24.

_____. "The Republic of Guinea-Bissau Starts to Build: Interview with President Luís Cabral on 8 July 1975," *Third World Coalition Newsletter*, no. 3 (Binghamton, N.Y.: Department of Sociology, SUNY, 1975), pps. 9, 13, and 14.

_____. "Ethnogenesis in Africa: Some Models of Unity and Diversity," *Reviews in Anthropology* 16 (1991): 245–255.

Lobban, Jr. Richard A., and Joshua Forrest. *Historical Dictionary of the Republic of Guinea-Bissau* (Metuchen, N.J.: Scarecrow Press, 1988). 2d ed.

Lobban, Jr. Richard A., and Marilyn Halter. *Historical Dictionary of the Republic of Cape Verde* (Metuchen, N.J.: Scarecrow Press, 1988). 2d ed.

Lobban, Jr. Richard A., W. Coli, and R. Tidwell. "Patterns of Cape Verdean Migration and Social Association," *New England Journal of Black Studies* 5 (1985): pps. 31–45.

Lopes, Carlos. *Guinea-Bissau: From Liberation Struggle to Independent Statehood* (Boulder: Westview Press, 1987).

Magubane, Bernard. "Amilcar Cabral: Evolution of Revolutionary Thought," *Ufahamu* 2, no. 2 (September 1971):71–87.

Marques, A. H. de Oliveira. *History of Portugal* (New York: Columbia University Press, 1976). 2d ed.

McNamara, Francis Terry. *France in Black Africa* (Washington, D.C.: National Defense University Press, 1989).

Meintel, Deirdre. "Cape Verdean Americans." In J. Rollins, ed., *Hidden Minorities* (Washington, D.C.: University Press of America, 1981).

_____. *Race, Culture, and Portuguese Colonialism in Cabo Verde* (Syracuse, N.Y.: Syracuse University Press, 1984).

Minter, William. *Portuguese Africa and the West* (Baltimore: Penguin Books, 1972).

Mondlane, Eduardo. *The Struggle for Mozambique* (Baltimore: Penguin Books, 1969).

Moran, Emílio. "The Evolution of Cape Verde's Agriculture," *African Economic History* 11 (1982): 63–86.

Moser, Gerald M. *Essays in Portuguese-African Literature* (University Park: Pennsylvania State University, 1969).

Murdock, George P. *Africa, Its People and Their Culture History* (New York: McGraw-Hill, 1959).

Niane, D.T., ed. *General History of Africa: Africa from the Twelfth to the Sixteenth Century,* vol. 4 (Berkeley: UNESCO, Heinemann, 1984).

Nebenzahl, Kenneth. *Atlas of Columbus and the Great Discoveries* (New York: Rand McNally, 1990).

Nielsen, Waldemar A. *African Battleline, American Policy Choices in Southern Africa* (New York: Harper and Row, 1965).

Ogot, B. A., ed. *General History of Africa: Africa from the Sixteenth to Eighteenth Century,* vol. 5 (Berkeley: UNESCO, Heinemann, 1984).

Oliver, Roland, ed. *The Cambridge History of Africa, ca. 1050 to ca. 1600,* vol. 3 (New York: Cambridge University Press, 1977).

Parsons, Elsie Clews. *Folklore from the Cape Verde Islands* (Cambridge, Mass.: American Folklore Society, 1923).

Patterson, K. David. "Epidemics, Famines, and Population in the Cape Verde Islands, 1580–1900," The International Journal of African Historical Studies 21, no. 2 (1988): 291–313.

Pélissier, René. *História da Guiná: Portugueses e Africanos no Senegâmbia, 1841–1936,* 2 vols. (Lisbon: Imprensa Universitária Editorial Estampa, 1989). Also published as *Naissance de la Guinée Portugais et Africains en Senegambie.*

Pereira, Daniel A. *Estudões da História de Cabo Verde* (Praia, Cape Verde: Instituto Caboverdiano do Livro, 1986).

Pereira, Duarte Pacheco. *Esmeraldo de Situ Orbis,* Memoria no. 19 (Bissau: Centro de Estudos da Guiné Portuguesa, 1956). First published in 1508.

Platzer, Michael, and Michael Cohn. *Black Men of the Sea* (New York: Dodd, Mead, 1978).

Renaudeau, Michel. *Cape Verde Islands* (Boulogne, France: Delroisse, 1985).

Rodney, Walter. *A History of the Upper Guinea Coast, 1545–1800* (New York: Oxford University Press, 1970).

_____. *How Europe Underdeveloped Africa* (Washington, D.C.: Howard University Press, 1974).

Romano, Luís. *Cabo Verde—Renascenço de uma Civilização no Atlântico Meádio* (Lisbon: Edição da Revista "Ocidente," 1970).

Rudebeck, Lars. *Guinea-Bissau: A Study in Political Mobilization* (Uppsala: Scandinavian Institute of African Studies, 1974).

Sampaio, João Melo de. "Cape Verde: Cooperation with the EEC." *The Courier,* No. 127 (May-June 1991): 23–26.

Silva, Baltazar Lopes da. *O Dialecto Crioulo de Cabo Verde* (Lisbon: Agência Geral do Ultramar, 1957).

_____. *Antologia da Ficção Cabo-Verdiana Contemporanea* (Praia, Cape Verde: Imprensa Nacional, 1960).

Spínola, António de. *Portugal e o Futuro* (Lisbon: Arcadia, 1974).

Traore, Amadou. "Cape Verde: A Mudança—Change," *The Courier,* No. 127 (May-June 1991): 10–21.

Tyak, David B. "Cape Verdeans in the United States." Ph.D. diss., Harvard University, 1952.

Urdang, Stephanie. *Fighting Two Colonialisms: Women in Guinea-Bissau* (New York: Monthly Review Press, 1979).

Vogt, John. *Portuguese Rule on the Gold Coast, 1569–1682* (Athens: University of Georgia Press, 1979).

Wagley, Charles, ed. *Race and Class in Rural Brazil* (New York: Columbia University Press/ UNESCO, 1952).

Walter, Jaime. *Honório Pereira Barreto: Biografia, Documentes* (Bissau: Centro de Estudos da Guiné Portuguesa, 1947).

Zurara, Gomes Eanes. *The Chronicle of the Discovery and Conquest of Guinea,* 2 vols. (London: Hakluyt Society, 1896 and 1899). First published in 1452.

About the Book and Author

The Cape Verde Islands, an Atlantic archipelago off the coast of Senegal, were first settled during the Portuguese Age of Discovery in the fifteenth century. A "Crioulo" population quickly evolved from a small group of Portuguese settlers and large numbers of slaves from the West African coast. In this important, integrated new study, Dr. Richard Lobban sketches Cape Verde's complex history over five centuries, from its role in the slave trade through its years under Portuguese colonial administration and its protracted armed struggle on the Guinea coast for national independence, there and in Cape Verde.

Lobban offers a rich ethnography of the islands, exploring the diverse heritage of Cape Verdeans who have descended from Africans, Europeans, and Luso-Africans. Looking at economics and politics, Lobban reflects on Cape Verde's efforts to achieve economic growth and development, analyzing the move from colonialism to state socialism, and on to a privatized market economy built around tourism, fishing, small-scale mining, and agricultural production. He then chronicles Cape Verde's peaceful transition from one-party rule to elections and political pluralism. He concludes with an overview of the prospects for this tiny oceanic nation on a pathway to development.

Richard A. Lobban, Jr., is professor of anthropology and the director of the Program of African and Afro-American Studies at Rhode Island College. Dr. Lobban's research is wide ranging and includes work on ancient African societies as well as studies of modern urbanization and development. He worked with Mozambican refugees in 1964 and walked across Guinea-Bissau with the nationalist guerrillas in 1973. In 1975 he witnessed the last days of colonialism and the beginning of independence in Cape Verde; he revisited the islands in 1992 to conduct research for this book. In 1993 he participated in the celebrations of the twentieth anniversary of independence in Guinea-Bissau. Dr. Lobban is also a founder of the Sudan Studies Association. His publications include *A Historical Dictionary of the Sudan,* coauthored with Carolyn Fluehr-Lobban and John Voll.

Index